014640341 Liverpool Univ

Designing, Delivering and Evaluating Learning and Development: Essentials for Practice

Edited by Jim Stewart and Peter Cureton

D1341397

The Chartered Institute of Personnel and Development is the leading publisher of
books and reports for personnel and training professionals, students, and all those
concerned with the effective management and development of people at work.
For details of all our titles, please contact the publishing department:
tel: 020 8612 6204
email: publishing@cipd.co.uk
The catalogue of all CIPD titles can be viewed on the CIPD website:
www.cipd.co.uk/bookstore

Designing, Delivering and Evaluating Learning and Development: Essentials for Practice

Edited by Jim Stewart and Peter Cureton

Chartered Institute of Personnel and Development

Published by the Chartered Institute of Personnel and Development
151 The Broadway, London SW19 1JQ

First published 2014

© Chartered Institute of Personnel and Development, 2014

All rights reserved. No part of this publication may be reproduced, stored in a retrieval system, or transmitted, in any form or by any means, electronic, mechanical, photocopying, recording, or otherwise, without the prior written permission of the publisher.

This publication may not be sold, lent, hired out or otherwise dealt with in the course of trade or supplied in any form of binding or cover other than that in which it is published without the prior written permission of the publisher.

No responsibility for loss occasioned to any person acting or refraining from action as a result of any material in this publication can be accepted by the editor, authors or publisher.

The right of the editors to be identified as the authors of the editorial material, and of the contributors as authors of their individual chapters, has been asserted in accordance with sections 77 and 78 of the Copyright, Designs and Patents Act 1988.

Designed and typeset by Exeter Premedia Services, India
Printed in Great Britain

British Library Cataloguing in Publication Data
A catalogue of this publication is available from the British Library

ISBN 9781843983606

The views expressed in this publication are the authors' own and may not necessarily reflect those of the CIPD.

The CIPD has made every effort to trace and acknowledge copyright holders. If any source has been overlooked, CIPD Enterprises would be pleased to redress this in future editions.

Chartered Institute of Personnel and Development

151 The Broadway, London SW19 1JQ
Tel: 020 8612 6200
Email: cipd@cipd.co.uk
Website: www.cipd.co.uk
Incorporated by Royal Charter. Registered Charity No. 1079797

Contents

List of figures and tables

About the authors

Dr Randhir Auluck is a Principal Lecturer in International HRM at Coventry University Business School. Previously, she worked at the National School of Government as a Leadership Development Consultant and Head of Knowledge Strategy. Randhir was advisor on an OECD strategic HRM study and has been a consultant on a variety of international projects, including being seconded to the French Government in Paris. She is a qualified social worker and has worked in the voluntary sector.

Peter Cureton is a Senior Lecturer at Liverpool John Moores University. For the CIPD he was an examiner for two PDS subjects, and is currently a Quality Assurance Panel Chair and a member of the Quality Advisory Group. He has practitioner experience in the UK and Europe in facilitating learning events and developing processes for consolidation. He is in the final stages of completing a doctorate in learning to be a manager in a contact centre.

Dr Clair Doloriert is a Lecturer at Bangor Business School and is currently Co-Director for the Centre for Business Research. She is the Deputy Personal Tutor for all Business School undergraduates and postgraduates. She is active in ethnographic research and her interests include organisational learning, knowledge management, employee engagement, organisational change, power and culture. She actively reviews articles for a number of journals, including: *Leadership Quarterly*, *Management Learning* and the *Journal of Organizational Ethnography*.

Dr Tricia Harrison is a Senior Lecturer at Liverpool John Moores University where she is the programme manager for MA Change Management. She has module responsibilities for International HRM/HRD, Organisational Behaviour and Strategic Human Resource Development. Her research interests include the development of professional practice, mental toughness, action learning and questioning. She has worked at Webster University, Geneva, Kingston University and Bournemouth University and has extensive HR consultancy experience and prior employment with Siemens.

Dr Niki Kyriakidou is a Principal Lecturer in HRM/OB at Leeds Metropolitan University, with a doctoral and master's degree in Human Resource Management and a bachelor degree in Political Sciences and Public Administration. Dr Kyriakidou's research interests revolve around International Human Resource Management, Leadership and Learning and Development. Her current publications are in the area of leadership and management; learning theories and practice; workplace learning; cross-cultural HRD; graduate employment; managing human resources in the Middle East and Mediterranean regions.

Amanda Lee is a Chartered Fellow of the CIPD with over 15 years' experience as an HRM practitioner in the NHS, construction and retail sectors. She has over 10 years' experience of managing and delivering postgraduate programmes and is currently Course Director for the MA HRM and MSc International HRM courses at Coventry University. Amanda is a part-time doctoral student and her research interests include issues associated with flexible working practices and managerialism in academia.

Michael McFadden began his career with Rolls Royce's Aero Engines Division. He subsequently held teaching and management roles in further education. Michael's experience of higher education was initially as a project manager for the Government's Aimhigher initiative before moving into business development for Coventry University. In this role he developed successful partnerships with HR practitioners from national employers in the design and management of their organisation's training programme. He is currently lecturing at Coventry University.

Michelle McLardy is a Chartered Member of the CIPD and Lecturer in Human Resource Management at Coventry University. She currently teaches on various human resource modules on both full- and part-time programmes including the BA HRM degree, CIPD Postgraduate Diploma in HRM and MA HRM, and is the programme lead on the Intermediate CIPD qualification. Her previous experience has included various roles within the private sector.

Sophie Mills is Senior Lecturer and Course Director for full-time postgraduate programmes in the HR&OB Department of the Faculty of Business, Environment and Society at Coventry University. She specialises in the areas of people and organisational development and is module leader for the CIPD accredited Level 7 Organisation Design and Organisation Development module. Her current research includes learning and practice in HRD, management education, academic career development and innovative approaches in teaching and learning.

Marian O'Sullivan is Principal Lecturer in Human Resource Management and Associate Head of the Department of Human Resources and Organisational Behaviour at Coventry University. Marian lectures in employee reward on both undergraduate and postgraduate courses and contributes to a range of applied research activities. Her previous work experience includes HR roles in a number of large public and private sector organisations and she was co-author of *Managing People in the Workplace*.

Nigel O'Sullivan is a Chartered Engineer and Chartered CIPD member. He has 30 years of industrial practice and also working alongside his industry career, he has 20 years of academic experience. His areas of expertise and interest are business, strategy and human resource development. These areas of interest enable him to undertake business and capability development in his industry role and bring a mixture of theory and practice to his role in teaching in academia.

Maureen Royce is a Principal Lecturer in HR at Liverpool John Moores University, where she manages undergraduate and postgraduate HR programmes. She is currently researching social exclusion in education and the professions. Maureen has been involved at board level in social enterprise organisations for some years and has interests in governance, board diversity and skills and developing community resilience through social capital. Formerly Maureen was an HR practitioner in the financial services and hospitality sectors.

Sally Sambrook is Professor of Human Resource Development, Director of the Centre for Business Research and former Deputy Head of School and Director of Postgraduate Studies at Bangor Business School. Sally is a founding member of the University Forum for HRD and served as a board member of the American Academy of HRD. Sally employs a critical and autoethnographic approach to HRD research, has published widely and holds various editorial roles on leading HRD journals.

Dalbir Sidhu is a Chartered Member of the CIPD with over 10 years' experience of organisation and leadership development. As a qualified coach, Dalbir has a breadth of experience in the L&D field offering a solution-focused consultancy. In addition to her progressive career in industry, Dalbir gained a master's in Strategic HRM and Change and is a lecturer and module leader at Coventry University, delivering modules on the CIPD postgraduate programmes.

Jim Stewart is Professor of HRD at Coventry University. He is a Chief Examiner for the CIPD as well as an External Moderator and Quality Assurance Panel Chair. Jim is also Chair of the University Forum for HRD. He has conducted research projects funded by the UK Government, European Commission, ESRC, UKCES and CIPD among others and is the author, co-author/editor of over 20 books on HRD. This is his third book for the CIPD.

Dr Crystal Zhang, academic member of the CIPD, is a Principal Lecturer in HRM and OB at Leeds Business School. She has a particular interest in talent management, cross-cultural learning/cognitive style, and international HRM. Her current publications are in the areas of learning and development, cross-cultural HRM, talent management and graduate employment. She has designed and delivered executive programmes in the UK, China and Africa, and acts as reviewer for publishers, academic journals and conferences.

Acknowledgements

The editors would like to thank a number of people for their support in bringing this book to completion. First, of course, are our contributing authors for staying with the project through our seemingly endless requests for additions, revisions and new information. Second, thanks are due to the team at the CIPD and especially to Katy Hamilton and Alex Krause for their patience as well as indispensable guidance. Finally, Jim Stewart as always would like to thank Pat for her continued forbearance through another writing challenge, and Peter Cureton would like to thank Audrey for her unwavering support with this and other projects.

Walkthrough of textbook features and online resources

LEARNING OUTCOMES

By the end of this chapter you will be able to:

- explain and critically evaluate a range of learning theories
- demonstrate understanding of the relevance and application of learning theories in instructional design
- analyse and assess the principles deriving from learning theories to support effective practice in design and delivery of learning and development interventions
- assess and evaluate the contribution of non-HR professionals and managers to ensure effective learning and development interventions.

LEARNING OUTCOMES

At the beginning of each chapter a bulleted set of learning outcomes summarises what you can expect to learn from the chapter, helping you to track your progress.

CASE STUDY 8.1

ETHICS AND EVALUATION IN PRACTICE: FREEPORT MCMORAN GOLD AND COPPER

Operating in Indonesia, Freeport had a tarnished reputation with the local community and they had been implicated in human rights abuse in the 1990s. The largely expatriate management of Freeport had lacked sensitivity to the needs and the culture of the Indonesian people. The company had also been accused of discrimination against Indonesian nationals in both recruitment and training. The relationship was indeed a difficult one. The initial response from Freeport was reactive and fractured in that money was given to schools, or clinics, consultative bodies were formed but each of these remained isolated interventions which did little to change the overall positioning of the organisation and the indigenous population. Prakash Sethi et al (2011) discuss the changes that followed a more integrated approach from Freeport, resulting in improved relations and reduced conflict. The approach involved a firm commitment to double and then double again the number of local people employed. This meant prioritising and creating access to training. One per cent of Freeport revenue was put aside to support community ventures which specifically targeted jobs or entrepreneurial activities. The holistic approach with clear targets combined with clear evaluation gave credibility to the interventions being made.

CASE STUDIES

A range of case studies from different countries illustrate how key ideas and theories are operating in practice around the globe, and are accompanied by questions or activities.

REFLECTIVE ACTIVITY 2.3

Think again about the recent learning experience you identified earlier. Does the process of learning you experienced reflect what is described by experiential learning theory? If so, do you now want or need to revise your personal theory? If not, can you identify weaknesses in experiential learning theory based on your experience of learning?

REFLECTIVE ACTIVITIES

In each chapter a number of questions and activities will get you to reflect on what you have just read and encourage you to explore important concepts and issues in greater depth.

EXERCISE 6.3

Proctor and Gamble (P&G), the world's leading consumer goods company, is determined to keep a balanced approach in these tough times and wanted to celebrate the power of its people. On 27 January 2009, they held an event to encourage employees to focus on their personal development. 'All About Me' also featured an information fair, where employees were encouraged to take advantage of the services and opportunities offered, including a mentoring and coaching programme (Business In The Community, **www.bitc.org.uk**)

How effective do you think information fairs and activities such as these are in promoting the benefits of coaching and mentoring?

EXERCISES

Take your learning to the next level by completing the exercises, which prompt you into thinking about how you would apply what you have just read, in practice.

EXPLORE FURTHER

CLUTTERBUCK, D. and MEGGINSON, D. (2005) *Techniques for coaching and mentoring*. Oxford: Elsevier Butterworth-Heinemann.

GOLD, J., THOPRE, R. and MUMFORD, A. (2010) *Leadership and management development*. London: CIPD.

ILES, P. and ZHANG, C. (2013) *International human resource management*. London: CIPD.

SIMMONDS, D. (2004) *Designing and delivering training*. London: CIPD.

STEWART, J. and GIGG, C. (2011) *Learning and talent development*. London: CIPD.

STEWART, J., GOLD, J., HOLDEN, R., ILES, P. and BEARDWELL, J. (2013) 'Encountering HRD', in GOLD, J., HOLDEN, R., ILES, P, STEWART, J. and BEARDWELL, J (eds) *Human Resource Development: Theory & Practice*, 2nd ed. Basingstoke: Palgrave Macmillan.

EXPLORE FURTHER

Explore further boxes contain suggestions for further reading and useful websites, encouraging you to delve further into areas of particular interest.

ONLINE RESOURCES FOR TUTORS

- Lecturer's Guide – Provides guidance on how to use the book in your teaching, discussing the context of each chapter and supplying suggested responses to in-text learning features.

- PowerPoint Slides – Design your programme around these ready-made lectures, including figures and tables from the text, as well as websites for further reading.

CHAPTER 1

Designing, Delivering and Evaluating Learning and Development

PETER CURETON AND JIM STEWART

LEARNING OUTCOMES

By the end of this chapter you will be able to:

- understand the structure and main themes of the book
- explain how the content relates to the CIPD's Advanced standard for Designing, Delivering and Evaluating Learning and Development
- understand how to use the book to maximise your own learning.

1.1 INTRODUCTION

In editing this book, we both reflected on how learning and development has changed in as little as a generation. Some of these changes have occurred as the discipline has assumed its own identity as a major contributor in the broad area of human resource management. Learning and development is now studied more formally. Whilst there had been many texts about training and development and learning prior to the late 1980s (for example, Nadler 1970 and Stammers and Patrick 1975), the subject had in many cases been included as part of organisational behaviour, or indeed subsumed into texts on human resource management. Other changes to the practice of training and development have occurred due to general changes in the world, notably through the development of information and communications technology (ICT).

The late 1980s proved to be a most interesting time. A scientist asked fundamental questions such as whether time could run backwards, and is the universe infinite or does it have boundaries (Hawking 2008). The war in Iraq ended; Australia celebrated its bicentennial; and the world population exceeded 5 billion people for the first time. In Britain, the formal ending of the First World War was noted as public houses were permitted to stay open all day, changing the licensing hours which had originally been introduced in 1914. It was common practice for retail shops to close on Wednesday afternoons for staff rest, an idea that may now seem anachronistic when viewed by younger generations. In the world of ICT, the first transatlantic fibre optic cable was laid, able to carry 40,000 telephone calls simultaneously. Commercial Internet services were launched in the United States and companies sought competitive advantage through forms of electronic data interchange. These developments were, however, also accompanied by the first major computer virus to infect computers connected to the Internet – the Morris WORM.

In 1988, Rosemary Harrison published *Training and Development* (CIPD), which was at that time widely regarded as *the* standard reader in the topic. The content provided a thorough analysis of the domain from a viewpoint that combined a pragmatic stance with a demonstration of the application of relevant theory in differing organisational contexts. Coverage ranged from the politics of training to a detailed treatment of the four-part systematic approach to training, all of which linked training to enhanced job performance. The term 'technology' was used, but at that time it related to '*general systems, procedures and methods*' (Harrison 1988, p256) through which individuals learned. The trainer was positioned as the person who directed and guided people in their learning, a traditional role. The Open University had very successfully used other technology such as radio, television and audio cassettes for individual learning, and the development of e-supported learning had begun in the form of computer-based training (CBT) and technology-based training (TBT, which added video images to the text on screen). Such approaches to learning seem rather old-fashioned now that the use of a range of devices, such as tablet computers with fourth generation mobile telephone standards and web 4.0 technologies, is part of everyday life.

1.2 STRUCTURE AND MAIN THEMES OF THE BOOK

So what has changed in the world of training and development in a generation? The most obvious change has seen the word training being replaced by learning. The CIPD changed the title of its annual survey on Training and Development to Learning and Development in 2006 and changed it again in 2010 to Learning and Talent Development. One of us recalls working as a consultant with a major bank in the north-west of England in the 1990s. The name of its Training and Development Centre was changed to Learning and Development, yet it could not shake off the tag of training in the minds of the staff. Perhaps this was due to the fact that they had simply replaced one word in the signage on the outside of the building. Although 'Learning' was then proudly displayed, the word 'Training' still appeared as a ghostly image as the sun had faded the brickwork, leaving an imprint of the previous word.

Other changes we have noted and consider in this book are the growth of coaching and the use of mentoring; the 'tightening' of short training courses – from five days to three days, from one day, to two hours and even the growth of so-called 'bite-sized learning', 20-minute sessions with examples of topics that provide helpful tips on how to use new routines in work. As organisations have downsized and reduced staff numbers, it seems that permitting staff to have time away from work for learning is more problematic. More learning is now delivered at and through work, learning is done on-the-job and near-job as the distinctions between work and learning soften. Individuals are encouraged to take greater responsibility for their learning as they use a range of technologies and social media to enhance their knowledge and skills. Access to learning is now available from every computer desktop.

Whilst the practitioner world has retained the title of learning and development, academics have preferred to use the term human resource development. They have questioned the fundamental purpose of human resource development and how it legitimates itself in an organisational setting. When human resource development is viewed through a critical management lens, questions about its purpose tend to fall into two areas. Firstly, does human resource development act as a mechanism to enable the emancipation of talented individuals to reach their potential by providing opportunities to develop their knowledge and skills? Or, secondly, is human resource development a servant of organisational senior managements to develop individuals solely to secure increased productivity by reinforcing accepted norm behaviours and standards? These issues continue to be debated in seminars and conferences, notably by the University Forum for Human Resource Development (UFHRD), an international association for universities, reflective practitioners, and learning-oriented organisations (Stewart et al 2009).

A principal change that we note in the last 25 years is the profusion of texts written (upwards of 500 we believe) about learning and development generally, as well as examinations of its many component elements. Learning and development can now truly be recognised as a significant field of study in people management. So, you may ask, why is there a need for yet another text at this time?

Designing, delivering and evaluating learning and development is a key practice for human resource management and especially for human resource development professionals. Engaging in associated activities, such as recording learning activity, organising learning schedules, managing the budget and confirming the value of learning probably accounts for the major time allocation and accountabilities for most practitioners. This book is aimed at human resource management generalists as well as learning and development specialists, together with students who have an interest in designing, delivering and evaluating learning and development. It is specifically written to support the CIPD's Advanced Standard for module 7DDE, the content of which was authored by Jim Stewart. The learning outcomes are mapped to each chapter as we note in the following section, in introducing each chapter. However, the text is not just for current postgraduate students working towards their postgraduate diplomas or master's degrees. It will be a useful text for those who have studied learning and development previously and wish to engage in continuous professional development (CPD), a topic that we cover in Chapter 8, to update their knowledge and skills. We are sure that they will be surprised at how the field has developed since they completed their studies. Students on other study programmes, including undergraduates, will also find it a valuable reference source, as learning and development has become an everyday part of general business and management curricula.

Learning practitioners who are not studying towards a professional qualification will also find useful ideas about the methods of other organisations, which should encourage them to reflect on the learning they provide and be reflexive about possible improvements to the range of learning opportunities that can be adopted. We have deliberately used examples from public, private and voluntary sector organisations to appeal to as broad an audience as possible. After all, professionals who are likely to move into different occupational sectors throughout their careers and maybe different countries need to understand how practice varies in other contexts.

Although the style of the book draws on UK practice and by implication that in North America, we are acutely aware of the growing globalisation of the labour market and have included examples from practice across the world. These examples will help to identify a range of challenges that learning and development professionals face in a multicultural world that requires them to operate in an inclusive way. If the 'war for talent' is over because 'talent won', employers need to focus on supporting individuals in their learning to allow potential to be used, not just for increased performance but for career development and employability, as well as personal well-being and growth.

1.3 OVERVIEW OF THE CHAPTERS LINKED TO THE CIPD'S ADVANCED STANDARDS

Whilst there is some consistency in the structure and presentation of each chapter, this is not uniform, which then allows each of the authors to explore the nuances of their topic appropriately.

1.3.1 CHAPTER 2 – INDIVIDUAL AND COLLECTIVE LEARNING

Clair Doloriert, Jim Stewart and Sally Sambrook

> **CIPD Learning Outcome 3**: Critically evaluate a range of learning and instructional design theories and principles and apply them to select and justify appropriate learning and development methods and delivery channels with the engagement and support of other professionals and managers.

The design and delivery of learning and development is predicated on understanding learning. Thus, that understanding is an essential foundation. The authors provide a critical exposition of a range of theories of individual and collective learning including cognitive, behavioural, social and constructivist models. A number of frameworks of instructional design are analysed for application of these theories, together with methods of learning and development appropriate to a range of purposes and audiences. The criteria for selecting and applying methods for use in a range of types of delivery channels, including the role of technology, are explored. The chapter also discusses approaches to and methods of engaging key stakeholders in design, including line managers, and especially their contribution to supporting learning and development.

1.3.2 CHAPTER 3 – THE EXTERNAL AND INTERNAL CONTEXT

Amanda Lee, Sophie Mills and Dalbir Sidhu

> **CIPD Learning Outcome 1**: Explain, evaluate and critically analyse the internal and external contextual factors impacting on the design, delivery and assessment of learning plans and interventions in organisations.

The practice of designing, delivering and evaluating learning and development occurs primarily in organisation contexts. Practitioners therefore need to understand factors, both internal and external, that influence those contexts. This chapter examines and analyses the role and impact of external factors such as economic and legislative conditions and internal factors on learning. These cover such topics as organisational plans and priorities, learning climate and resource availability, and how these affect the attitudes of individuals to their learning. This introduces workplace and work-based learning strategies and notions of formal and informal learning. Developments in ICT, such as e-learning, social media and games, and the opportunities and limitations of these for the design and delivery of learning are also addressed. Suggestions for strategies of blended learning are explored. More generally, external and internal barriers, inhibitors and facilitators of learning and development are identified and evaluated. The authors demonstrate how such potential restraints can inhibit the development of a high-performance work culture and the contribution that key stakeholders can make.

1.3.3 CHAPTER 4 – ESTABLISHING LEARNING NEEDS

Dr Tricia Harrison and Dr Randhir Auluck

> **CIPD Learning Outcome 2**: Evaluate, select and apply a range of approaches and processes for establishing learning and development needs at organisational, group/team, occupational and individual levels in collaboration with relevant stakeholders.

The design, delivery and evaluation of learning and development needs to be built on clear understanding of learning needs at a number of levels. This chapter begins by examining and analysing the role and responsibilities of a range of stakeholders in identifying learning and development needs. The strengths and limitations of approaches to and methods of identifying learning needs at organisational, occupational and individual levels are then explored and critically evaluated. These are illustrated with relevant examples. As part of this, the role of data and the forms it takes in organisational settings and contexts to identify learning needs is critically examined. Human resource development practitioners may need to be proactive in seeking such data. Approaches to and methods of building support for learning among a range stakeholders are described and explored as the identification of learning needs is located within wider development processes.

1.3.4 CHAPTER 5 – DESIGNING LEARNING INTERVENTIONS

Dr Crystal Zhang and Dr Niki Kyriakidou

> **CIPD Learning Outcome 4**: Design learning plans and interventions to meet identified needs in a timely, feasible and cost-effective way.

The design stage of designing, delivering and evaluating learning and development follows logically from the specification of learning needs. Factors that determine and influence learning and development plans, such as the purpose and timeliness of learning and its associated costs are explored and analysed in this chapter. It will develop the examination of learning theory in Chapter 2 to include learning from both an organisation and learner perspective. This considers ways of meeting organisational, occupational and individual level learning needs in a timely way that reflects an organisation's culture and the diverse needs of individuals. The value of training is analysed, not just in economic terms, but by reflecting how people of different age groups view learning. This is discussed alongside the need for innovative learning to tackle global challenges on sustainable employability. Various and varying components and features of organisational, departmental, team and individual learning plans are described and explored together with the importance of specifying learning outcomes. The chapter also examines methods and processes for estimating and justifying costs, and for planning, designing and managing implementation of feasible learning interventions and events.

1.3.5 CHAPTER 6 – DELIVERING AND FACILITATING LEARNING

Michelle McLardy and Nigel O'Sullivan

> **CIPD Learning Outcome 5**: Demonstrate skills of delivery and facilitation of learning through a range of methods and for employees at a range of organisational levels and a range of occupational groups.

The skills associated with facilitating learning of groups and individuals are examined in this chapter. Given the changes we noted in the previous section, the chapter begins by considering methods of providing one-to-one coaching and mentoring, as these are increasingly used in organisations. More traditional forms of learning delivery through the use of presentational and instructional skills are also included. The ideas and suggestions based on practice are applied in ways that help to create appropriate and effective learning climates. Feedback is a key element of learning, and approaches to and techniques of giving and receiving feedback are considered. In addition the chapter provides guidance on how to support learning of groups and individuals through blended approaches, and how the use of technology after an intervention back on the job can support the consolidation of learning. This is a necessary and often overlooked part of a learning and development professional's responsibilities.

1.3.6 CHAPTER 7 – EVALUATING LEARNING AND DEVELOPMENT

Marian O'Sullivan and Michael McFadden

> **CIPD Learning Outcome 6**: Design and implement appropriate evaluation methods to assess the success and effectiveness of learning plans and interventions.

Establishing impact and benefits through evaluation is often considered as the final stage of designing, delivering and evaluating learning and development practice.. This chapter challenges this approach and considers activities that need to be built into the learning design to ensure quality, starting with a consideration of the purposes of evaluation. It describes and critically analyses a range of approaches to and methods and techniques of evaluation including return on investment, value added and stakeholder satisfaction. A number of models and frameworks of evaluation are examined, as are a range of sources and types of data for evaluation purposes. These are critically examined and problems and limitations discussed, particularly why they have not been used extensively in organisations, despite knowledge of this crucial activity being in existence for more than two generations. This discussion focuses on problems of measurement and the politics of evaluation, among other factors. The role and contribution of formative and summative assessment in learning evaluation is explored and how these can be used for continuous improvement.

1.3.7 CHAPTER 8 – ACTING PROFESSIONALLY AND ETHICALLY

Peter Cureton and Maureen Royce

> **CIPD Learning Outcome 7**: Act ethically and professionally with a demonstrated commitment to equality of opportunity and diversity in the design and delivery of learning and development and to continuous personal and professional development.

The CIPD rightly emphasises the need for HR practitioners to act professionally and ethically and so this chapter will examine those qualities in the context of designing, delivering and evaluating learning and development. Definitions and understandings of ethics, including philosophical bases of cognitivism and consequentialism, are described and evaluated. An examination of the similarities and differences of notions of equality and diversity also forms part of the chapter, as we take a broad perspective on inclusivity and the notion that this topic is part of an organisation's 'mainstream' activities. Notions of professionalism and professional practice are examined and analysed through a consideration of both aspects of integrity and practice through the four-part systematic approach to training. The implications for and application of these concepts and associated debates in professional practice associated with design, delivery and evaluation of learning and development are explored. Rationales for and processes of CPD, including evaluation of a range of CPD methods, are considered. Challenges in CPD, particularly for human resource development professionals, form the final part of the chapter.

1.3.8 CHAPTER 9 – THEMES AND THE FUTURE OF DDE

Jim Stewart and Peter Cureton

The final chapter draws together the main themes and emerging issues from the book by proposing some personal viewpoints rather than summarising the contributions from the other authors. In highlighting the key points from the chapters, it picks up key current debates and challenges in the designing, delivering and evaluating of learning and development and human resource development discourse. The chapter also includes speculations about the future of designing, delivering and evaluating learning and development. This is intended to stimulate further thinking and challenge practitioners and academics to consider how they might make a contribution to future theory and practice. Not only should this encourage reflection about current practice but we exhort professionals to engage with and plan the continuous development of their knowledge and skills.

1.4 HOW TO USE THIS BOOK

The book adopts an approach that encourages a critical examination of taken-for-granted assumptions of designing, delivering and evaluating learning and development practice. It supports this questioning by providing alternative perspectives on and accounts of practice. Whilst the book is loosely structured around a systematic approach to learning and development, readers may choose to start with a specific chapter to further their knowledge of a particular theme.

We have included case studies from practice, vignettes and activities to encourage readers to consider how suggestions might apply in their contexts. We hope they find new ideas here, or perhaps confirmation of ideas that have been developed through practice. It may also be an opportunity to refresh ideas that may have been forgotten that might be relevant now. In addition, the book supports application and development of practice through a range of pedagogical features which will be applied throughout the book and in all chapters. We also include suggested reading at the end of each chapter and web-based support for study can be found at the CIPD website.

As editors of this book, we hope that readers continue to develop their practice continually to respond to evolving work contexts and expectations. We believe that they must recognise the many and diverse ways in which learning makes contributions to the development and advancement of both organisations and individuals. If enhanced professional practice is successful in building a number of different capabilities through effective use of designing, delivering and evaluating learning and development technologies, the reputation and standing of learning and development can only be enhanced.

CHAPTER 2

Individual and Collective Learning

CLAIR DOLORIERT, JIM STEWART AND SALLY SAMBROOK

LEARNING OUTCOMES

By the end of this chapter you will be able to:

- explain and critically evaluate a range of learning theories
- demonstrate understanding of the relevance and application of learning theories in instructional design
- analyse and assess the principles deriving from learning theories to support effective practice in design and delivery of learning and development interventions
- assess and evaluate the contribution of non-HR professionals and managers to ensure effective learning and development interventions.

2.1 INTRODUCTION

Design, delivery and evaluation of learning and development (DDE) as professional practice are predicated on understanding learning. Therefore, understanding learning is an essential foundation. There have been and continue to be many attempts to provide understanding in the form of various theories of learning. These theories can be categorised according to the level at which they analyse and emphasise the learning process, whether at individual, social interaction or organisational level. This chapter will provide a critical account of leading theories of individual and collective learning including cognitive, behavioural and social and constructivist models. Guidance on applying theories across a range of delivery channels will emerge, as will approaches to engaging others in design and delivery of learning and development. This guidance will be achieved through the process of applying the reflective activities and exercises included in the chapter. Chapters 5 and 6 will explore these matters in more detail and so the main focus here will be on the theoretical foundations of the practice of DDE, beginning with some definitions.

2.2 DEFINING LEARNING

A useful place to start is to explore formal definitions. The Oxford English dictionary defines learning as 'the *action* of receiving instruction or acquiring knowledge' (OED 2013 *italics added*), whereas the American Psychological Association defines it as 'a *process* based on experience that results in a relatively permanent change in behaviour or behavioural potential' (APA 2013 *italics added*). Within the business literature, Bass and

Vaughan (1976), in their early work on training in industry, define learning as 'a relatively permanent change in behaviour that occurs as a result of practice or experience'. Reynolds et al (1997) define learning as 'a change in attitudes, knowledge or skill. The change can be physical and overt, or it can be intellectual or attitudinal' (p128).

Traditionally, learning theories have developed from research in the long-established disciplines of psychology, anthropology, linguistics and education. More recently, contemporary academic fields such as human resource management (HRM) and artificial intelligence (AI) have become interested in learning theory and their own contextualised understandings of it, for example in the context of business performance for HRM. From an HRM perspective, Torrington et al (2005) consider the results of learning 'to be changed or new behaviour resulting from new or reinterpreted knowledge that has been derived from an external or internal experience' (p385). From an AI perspective: (1) learning involves memory storage and organisation such that memory can be retrieved at the opportune time; (2) learning also involves the acquisition of concepts; (3) learning is based on the compilation of know-how; and (4) like human beings, a machine should be capable of inventing new theories to explain or summarise a body of facts or a series of events (adapted from Houdé 2004, pp226–227).

Clearly, there are a variety of definitions of learning. Some see learning as an action, others see it as a process (suggesting some degree of order and linearity), behaviour change or experience. Harrison (1997, p225) notes that some definitions treat 'learning' as a noun (eg OED 2013, as quoted previously); however, using 'learning' as a verb makes it more dynamic (learning as practice, experience, change). Kim (1993, p38) also notes that a number of theorists make the connection in their definitions between (1) the acquisition of skill or *know-how* (what people learn) and (2) the acquisition of *know-why* (how they understand and apply that learning). In the above examples learning can be seen as resulting in changed attitudes, skills, knowledge and/or behaviour. The fact that learning theory is now moving into the domain of artificial intelligence demonstrates the sheer scope, application and longevity of this 'science', although we will see through our historical review of individual learning theory that as far back as the 1950s learning psychologists have been using the analogy of computers/information processing to help inform understanding of the learning process.

 EXERCISE 2.1

Consider the various definitions given in section 2.2 and respond to the following questions:

1   How can learning be facilitated according to each definition?

2   What factors can inhibit learning according to each definition?

3   Which definition of learning will have most utility in designing and delivering learning interventions?

2.3 INDIVIDUAL LEARNING THEORY

Over the course of a century, individual learning theory has developed from single and multi-disciplinary research methodologies, producing many competing views.

REFLECTIVE ACTIVITY 2.1

Think about a learning experience you have had recently, eg a driving lesson, a class or course you attended, a new task at work, trying a sport for the first time, finding a route to a destination you visited for the first time, getting to know a new friend or colleague.

What prompted you to learn? What did you do in order to learn? What happened to and with you as you learned? How did you establish if you were successful or not? Based on your answers to these questions, what is your personal theory of how people learn?

2.3.1 TRADITIONAL THEORIES OF INDIVIDUAL LEARNING

Traditional theories of individual learning, including behaviourism, cognitive approaches, and social learning theory, tend to have roots in psychology, whereas more contemporary theories and models, including adult learning, experiential learning and learning styles, span various disciplines. We have tabled some of the key theories as presented in HR-related textbooks in Figure 2.1. These suggest a range of theoretical positions, discussed in the following sections.

Figure 2.1 An overview of some of the key theories described in HR-related texts

Author/Year	Traditional theories ← — — — — — — — — — — — — — → Contemporary theories				
Marchington and Wilkinson (2000)	Learning by association	Cognitive	Cybernetics	Social learning theory	Learning from experience
Reid and Barrington (2001)	Reinforcement theories	Cognitive theories and problem-solving	Cybernetic and information theories		Experiential learning
Torrington et al (2005, 2011)	Behaviourist	Cognitive	Constructivist	Social learning theory	Learning from experience
Harrison (2005)	Learning as conditioning	Learning as information processing		Learning as a social process	Learning as experience
Sadler-Smith (2006)	Behaviourist theories	Cognitive (information processing) approaches		Social learning theory	Experiential learning

2.3.1.1 Behaviourism

Behaviourism, also known as the 'behavioural approach', was the dominant way of researching, theorising and conceptualising learning in the early twentieth century. There are a number of psychologists who have contributed to this approach, as shown in Figure 2.2.

Psychologists working under the behavioural approach placed importance on conducting systematic and controlled laboratory experiments to advance knowledge and understanding. This was done through observing behaviour and ignoring non-observable intervening cognitive/mental processes (such as thinking and emotion) in the learning process. Observational experiments were mostly on animals, although it was argued, at the time, that the findings were transferable to the human context. This approach has received much criticism more recently, especially concerning its relevance for adult and workplace learning. The 'language' used focused on 'stimulus – response' connections (often the note form of S–R is used).

Figure 2.2 Key psychologists contributing to behaviourism

Psychologist	Dates	Famous work	Contribution
Thorndike (America)	1874–1949	Puzzle-box experiment – using cats to work out how to escape the box by pressing levers	Introduced the notion of the S–R unit for describing learning behaviour Introduced concept of reinforcement and 'law of effect'
Pavlov (Russia)	1849–1936	Pavlovian experiment – using dogs	Developed theory of 'classical conditioning'
Watson (America)	1878–1958	Little Albert experiment – using rats and noise to create fear in children	A case study providing empirical evidence of classical conditioning in humans. Advocated behaviourism as 'the way' of researching into learning
Skinner (America)	1904–1990	Operant experiment (Skinner box – teaching pigeons to play ping-pong)	Theorised direct link between action and consequences as the basis of learned behaviour through operant conditioning

Thorndike was the first to use S–R theory for understanding learning. From his puzzle-box experiments he developed the *Law of Effect*, which stated that any behaviour that is followed by pleasant consequences is likely to be repeated, and any behaviour followed by unpleasant consequences is likely to be stopped (Thorndike 1898).

Pavlov's *classical conditioning theory* (Pavlov 1928) is a good way of exemplifying the S–R theory. Pavlov showed, through his animal experiments, how naturally occurring behaviour can be altered through learning. Pavlov used a bell sound (stimulus) and food (reinforcer) to trigger salivation in a dog (response). He found that after a number of trials the dog would salivate on hearing the bell without seeing/smelling the food. The dog had learned an association between the bell (stimulus) and the food (reinforcer). Classical conditioning is also known as *respondent conditioning* because it tests learning based on bodily *responses* that are reflexive such as knee jerks, pupil contractions and salivation.

Although Watson (1978–1958) did not invent behaviourism, and did very little laboratory research (Bolles 1975), his contribution to behaviourism is important to note because he became widely known as its chief spokesman and protagonist. In the 1910s to 1920s he successfully demanded that American psychologists become behaviourists, and because of this the behaviourism movement is largely attributed to him.

As behavioural theory developed, Skinner (1938) emphasised the importance of an animal operating in its environment in determining resultant behaviour outcomes (Gregory 1987). His work was based on Thorndike's law of effect (McLeod 2007). Operant conditioning theory, therefore, associates behaviour with either a pleasant or an unpleasant consequence. Operant conditioning helps to explain how new patterns of behaviour become established. The effects of consequences on behaviour can be stated as:

- Behaviours will increase in frequency if they are rewarded.
- Behaviours will increase in frequency if they result in the avoidance of an unpleasant event, or in something unpleasant being terminated.
- Behaviours will decrease in frequency if they lead to something unpleasant happening.
- Behaviours will decrease in frequency if they have been rewarded in the past but are subsequently no longer rewarded (Skinner 1953).

Harrison (2009) summarises S–R theory in general and sees learning as a conditioning process that operates through an interaction in the individual of four processes: drive, stimulation, response and reinforcement.

Behaviourism often centres on how children learn through positive reinforcement when their behaviour pleases their parents (reward) and negative behaviour that contradicts the expectations of their parents (punishment). This might be translated into the work context, exploring how employers manipulate the learning of their employees and how employees please (or otherwise) their employers.

There are widely accepted criticisms of the behavioural approach. By focusing on observable behaviour, particularly in animals, the behavioural approach only provides a partial view of learning in humans. It does not explore those areas which are 'particular and special to humans' (Mullins 1999, p361) such as personality, desire, free will and incidental/accidental learning. It is also important to note in the context of these criticisms that behaviourist psychology was not primarily focused on producing a theory of learning. The goal was more ambitious in seeking an explanation of animal behaviour, including that of humans. The basic argument of behaviourism is that behaviour is learned, and the process of learning behaviour is through application of the 'law of effect' and 'operant conditioning'.

2.3.1.2 Cognitive approach, cybernetics and constructivism

The cognitive approach is multi-disciplinary, spanning psychology, anthropology and linguistics and is rooted in Gestalt psychology (developed in Germany in the early twentieth century). It is an attempt to explain and understand learning through the internal workings of the mind. Cognitive theories focus on the conscious mind (unlike behaviourist theories which focus only on what can be observed and measured or psychoanalytic theories that focus on the unconscious mind). Under a cognitive approach, learning involves the transformation of information gained from the environment into knowledge that is stored in the mind. Cognitive psychologists are interested in the brain as an information processing system that can produce high-quality knowledge (Harrison 2009), studying internal 'human' processes including perception, attention, language, memory and thinking.

A current example of the cognitive approach is the tool many organisations use to develop their improvement teams, training staff in the skills of Six Sigma and Lean improvement initiatives. Many organisations are now recognising the benefits of developing staff with specific improvement skill sets so they can lead improvement initiatives and also help people within their organisations become Green Belt and Black Belt Lean practitioners. These training programmes are seen by many organisations (eg GE and Unipart) as key investments in skills development engineered specifically to improve the organisation's performance and profitability. Much of this is built on the work of the quality gurus (eg Deming 1986) and the Toyota Motor Company.

Taylor and MacKenney (2008) propose that cognitive learning theory can be separated into four classes: behavioural, developmental, information processing, and linguistic orientation.

From a behavioural perspective, Estes (1961) and Bower (1961) showed that a simple conditioning model could demonstrate paired-associate learning, which involves learning a sequence of information in the correct order. Such work draws on S–R theory (from the behavioural approach) but focuses on the internal workings of the mind rather than observation so falls under the heading of cognitive learning theory.

Developmental theory can be represented by two significant early cognitive psychologists, Jean Piaget (1896–1980) and Lev Vygotsky (1896–1934). Their research is complex, extensive and focused on a child's active construction of understanding. Their work highlighted the importance of examining changes in children's thinking at various stages of their development.

From an information processing theory (IPM) perspective, theorists tend to view the computer as a metaphor for human mental activity (Newell et al 1958; Feigenbaum and Feldman 1963). In broad terms, the difference between the information-processing approach and Piaget's developmental approach is that Piaget had primarily been concerned with the characterisation of tasks and the sequence in which the child learns to solve these tasks; in contrast, the information-processing approach has been concerned with the processing apparatus necessary to handle even the most elementary forms of cognition (Taylor and MacKenney 2008). The most important feature of the information-processing approach has been the attempt to simulate by a computer program the detailed processing in which a human subject engages in problem-solving (ibid).

Information processing theory is often associated with the learning of skills. For example, when we learn to drive a car, this usually starts slowly, learning how to control the impact of steering effectively. As the driver turns the steering wheel, the effect this has allows the driver to adjust their actions to correct any over- or under-steering they may have undertaken. This monitoring and information feedback to the driver is important and becomes part of the learning. As the driver gains experience, this allows the driver to steer more accurately, increase the speed of the car and drive more effectively. As the driver becomes more proficient, she/he can make judgements on the road about her/his speed and make sure that she/he is not driving too fast or too slowly when negotiating bends and corners (Reid et al 2007). In an organisational context many skill-based apprenticeships rely heavily on this type of learning to ensure employees learn these skills. For example, in the manufacturing sector, the skills necessary to learn machining or hand craft skills are important examples of this type of skills development.

Within information processing theory, cognition may be divided into a number of stages (Sadler-Smith 2006, p107):

- input processing (ie attention and pattern recognition in the sensory register)
- temporary storage and active processing (ie in a short-term or working memory)
- encoding and more-or-less permanent storage (ie in the long-term memory)
- output (ie manifested in problem-solving, reasoning and language).

This theory offers detailed descriptions of cognitive processes through analysing the four main types of feedback:

- intrinsic feedback (information that comes from within bodies such as muscles, skin and balance)
- extrinsic feedback (information that comes from the environment such as visual and auditory stimuli)
- concurrent feedback (information that arrives during behaviour and is used to control behaviour as it occurs)
- delayed feedback (information that is received after having completed a task and is used to influence future performance).

Information processing research has evolved in two different ways, into cybernetics and into constructivism. These are not really opposing but serve different disciplines with their own needs for knowledge: the first is a 'scientific' framework for understanding organisation, pattern, and communication in animals and machines; the second is a subjectivist framework for understanding how different learners engage differently and uniquely with knowledge.

In constructivism, perhaps more relevant to workplace learning, contemporary cognitive learning theorists appreciate that individuals do not just take in information at face value but they negotiate with and make sense of information (Taylor and MacKenney 2008; Ormrod 2011). Learning is a process of actively constructing knowledge rather than passively absorbing information through the five senses (Collins and Green 1992; Driver 1995; Taylor and MacKenney 2008). Individuals receive and react to information through individual and social (collective) constructivism.

The cognitive approach attracts criticism in the research literature. Whilst rich and interesting, it can be complex, vague and difficult to research. Its focus on learning as an individual mental event ignores social processes and embodiment, and its treatment of teaching as a technical-rational activity ignores the element of reflective practice and artistry involved (Jordan et al 2008).

REFLECTIVE ACTIVITY 2.2

Thinking back to your personal theory of how people learn, assess whether it is closer to the behaviourism or cognitive approach.

Do you now want or need to revise your personal theory?

2.3.1.3 Social learning theory

Developed from the behavioural approach, social learning theory (Bandura 1977a) proposes that learning cannot be considered a purely individual activity; rather it is situated in social institutions, social groups and social class. According to Bandura (1977a, 1986) individuals, their behaviours and their social environment are dynamically bound together in a process of reciprocal determinism. Social learning theory argues that correct (and incorrect) behaviours are learned through experience and through the examples of others. Central to this theory is a learner's capabilities for reflection and self-determination (Bandura 1977a). Socialisation is accomplished without intentional intervention, by giving rewards such as praise, encouragement and recognition for correct behaviour. It is also achieved by negative reinforcements and punishments, such as being excluded for unacceptable behaviour.

Jordan et al (2008) identify key ideas of social learning theory:

- Learning does not occur in isolation; it is socially constructed.
- Learning has both sociological and psychological implications.
- Society regulates social life through institutions and systems.
- Learning is a process of socialisation mediated through membership of various groups. Education reproduces class and structural inequalities in society (Bandura 1986).
- Intra- and inter-group processes are important in forming individual identity.
- There is a dynamic relationship between individual self-esteem, the social environment and the learner's action.
- There is a tension between structure (the extent to which societal structures shape individuals) and agency (the extent to which individuals determine their own destiny) (p79).

EXERCISE 2.2

1   Compare and contrast the theories as explained in the text. Identify the main similarities and differences.

2   Derive a list of at least five principles of learning that are supported by each of the theories.

3   Consider how the five principles can be applied to produce effective designs and delivery of learning interventions.

4   Discuss the results of question 3 with colleagues and produce an agreed

list of principles to apply in designing and delivering learning interventions.

5   Consider and identify with your colleagues the implications of these principles for the roles of various people in facilitating learning: eg individual employees; their colleagues; their line managers; professional HRD staff.

2.3.2 CONTEMPORARY THEORIES OF INDIVIDUAL LEARNING

As Iphofen (1998) states, the theorisation of learning has progressed from basic stimulus-response ideas towards interest in more authentic accounts produced in learning dialogues. Organisational and HRM researchers suggest that traditional approaches may be appropriate to instructional situations such as school education, but are not as appropriate for adult learning in and at work, partly due to the nature of adult learning and partly due to the nature of the work environment (Harrison 1997; Gibb 2008; Marchington and Wilkinson 2012). So, new and alternative theories have been developed.

2.3.2.1 Andragogy

Andragogy emerged in the late 1970s as a response to criticisms of traditional theories (Knowles et al 1998). It is a set of core adult learning principles that apply to all adult learning situations (Knowles et al 2011), but these approaches can be contextualised for various adult learning purposes (such as workplace training).

Knowles et al (2005, p39), drawing on the much earlier work of Lindeman (1926), propose the foundations of adult learning theory as follows:

1   Adults are motivated to learn as they experience needs and interests that learning will satisfy; therefore, these are the appropriate starting points for organising adult learning activities.

2   Adults' orientation to learning is life-centred; therefore, the appropriate units for organising adult learning are life situations, not subjects.

3   Experience is the richest resource for adults' learning; therefore, the core methodology of adult education is the analysis of experience.

4   Adults have a deep need to be self-directing; therefore, the role of the teacher is to engage in a process of mutual inquiry with them rather than to transmit his or her knowledge to them and then evaluate their conformity to it.

5   Individual differences among people increase with age; therefore, adult education must make optimal provision for differences in style, time, place, and pace of learning.

The three dimensions of adult learning theory in practice are: (1) goals and purposes for learning; (2) individual and situation differences; and (3) andragogy. In practical terms, andragogy means that instruction for adults needs to focus more on the process and less on the content being taught. Strategies such as case studies, role-playing, simulations, and self-evaluation are most useful, and instructors adopt a role of facilitator or resource rather than lecturer or grader.

2.3.2.2 Experiential approach

A key premise of andragogy is experience; experience (including mistakes) provides the basis for learning activities. Experiential learning views learning as a cycle whereby the learner is proactively involved in 'constructive learning'. This constructive learning occurs through experience and discovery (Gibb 2002, p87). The proactive nature of experiential learning is seen as a way of embracing the diverse needs of adult learners by directly integrating the learner with their learning.

Rogers (1969) was one of the earliest advocators of experiential learning. His research identifies four components of experiential learning: personal involvement, self-initiation, pervasiveness and evaluation by the learner (p5). Rogers proposes that there is a need to create *communities of learners*, where the educator is *facilitating* change and learning, *not* instructing learners. More recently Kolb et al (1984) (see also Osland et al 2007) contribute an experiential cycle to the literature, as illustrated in Figure 2.3. This cycle has become extremely popular in management and organisational behaviour texts as well as in practice.

Figure 2.3 Experiential learning cycle (Kolb et al 1984, p49)

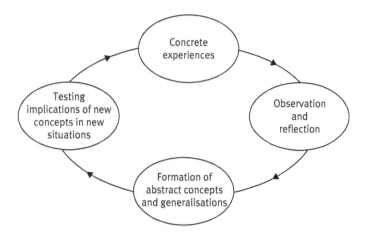

Kolb et al's (1984) experiential cycle has certain characteristics (p50). It has no specific starting point, and no specific ending point. Learning is individual both in its direction and in its process. For learning to occur, the four stages of the cycle must be completed. The direction of learning is governed by the learner's needs and goals, but needs to be clarified to prevent learning from becoming erratic and inefficient.

As shown in Figure 2.3, there are four stages to this cycle.

- The *concrete experience* stage is based on the learner's perception of the objective world and can be planned or accidental.
- *Reflective observation* is when the learner actively thinks about this experience, its basic issues and its significance.
- The *abstract conceptualisation* stage is when the learner generalises from their reflections, and analyses this in order to develop ideas, theory or principles which they

can then apply to other, similar problems or situations. This subsequently leads to more successful behaviours in these situations.

- Finally the *active experimentation* stage is when the learner tests the implications of their learning (such as new concepts) in new situations. This creates new concrete experience, and so the cycle begins again.

An example of this approach is where individuals in organisations are required to use learning logs to reflect on their experiences and what they have learned. Organisations that run apprenticeship schemes will need their apprentices to keep learning logs and also complete assessments which require them to reflect on what they have learned and give examples of this learning within the context of the subject area of the apprenticeship scheme. Also many professional institutes, including the CIPD, now insist that their members keep learning logs and develop continuous improvement plans.

Harrison (1988) criticises this cycle for providing an oversimplified explanation of the learning process. However, it highlights the importance of reflection and internalisation (Mullins 2013) and emphasises the significance of the combination of an individual's behaviour and the evaluation of their actions.

 REFLECTIVE ACTIVITY 2.3

Think again about the recent learning experience you identified earlier. Does the process of learning you experienced reflect what is described by experiential learning theory? If so, do you now want or need to revise your personal theory? If not, can you identify weaknesses in experiential learning theory based on your experience of learning?

2.3.2.3 Learning styles

Kolb's experiential cycle, which shows *how* the learning process may occur in individuals, has been further developed into a learning styles instrument, which attempts to classify learners into four learning style categories. Others have also proposed learning styles instruments, including Honey and Mumford (1992). Figure 2.4 compares the Kolb et al (1984) and Honey and Mumford (1992) instruments. Kolb's concrete experience is very similar to Honey and Mumford's activists; likewise reflective observation is similar to reflectors, abstract conceptualisation is similar to theorists, and active experimentation is similar to pragmatist.

Honey and Mumford's questionnaire is a self-development tool that individuals can use to identify specific work-related behaviours. Unlike Kolb et al's, it does not ask managers how they learn. Managers are encouraged to focus on strengthening weaker styles in order to realise a greater learning potential (Honey and Mumford 2006). Both instruments, however, highlight differences in learners and learning style combinations and provide a greater understanding of teaching and learning techniques in workplace learning. Some have commented that these categories are idealistic, reductionist and are not representative of real learners. Marchington and Wilkinson (2012) argue that the 'reality' is that learners are usually a combination of the different types. These tools are useful though for generating an awareness of the potential differences in the way people learn and this understanding is insightful and enriching in itself.

Figure 2.4 Comparing experiential instruments

Learning Styles Inventory (Kolb et al 1984)	Learning Styles Questionnaire (Honey and Mumford 1992)
An orientation towards *concrete experience* means that individuals adopt an intuitive stance, relying upon their personal judgement rather than systematic analysis. These individuals enjoy relating to people, being involved in real situations, and adopt an open-minded approach to life.	*Activists* learn best by active involvement in concrete tasks, and from relatively short tasks such as business games and competitive teamwork exercises.
An orientation towards *reflective observation* leads individuals to view situations carefully, considering their meaning, and drawing out the implications of ideas. These people prefer to reflect on issues rather than acting, looking at questions from different points of view, and they value patient and thoughtful judgement.	*Reflectors* learn best by reviewing and reflecting upon what has happened in certain situations, where they are able to stand back, listen and observe.
An orientation towards *abstract conceptualisation* implies the learners emphasise the use of logic, ideas and concepts, opposing intuitive judgements. These individuals are good at systematic planning and quantitative analysis, and they value precise formulations and neat, conceptual systems.	*Theorists* learn best when new information can be located within the context of concepts and theories, and are able to absorb new ideas when they are distanced from real-life situations.
An orientation towards *active experimentation* means that the individual enjoys practical applications, active involvement in change, and pragmatic concern with what works in practice. Achieving results is important for this group of learners, and they value having an impact on their working environment.	*Pragmatists* learn best when they see a link between new information and real-life problems and issues, and from being exposed to techniques that can be applied immediately.

Source: developed from Kolb et al (1984, p50); Honey and Mumford (1992, pp175–177); Mullins (1999, p364); Marchington and Wilkinson (2000, p166)

EXERCISE 2.3

1   Compare and contrast the theories as explained in the text. Identify the main similarities and differences.

2   Derive a list of at least five principles of learning that are supported by each of the theories.

3   Consider how the five principles can be applied to produce effective designs and delivery of learning interventions.

4   Identify the implications of the principles for different people in organisations: eg employees, line managers, HR staff, HRD professionals.

5   Compare the results of Question 3 with those from Exercise 2.2.

6   Revise the results of Exercise 2.2 to produce a new list of five principles to apply in designing and delivering learning interventions.

7   Discuss the results of Question 5 with colleagues and produce an agreed list of principles to apply in designing and delivering learning interventions.

2.4 COLLECTIVE LEARNING

Some texts on individual learning state that the theory can also refer to collective learning (Harrison 2009; Marchington and Wilkinson 2012). Since groups comprise individuals, we agree that many aspects of individual learning can be applied to the collective. However, the relationships, dynamics and tensions within groups distinguish and complicate it beyond individual learning. Sadler-Smith (2006) defines collective learning as a term used to 'distinguish the learning that takes place at the supra-individual (ie above the individual) level. Collective learning can encompass dyads, teams, communities, networks, organizations and even whole societies' (p180). We categorise collective learning at group and organisational level.

2.4.1 GROUP-LEVEL LEARNING

Group learning is defined by Argote et al (2001) as '[t]he activities through which individuals acquire, share, and combine knowledge through experience with one another' (p370). It is a term used to include all forms of groups including formal, informal, planned, emergent, primary and secondary. Formal groups in a work context are often referred to and defined as teams. At a general level, groups can be personal, social, cultural or geographic. Groups can be work-related, including professional membership groups, formal work teams, informal communities of practice, and even virtual/technological groups. Group-level learning can be categorised as group learning and team learning. Before exploring these, we summarise key theories on group (or team) development in Figure 2.5, as it is helpful to have an overview of the issues and challenges of becoming and being a group that can ultimately affect successful learning at both collective and individual levels. Mohrman et al (1995) argue seven benefits of working within a group, while Steiner (1972) describes three forms of group task that require different capabilities from group members. Huczynski and Buchanan (2001, 2013) define formal and informal groups and describe how each may emerge. One of the most frequently cited and well-known theories on groups is Tuckman and Jensen's (1977) five stages of group development. Finally, Figure 2.5 illustrates some of the issues that a group may face (Cohen et al 1995).

2.4.1.1 Team learning theory

Pearn (1998) proposes that 'team learning links performing and learning, which includes the way teams select their vision and goals' (p139). Senge (1990) identifies team learning as one of five disciplines necessary to realise *a learning organisation*. Senge (1990) defines team learning as, 'the process of aligning and developing the capacity of a team to create the results its members truly desire' (p236). Senge argues there are two requirements for teams to learn effectively: shared vision (a vision that many people are committed to, because it reflects their own personal vision) and personal mastery (approaching one's life as a creative work). Both definitions see team learning as a process, and imply some degree of commonality of purpose.

Dechant et al (1993) propose an empirical 'dynamic open systems' model of team learning, illustrated in Figure 2.6. Collective thinking and action are at the heart of the model, along with four learning processes that are central to the learning system (p7). These are:

- Framing: the group's initial perception of an issue, situation, person, object etc based on past understanding and present input.
- Experimenting: group action taken to test hypotheses, discover and assess impact.
- Crossing boundaries: the team as a whole communicates and moves ideas, views or information between and among other people. Boundaries can be physical, mental or organisational.

Figure 2.5 Comparing group theory

Benefits of working within a group	Types of group task	Types of group	Stages of group development	Issues facing workgroup
(Mohrman et al 1995)	(Steiner 1972)	(Huczynski and Buchanan 2001, pp297–298)	(Tuckman and Jensen 1977)	(Cohen et al, 1995, p142)
Allows organisations to develop and deliver products and services quickly and cost-effectively while maintaining quality. Promotes improved quality management. Groups can undertake effective process reengineering. Production time can be reduced if tasks performed concurrently by individuals are performed concurrently by people in groups. Group-based organisations with flat structures can be monitored, co-ordinated and directed more effectively if the functional unit is the group rather than the individual. Groups can manage increased organisational information and knowledge better than individuals.	**Additive Task** Dependent on the sum of all the individual efforts within the group. **Conjunctive Task** Dependent on the effort and performance of the group's least capable member. **Disjunctive Task** Dependent on the group's most capable member.	**Formal Group** One which has been deliberately created to achieve some part of an organisation's collective purpose. **Informal Group** A collection of individuals who become a group when members develop interdependencies, influence one another's behaviour and contribute to mutual need satisfaction, eg community of practice.	**Forming** The orientation phase when individuals have not gelled. Members are dependent on some leader for structure and ground rules. Task-wise members seek orientation. **Storming** The conflict phase which involves members' bargaining with each other. The task function is organisation, and how best to organise to achieve the group's objective. **Norming** This is the cohesion stage when members develop closer relationships. Task-wise members are more open about goals and there is an increase in data flow. **Performing** At this stage the group's concern is with achieving the job in hand. Task-wise there is a high commitment to objectives. **Adjourning** This is the final stage. The group may disband due to achieving objectives or members leaving.	Atmosphere and relationships. Member participation. Goal understanding and acceptance. Listening and information-sharing. Handling disagreements and conflict. Decision-making. Evaluation of member performance. Expressing feelings. Division of labour. Leadership.

● Integrating perspectives: group members synthesise their divergent views such that apparent conflicts are resolved through dialectical thinking, not compromise or majority rule.

Their research proposes four learning phases that teams advance along (some advance further than others) based on the extent to which they utilise the four learning processes. The more they utilise the processes, the more they advanced in their collective development and learning towards an evolutionary pattern of learning processes. The phases are summarised in Figure 2.6.

Figure 2.6 Phases of team learning advancement, adapted from Dechant et al (1993)

Phase	Brief summary	Reframing	Experimentation	Information
Phase 1 Fragmented learning	Marks the start of a group's work together. Learning has not yet moved beyond the individual.	It is inhibited because members hold different frames or views and vary in commitment levels. Members are not typically open to reframing based on the perspectives of others.	Very little experimenting is done, few risks are taken.	Very few boundaries crossed although some information may be looked for and looked at in the process of task-setting.
Phase 2 Pooled learning	Clusters of individuals learn within groups. There are the beginnings of a collected pool of knowledge but little attempt to develop a collectively held and understood view.	Any reframing that occurs is mainly individual in nature; people may listen to others, but they are not as likely to change their own frameworks for understanding reality.	Experimenting is not the norm and done with caution.	Individuals may go outside the group to collect information and bring it back.
Phase 3 Synergistic learning	Members have evolved a language of shared meaning, including their own team models and metaphors.	Collective reframing is a characteristic of this phase. Meaning schemes are altered or discarded as a result of collective reframing among group members.	Group experimentation is a characteristic of this phase, particularly in high-risk levels of personal and social interaction for which there are no easily recognised rules.	When members cross boundaries, they interact with others in a two-way fashion.
Phase 4 Continuous learning	All team learning processes are used easily and regularly. Members' perspectives are easily integrated and evolved into consensual understanding.	Collective reframing has become the norm.	The team experiments individually and as a body within the larger organisation, thus extending learning to others.	The group has developed the habit of seeking out and valuing diversity, internally and externally, in order to broaden its perspective.

2.4.1.2 Group learning theory

Broadening the scope from team learning, Kasl et al (1993) develop four phases of *group* learning. They specifically chose the label 'group learning' as opposed to 'team learning' as their intention was 'to communicate the possibility that [their] model is applicable to groups who are not functioning as units of organizations, such as community action groups, research teams, self help groups' (pp143–144). However, their empirical study of two profit-oriented corporations helps us understand group learning in dynamic organisational-related contexts. Their four phases of group learning are (pp144–145):

- Phase 1: Contained learning: a group exists, but learning, if any, is contained within individual members.
- Phase 2: Collected learning: individuals begin to share information and meaning perspectives. Group knowledge is an aggregate of individual knowledge. There is not yet an experience of having knowledge that is uniquely the group's own.
- Phase 3: Constructed learning: the group creates knowledge of its own. Individuals' knowledge and meaning perspectives are integrated, not aggregated.
- Phase 4: Continuous learning: the group habituates processes of transforming its experience into knowledge.

Kasl et al (1993) describe these phases as being developmental to indicate progression and growth in learning – although groups have been known to regress. They propose that groups are propelled from one phase to the next when they meet the following conditions (p155):

- Groups move from the contained to the collected phase when particular learning conditions are present, including mutual trust, respect and regard among the participants, as well as the perception that association in the context of a group can bring personal benefit.
- Groups move from the collected to the constructed phase when members listen carefully and respectfully to each other, and understand each other with enough depth that multiple perspectives can be integrated to construct meaning.
- The energy that propels a group from constructed to continuous learning is created when the group frames its identity as a learning group, and becomes conscious of monitoring its processes as learning processes, rather than the processes of interpersonal interaction and role fulfilment that are described in the group dynamics literature.

With reference to their first proposition, Kasl et al (1993) identify mutual trust, respect and regard as necessary for movement. Others have discussed the importance of trust in team learning. Lawler (1992) implicated trust as being vital in the implementation of self-managed work teams and Edmondson (1999) showed that work groups with high levels of trust amongst their members are more likely to engage in learning behaviours than other groups.

 REFLECTIVE ACTIVITY 2.4

What examples of group learning can you identify from your own experience? Do these examples support or question theories of group learning?

2.4.1.3 Organisational-level learning

Whether organisations can actually learn is a widely debated question. Popper and Lipshitz (1998) refer to this as the problem of anthropomorphism in organisational learning, ie attributing human qualities to non-human entities. March and Olsen (1976) explain that learning implies thought and that the concept of organisational learning attributes human characteristics (learning) to organisational structures. Hedberg (1981) is persuasive in his argument for organisations as learning entities because '[even though] organizations do not have brains... they have cognitive systems and memories. As individuals develop their personalities, personal habits and beliefs over time, organizations develop world views and ideologies. Members come and go, and leadership changes, but organizations' memories preserve certain behaviours, mental maps, norms, and values over time' (p6).

Accepting the argument that organisations can learn, two streams of literature have developed since the late 1970s to understand this: organisational learning (OL) and the learning organisation (LO). There are several significant differences between these two sub-fields and it is important to be mindful of these as they have implications for designing, developing and evaluating learning within the workplace. For simplicity we have summarised the key differences in Figure 2.7.

Figure 2.7 Organisational learning versus learning organisation

	Organisational learning (OL)	Learning organisation (LO)
Characteristic definition	'Organisational learning means the process of improving actions through better knowledge and understanding' (Fiol and Lyles 1985, p803).	'A learning organization is one where people continually expand their capacity to create the results they truly desire, where new and expansive patterns of thinking are nurtured, where collective aspiration is set free, and where people are continually learning together' (Senge 1990, p3).
Nature of field	OL is an academic field of research that seeks to understand how learning processes occur at and within organisational settings (Easterby-Smith 1997; Tsang 1997).	LO is a practitioner/consultancy-based 'toolkit' that seeks to create an ideal type of organisation (Easterby-Smith 1997; Tsang 1997).
Type of contributors	Contributors are typically academic researchers (Easterby-Smith and Araujo 1999).	Contributors may be highly experienced (or lesser experienced) professionals, management consultants or 'gurus'.
Key theory and models	Describes a process, be it a process of improving actions, change or knowledge acquisition (Sun 2003). Models are descriptive and scientifically driven.	Prescribes a toolkit/intervention for working towards an ultimate organisational vision. Models are prescriptive, idealistic and intuitive, but can be insightful.
Dissemination	Research is usually disseminated via peer-reviewed academic journals, conferences and lectures.	Usually disseminated through paid consultancy, 'self-help' books, personal or consultancy blogs/websites, etc.
Impact on design, development and evaluation of learning	Less impact but design of learning interventions can take account of organisational learning processes to enhance those.	More impact through prescriptions and recommendations for interventions to promote and achieve learning organisation state.

2.4.2 ORGANISATIONAL LEARNING

There is a wide range of theories and models of organisational learning. Models vary from simple levels of organisational learning to complex feedback cycles, and according to whether they have been informed by the traditional or more contemporary individual learning theories that we discussed earlier in the chapter.

2.4.2.1 Cyclical model of organisational learning

March and Olsen (1976) were among the earliest contributors to organisational learning theory. Their four-stage cyclical model linked individual beliefs (stage 1) to triggering individual action (stage 2). Organisational learning begins when the individual's actions contribute to organisational action (stage 3). An organisation's actions are shown to induce environmental responses (stage 4). Environmental responses are conveyed back to the organisation, which in turn alters individuals' cognitive maps, and therefore influences individuals' future actions. Importantly, March and Olsen's model addressed the issue of incomplete learning cycles. They identified four cases that weaken or break the learning cycle:

- Role-constrained learning (this can occur when individual learning has no effect on individual action, due to the constraints on the individual's role).
- Audience learning (this can occur when the individual affects organisational action in an ambiguous way).
- Superstitious learning (this can occur when the link between organisational action and environmental response is broken).
- Learning under ambiguity (occurs when the individual affects organisational action, which in turn affects the environment, but the connections among the events are not clear).

2.4.2.2 Single-loop and double-loop organisational learning

Argyris and Schön (1978) offer one of the most well-known organisational learning models. This draws upon ideas from cybernetic cognitive learning theory discussed earlier. In cybernetics, the notion of feedback is a critical component of learning, and Argyris and Schön extend the idea of feedback to the organisational level. Argyris and Schön (1978) viewed learning as occurring under two instances. First, when an organisation achieves what it initially set out to achieve, there is a 'match between its design for action and actuality of outcome' (Argyris and Schön 1995, p8). Second, when something goes wrong but is rectified, 'a mismatch is turned into a match'.

Single-loop learning occurs when either matches are created, or when mismatches are detected and then corrected by changing some actions, which in turn alter consequences to create matches. Single-loop learning occurs within the set of existing governing variables. Governing variables, which reflect an organisation's values, heavily influence a desired outcome and create certain limitations on how the desired outcome can be achieved. Simply stated, single-loop learning is concerned with accepting change without questioning underlying assumptions and core beliefs.

Double-loop learning occurs through altering the organisation's governing variables. Here, mismatches are identified and then, through altering governing variables, actions are altered to correct mismatches. As Harrison (1988) explains, double-loop learning is 'concerned to question why [a] problem arose in the first place and tackle its root causes' (p238). Argyris (1999) emphasises that single- and double-loop learning only occur when the solution to a problem has actually been produced.

Deutero-learning is the highest level of learning in Argyris and Schön's typology, and can be described as the ways in which an organisation develops the ability to pre-empt changes in its environment (Birdthistle 2003), and learns how to learn (Worrel 1995).

Deutero-learning is concerned with the why and the how of changing the organisation. Deutero-learning facilitates the learning and improving of organisational processes through building on the single-loop and double-loop learning processes. Argyris and Schön acknowledge that learning in organisations is normally restricted to single-loop learning, and not double-loop learning. They also suggest that deutero-learning is predominantly used for reflection about single-loop learning and not double-loop learning.

Argyris and Schön are not unique in offering a typology of learning levels. Figure 2.8 (adapted from Fiol and Lyles 1985, and Perin and Sampaio 2003) shows the many different contributions which have separated organisational learning into three levels. Despite varying terminology, these have many similarities.

Figure 2.8 Typologies of levels of learning

Author/s	Three Levels of Learning		
Bateson (1973)	Learning level I	Learning level II	Deutero-learning
Argyris and Schön (1978)	Single-loop learning	Double-loop learning	Deutero-learning
Hedberg (1981)	Adjustment learning	Turnover learning	Turnaround learning
Shrivastava (1983)	Adaptive learning	Assumption-sharing	Development of knowledge base
Fiol and Lyes (1985)	Lower-level learning	Higher-level learning	
Pautzke (1989)	Raising effectiveness	Learning from experience	Change in knowledge structures
Garratt (1990)	Operational learning cycle	Policy learning cycle	Integrated learning cycle
Klimecki et al (1991)	Improvement learning	Change learning	Learning to learn
Sattelberger (1991)	Organisational change	Organisational development	Organisational transformation
Staehle (1991)	Assimilation	Accommodation	Equilibration
Pawlowsky (1992)	Idiosyncratic learning	Adaptation to environment	Learning to solve problems
Morgan (1986)	Single-loop	Double-loop	Holographic learning
Probst and Buchel (1997)	Adaptive learning	Reconstructive learning	Process learning

2.4.2.3 The 4I framework of organisational learning

Crossan et al (1999) propose a cyclical model with feedback and feed forwards pathways. Their 4I framework is dynamic in that it links individual (cognition) with group (socialisation) and organisation (institutionalisation) levels. It also links four micro processes (intuiting, interpreting, integrating and institutionalising – the 4I's) to three organisational levels (individual, group and organisation). Crossan et al view organisational learning as the principal means of achieving strategic renewal within an enterprise and their interest in strategic renewal is the underlying reason for the development of their framework.

Their framework is based on four key premises. Firstly, organisational learning involves a tension between assimilating new learning (exploration) and using what has been learned (exploitation). Secondly, OL is multi-level (individual, group and organisational). Thirdly, the four social and psychological processes of intuiting, interpreting, integrating and institutionalising link the three levels of OL. Finally, cognition affects action and vice versa (p523). Figure 2.9 summarises the four processes, the levels at which they occur, and the input and outcomes of the learning processes identified by Crossan et al (1999).

Figure 2.9 4I processes

Level	Description of 'I' Process	Inputs/Outcomes
Individual	**Intuiting:** The pre-conscious recognition of the pattern and/or possibilities inherent in a personal stream of experience. This process can affect the intuitive individual's behaviour, but it only affects others as they attempt to (inter)act with that individual.	Experiences Images Metaphors
Group	**Interpreting:** The explaining of an insight or idea to oneself and to others. This process goes from the pre-verbal and requires the development of language.	Language Cognitive map Conversation/dialogue
Group	**Integrating:** The process of developing shared understanding amongst individuals and the taking of coordinated action through mutual adjustment. Dialogue and joint action are crucial to the development of shared understanding. This process will initially be ad hoc and informal, but if the co-ordinated action-taking is recurring and significant it will become institutionalised.	Shared understandings Mutual adjustment Interactive systems
Organisation	**Institutionalising:** The process of ensuring that routine actions occur. Tasks are defined, actions specified and organisational mechanisms put in place to ensure that certain actions occur. Institutionalising is the process of embedding learning that has occurred at individual and group level into the institutions of the organisation, including systems, structures, procedures and strategy.	Routines Diagnostic systems Rules and procedures

Source: derived from Crossan et al (1999, p525); Crossan and Hulland (2002, p1090)

 REFLECTIVE ACTIVITY 2.5

Think about and analyse your current/recent experience of working in an organisation. Can you identify any examples of organisational learning? What were the circumstances and how do you know organisational learning occurred? If you cannot identify any examples, can you say organisational learning never occurred? Try to justify that statement.

Lawrence et al (2005) introduce the role of social political processes into Crossan et al's model of organisational learning. They link *episodic power* (discrete, strategic political acts initiated by self-interested actors) to interpreting and integrating stages, and *systemic power* (routine, ongoing organisational practices) to institutionalising and intuiting stages; see Figure 2.10.

Figure 2.10 The politics of organisational learning

Process	Interpretation	Integration	Institutionalisation	Intuition
Key requirements	Managing ambiguity and uncertainty in the adoption of language and the construction of cognitive maps.	Translating new ideas consistently across members in order to achieve collective action.	Overcoming the resistance to change of organisational members.	Developing organisational members with experience and identities that facilitate expert-level pattern recognition.
Associated forms of power	Influence	Force	Domination	Discipline
Mode	Episodic	Episodic	Systemic	Systemic
How it works	Affecting costs/ benefits of behaviours	Restricting available behaviours	Restricting available behaviours	Affecting costs/ benefits of behaviours
Examples	Moral persuasion Negotiation Ingratiation	Agenda-setting Limiting decision alternative Removing opponents	Material technologies Information systems Physical layout	Socialisation Training Team-based work

Source: adapted from Lawrence et al (2005, p185)

CASE STUDY 2.1

Sheila Ghosh is an HRD Manager currently tasked with designing and managing implementation of learning and development interventions to support a change programme intended to deliver improved customer service in her organisation. This is a regional brewing company with just over 1,500 staff. The majority of these, nearly 80%, work in retail operations managing and delivering services to the 'eating and drinking public'. Retail operations consist of managed and tenanted pubs and restaurants. The remainder of the staff work in head office, which consists of the brewing operation, a 'free sales' department and central functions such as finance, IT, logistics and HR. The company has high commitment to learning and development from everyone up to and including board level. It has achieved IIP Gold and at the last reckoning invested 7% of total payroll expenditure in learning and development.

The HRD function is well resourced with professionally qualified staff and learning facilities, which include a training pub at head office and an intranet supporting a learning platform with extensive online resources.

The improving customer service strategy has made extensive progress in developing sets of specified service standards. These standards cover every function in the company and define service levels for internal as well as external customers. So, the learning interventions have to cover and be relevant to all employees in the company, including senior managers as well as front-line servers in retail operations. Sheila knows that whatever she designs and delivers has to go beyond simply communicating the agreed service standards to also produce commitment to meeting them among the majority of staff.

Questions

1 What principles of facilitating learning can Sheila apply in designing appropriate learning interventions to meet the broad objectives of the interventions?

2 What role and contribution should Sheila expect and/or require from employees, managers, HR staff and her HRD professional colleagues in designing and delivering these learning interventions? How should these contributions affect and shape the design and delivery of the interventions?

3 What indicators of success should Sheila plan to use in evaluating the learning interventions?

Although Lawrence et al (2005) believe power (of type: influence, force, discipline, and domination) is omnipresent in an organisation, their model represents the combination that is *most likely* to facilitate organisational learning. Interestingly, an important implication raised is the need for a more nuanced understanding of the roles of the (innovation) champion for organisational learning – different champions (with different skills) may be required for different levels because of the various political dimensions. Lawrence et al (2005) conclude that 'managers must recognise that organisational politics and organisational learning are not antithetical; in order to learn, organisations need active, interested members who are willing to engage in political behaviour and that pushes ideas forward and ensures their interpretation, integration, and institutionalisation; without political behaviour, new ideas may be generated by individuals, but organisations will never learn' (p 190).

EXERCISE 2.4

1 Review the arguments on collective learning explained so far and answer the following questions.

(a) What are the areas of similarity and difference between the various accounts/theories/models?

(b) How does each of them relate to and connect with the theories of individual learning examined earlier?

(c) Which in your view seems the most valid? And provides the most utility?

(d) What are the implications of your chosen account/theory/model for designing and delivering learning interventions?

(e) What are the implications for various roles in organisations, eg management and HR professionals?

2 Discuss your response to Questions 1(d) and 1(e) with some colleagues.

3 Agree a set of principles on collective learning that can be usefully applied in design and delivery of learning interventions.

2.5 WORKPLACE LEARNING THEORY

According to Harrison (2005), in the past the terms 'training and development', 'employee development', and 'human resource development' have been used to describe what she refers to as the learning and development field. To summarise her critique of these terms (p5):

- Training and development – is still popular; however, training is only one way of achieving development.
- Employee development – is politically incorrect because it implies power inequity: 'master-servant' relationship.

- Human resource development – is popular amongst academics but has never caught on amongst practitioners, possibly because referring to people as resources is viewed negatively.

However, Harrison also suggests that 'learning and development' is not necessarily the definitive solution as 'what is gained in scope is lost in generalisation' (p5). She defines [workplace] learning and development as an organisational process to aid the development of knowledge and the achievement of organisational and individual goals.

2.5.1 SPACES AND FORMS OF WORKPLACE LEARNING

Vaughan (2008) suggests that when it comes to workplace learning, there is potential for two different directions. The first draws on traditional individual learning theory, focusing on the articulation between education and work in order to recognise and provide credentials for all forms of learning. Second, it draws on experiential, collective and social learning theory, focusing on the workplace as a learning environment where learning is a process embedded in production and organisational structures and is therefore about participation in communities of practice. However, she and others (eg Mitchell et al 2001) suggest that a combination of both approaches through an ongoing refinement and extension of theories and approaches would be the ideal.

Sambrook (2006) discusses the spaces for workplace learning. She identifies important differences between learning *at* work, learning *in* work and learning *outside* of work. She states that learning may occur *outside* of work, *at* the place of work, or embedded (with)*in* work processes, as shown in Figure 2.11.

Figure 2.11 Learning outside, at and in work

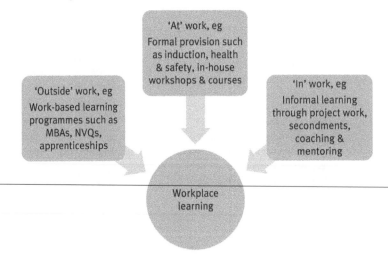

Source: adapted from Sambrook (2006, p98)

Learning outside of work tends to occur at universities, technical colleges and private training centres. Sambrook (2006) further suggests that there is some degree of overlap between learning outside of work and learning *at* work. Although content of university courses etc is delivered outside of the workplace, some of the experiential learning and sense-making occurs back at the workplace. Both learning outside of work and at work are more formal, explicit and deliberate learning activities whilst learning *in* work is more informal, implicit and accidental (sometimes referred to as learning on the job), and is hidden within the process of working.

Complementing Sambrook's work, Vaughan (2008) offers an extensive (but not exhaustive) description of forms of workplace learning (p4):

- Off-the-job training where learning assignments are related to problem-solving and task-centred activities linked to the strategic business intent of the organisation.
- Structured learning in the workplace (alternance), managed and validated by external educational providers in partnership with employers/managers/supervisors, learning professionals, and worker-learners.
- Informal, pervasive learning that forms the foundations of the context informing work practices, routines and behaviours so that communities are formed or joined and personal identities are changed.
- Forms of intentional, structured and organised learning on the job that have an explicit pedagogic strategy. These aim to develop competencies of employees by supporting, structuring and monitoring their learning through different principles such as:
    - Structuring of workplace learning into the workplace – such as job rotation, sequencing of learners' activities, increasing variety and complexity of work tasks, creating opportunities for learner awareness of skill and performance.
    - Participative modes of action-reflection – such as a group working together for certain periods of time and focused on work-based issues brought by each individual to the group; new ways of thinking about feedback, questioning, talking, reflecting, and making sense of experience; individuals sharing their learning with others in the team and that shared learning being used to make changes in the organisation.
    - Social learning and mutual construction of knowledge and critical awareness of worker roles.

Informed by Sambrook (2006) and some of her earlier contributions (Sambrook and Betts 2001; Sambrook 2003) we deliberately refer to the all-encompassing term 'workplace learning' rather than, arguably, misusing the narrower terms learning at/in work. Indeed, these 'boundaries' are increasingly blurred with the escalating use of online and mobile learning resources.

2.5.2 TECHNOLOGY AND WORKPLACE LEARNING

Sambrook (2006) identifies the importance of information and communication technologies (ICTs) in providing yet another space for learning outside, at and in work. These can include distance education through online degree programmes (outside work), formal courses on a company intranet (at work) and use of social media sites such as Twitter and Facebook to facilitate knowledge-sharing and other interactions between team members who are geographically separated (in work).

2.5.3 DESCRIPTIVE MODELS OF WORKPLACE LEARNING

There are few descriptive models (depicting what actually happens), given the tendency for prescriptive models that, arguably, lend themselves more conveniently to tools for planning and designing workplace learning. This said, drawing on two research projects, Sambrook's (2006) empirical model of workplace learning shown in Figure 2.12 is comprehensive and holistic, and in particular focuses on the links between workplace learning and ICT-based learning.

The model highlights the sheer intricacy of workplace learning. First, it identifies factors at organisational, functional and individual levels, illuminating the complex combinations of soft (cultural), hard (structural, technological) and human organisational processes and functions (eg motivation, trust, resources) that can play a role in workplace learning success. It then identifies factors influencing the design and delivery of effective learning interventions in general, followed by learning materials themselves and then specifically ICT-based learning materials.

Figure 2.12 A descriptive model of workplace learning

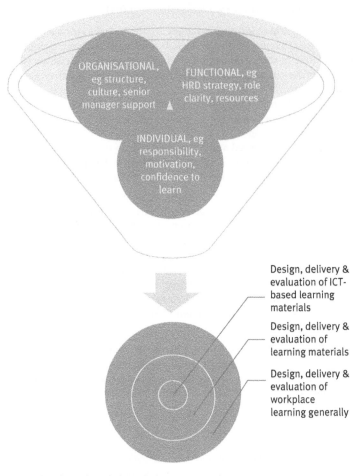

ORGANISATIONAL, eg structure, culture, senior manager support

FUNCTIONAL, eg HRD strategy, role clarity, resources

INDIVIDUAL, eg responsibility, motivation, confidence to learn

Design, delivery & evaluation of ICT-based learning materials

Design, delivery & evaluation of learning materials

Design, delivery & evaluation of workplace learning generally

Source: adapted from Sambrook (2006)

EXERCISE 2.5

In the context of your organisation's requirements (it may be appropriate to consider a departmental perspective), develop an appropriate learning plan for the next two years. Include the following in your development plan:

- learning required, eg health and safety training for all staff members, leadership development
- level required, eg whether the training addresses individual, group and/or team learning
- method of learning, eg in work, at work, outside work, formal or informal learning
- learning theory associated with the training need, eg behavioural, cognitive, social, experiential etc
- learning style, eg assess how this is likely to be relevant, considering Kolb's or Honey and Mumford's theories
- outcomes, eg how do these contribute to achieving the organisation's overall business objectives?

2.5.4 PRESCRIPTIVE MODELS FOR WORKPLACE LEARNING

There are various prescriptive, normative models for workplace learning. For example, Vaughan (2008) prescribes structures and climate for workplace learning and states that workplace learning works best when (p24):

- workplace learning is aligned with or reflects the (desired) workplace culture
- the strategic directions of the business and the nature of its challenges and opportunities are reflected in the aims and processes of workplace learning
- learning is adequately resourced with the right people and the right tools
- the organisation is committed to everyone's learning
- there is sufficient time for learning to be meaningful
- innovation and thoughtful risk-taking are encouraged
- opportunities to learn are part of everyday work (not add-ons)
- formal and informal learning are integrated
- learning is recognised
- talent is identified and nourished.

EXERCISE 2.6

1   Review the arguments on workplace learning and answer the following questions.

   (a)   Which theory/model in your view seems the most valid? And provides the most utility?

   (b)   What are the implications of your chosen theory/model for designing and delivering learning interventions?

   (c)   What are the implications for the role and contribution of various people in facilitating learning, eg managers and HR professionals?

2   Discuss your responses to Questions 1(b) and 1(c) with some colleagues.

3   Agree a set of principles on workplace learning that can be usefully applied in design and delivery of learning interventions.

4   With your colleagues, compare the results of Question 3 with the results of Exercise 2.4.

5   Produce an agreed list of principles on collective learning to apply in designing and delivering learning interventions.

2.6 CONCLUSION

This chapter has shown that there are various theories that seek to explain and understand learning. These theories examine learning at varying levels: the individual, the group and the organisation. At each level there are disagreements and differences as well as agreement and similarities in the explanations and understanding advanced by the various theories. So, we can conclude that there is no single right or correct theory of learning at any level. However, there is probably enough agreement and similarity to enable some useful if not necessarily proven general principles to be applied in designing, delivering and evaluating learning and development. These principles are likely to be significant and have varying application at each level, ie what will help learning at the individual level might not be relevant at the group or organisational level. So, learning and development interventions have to take account of each and every level if they are to be fully effective. They also have to involve and maximise the contribution of various roles in organisations. These include individual employees, line managers, HRD professionals and

HR staff. Overall, we can say that learning is not yet well enough understood for HRD professionals to ever guarantee the outcomes of learning and development interventions and so to be able to say that learning interventions will always directly contribute to achieving desired or set organisation objectives. However, learning is well enough understood for HRD professionals to take account of and apply learning theory when designing and delivering learning and development interventions.

CASE STUDY 2.2

Rajesh Khan is the owner-manager of Books4U, a small but rapidly growing company that supplies discounted books over the Internet. Books4U is located in a small business park on the edge of a small city in a rural area. Rajesh established the organisation three years ago, initially with just four employees, two of whom are now Team Leaders. Today, the company employs around 30 staff, with 10 working on a part-time basis to suit their domestic arrangements.

Business has recently been expanding and this had led to a period of overtime for full-time employees and asking part-time employees to work extra hours. This is causing some difficulty for them, as mentioned by one or two of the longest-serving staff, but they are committed to this exciting, growing company and have asked the owner-manager to consider employing more staff, even on a temporary basis. However, the local labour market lacks the IT and Internet customer service skills Rajesh's employees require and hiring new recruits will result in the need for training and development. As existing staff are so pressured to meet tight deadlines for delivery, it will be difficult for them to train new recruits. Tensions are rising, mistakes are increasingly being made and staff are leaving, taking valuable knowledge with them.

Rajesh set up Books4U to provide a steady income without having to work excessive hours – his vision was more for quality of working life for himself and his employees rather than dreams of rapid expansion and growth. He is not sure he wants to expand any further but the current level of staffing cannot cope with demand. As the business grows, Rajesh is increasingly involved in more strategic decisions, dealing with financial matters, and has less time to focus on important HR issues.

Questions

1   What types of individual and collective learning are required for existing and new employees to meet the business needs?

2   Given the current business situation, what types of learning might be required to assist succession planning and management development of the Team Leaders?

3   Draw up a learning plan to help deliver the business strategy.

4   Advise Rajesh on how to manage learning within his company.

EXPLORE FURTHER

HISLOP, D. (2013) *Knowledge management in organizations: a critical introduction.* 3rd ed. New York: Oxford University Press.

HONEY, P. and MUMFORD, A. (2006) *The learning styles questionnaire, 80-item version.* Maidenhead: Peter Honey Publications.

ILLERIS, K. (2011) *The fundamentals of workplace learning: understanding how people learn in working life.* London: Routledge.

KNOWLES, M.S., HOLTON III, E.F. and SWANSON, R.A. (2011) *The adult learner.* 7th ed. London: Elsevier.

SADLER-SMITH, E. (2006) *Learning and development for managers: perspectives from research and practice.* London: Blackwell Publishing.

STEWART, J. and RIGG, C. (2011) *Learning and talent development.* London: CIPD.

CHAPTER 3

The External and Internal Context

AMANDA LEE, SOPHIE MILLS AND DALBIR SIDHU

LEARNING OUTCOMES

By the end of this chapter you will be able to:

- explain, evaluate and critically analyse the role of external and internal factors and their impact on the design, delivery and assessment of learning plans and interventions in organisations
- outline developments in information and communication technologies (ICT) and examine the opportunities and limitations they present for the design and delivery of learning
- examine barriers, inhibitors and facilitators of learning and development (L&D) approaches.

3.1 INTRODUCTION

The practice of designing, delivering and evaluating learning and development occurs primarily in organisational contexts. It is therefore necessary for practitioners to have an understanding of factors influencing those contexts. This chapter will examine and analyse the role and impact of external factors such as economic, political and legislative conditions and internal factors such as organisational plans and priorities, learning climate and resource availability. Developments in ICT and the opportunities and limitations of these for design and delivery of learning and development will also be explored. Finally, external and internal barriers, inhibitors and facilitators of learning and development will be identified and discussed.

3.2 THE EXTERNAL CONTEXT

Whilst there are a number of external conditions which impact and influence the development and design of any learning and development intervention, it is important to consider the general external environment and the influences this may have upon L&D. L&D is governed by varying conditions which if prevalent together can either inhibit investment in learning, or can facilitate it and promote its importance.

A useful method for exploring external influences is to undertake a PESTLE analysis. This is a tool for understanding the wider environment which impacts upon an organisation (CIPD 2010). Table 3.1 uses a PESTLE analysis to provide an overview of the high-level external influences impacting the design and delivery of training.

Table 3.1 PESTLE analysis of external influences

Political	Economic	Social/Cultural
• Changes in government training initiatives • Development of NVQs • Increase in apprenticeships and vocational learning	• Downturn in the economy • Impact of the recession • Wider competition • Trends in labour markets	• Widely accepted flexibility in training approaches • Increase in education, qualifications and skills • Stronger emphasis on education and learning
Technological	**Legal**	**Environmental**
• Developments in ICT • Pace of communication and learning accelerated • Widely accessible modes of learning	• Mandatory training, eg health and safety • Updates in legislation and code of conduct	• Resource management • Poor infrastructure limits • The accessibility of training

3.2.1 ECONOMIC CONDITIONS

With a downturn in the economy and the impact of recession, the first cuts in budgets tend to be for training initiatives and development projects. A report by the UK Chartered Institute of Personnel Development (2009) concluded that 32% of working professionals from a survey sample of 859 had reported a drop in L&D funding over the 12 months in the midst of the recession. This creates a challenge for organisations, in particular HRD professionals, to ensure training and learning and development initiatives remain on the strategic agenda, especially those which are business critical.

During the course of a recession, organisational priorities are focused primarily on survival and the investment in training is lessened. The cultural mentality of short-term survival makes organisations more task- rather than people-focused. This shift in thinking will inevitably impact upon the future sustainability of the skills and knowledge of the workforce. As the value of learning and development during a period of competitive challenge and uncertainty is not widely recognised, it is even more pertinent for HRD to focus on strategically partnering with the organisation by offering a variety of both cost-effective and innovative ways to deliver learning solutions. Engaging and influencing senior management and stakeholders to champion the continuation of training will strengthen the workforce's capability to future-proof the organisation.

Economic growth also dictates the amount of investment an organisation channels into training, therefore the direction of the economy is an interesting factor to consider in the context in which training is offered. Although there has been continual growth in the service sector, the UK Government is keen to increase the economic role played by manufacturing. This will require a more focused view on the particular and specialist skills required for those working in manufacturing and, coupled with the developments in technology, the need to offer further product-specific and resource-efficient training interventions.

There has been a gradual shift from residential-based or standard one-day training sessions offered by external suppliers, towards in-house, tailored and bespoke bite-sized learning which can be more readily and instantly applied to the organisational learning climate and culture. Work-based and job-related training is not viewed as an expense as it is integrated within the workplace and seen as value-adding. In addition, visible links can be made from the learning which aligns organisational culture, values and needs. Thus there are a number of internal influences that also need to be considered.

Furthermore, work-based learning, such as the evolution of apprenticeships, is gradually increasing due to a multiplicity of reasons. The National Apprenticeship Service reveals that online apprenticeship applications have increased by nearly a third (32%) year on year, with over 1.4 million (1,403,920) applications made for vacancies in 2012 (http://www. trainingzone.co.uk/news/news-32-increase-online-apprenticeship-applications). One reason for this stems from the political agenda set by the Government to increase work skills, lifelong learning and also the movement by both vocational and academic institutes towards continuous professional development. Therefore the design and development of any training must demonstrate a strong link to the role and include a multitude of transferable skills.

3.2.2 LEGISLATIVE CONDITIONS

Legislative influences play an important role in prioritising the need for training, and also have a bearing on how training is developed and designed to maximise its impact on performance while also adhering to protocol and set regulations. Legislative requirements, such as health and safety regulations, and the ways in which these impact and pose a risk to the organisation will be a determinant of the approach and delivery method. There are serious implications for an employer neglecting to undertake health and safety training, which can include both direct financial losses due to accidents, and the possible legal actions that might arise from potential negligence. A programme of employee training to develop a safe working environment can be both timely and cost-effective.

Given the range of external influences on the design and delivery of training, how training is offered within an organisation needs to be 'fit for purpose' and a number of internal influences as discussed below will also need to be taken into account. There is a wider shift to deliver core mandatory training such as health and safety, code of conduct and regulations such as employment law and equalities law via a more consistent approach within the workplace, which can be regulated and monitored and also minimise the impact of time away from the workplace.

With developments in ICT, e-learning is one method of delivering mandatory training which often is used to update on legislative knowledge or health and safety requirements. ICT will be discussed in more detail later in this chapter. As summarised in the PESTLE analysis earlier, trends such as the tightening and loosening of the labour market and the skills and competencies available will influence the extent to which an organisation invests in training. Within a tight labour market, where the choice of candidates is limited, the costs of employing can be high. However, the level of skill and competence may be low and, given the limited choice, employers may not be able to recruit to the right level of competence; hence the requirement to offer more extensive training to bring skills up to the right standard. Whereas in a loose labour market, the employer is offered a wider choice and can seek a higher level of skills and competence, lessening the requirement to offer more extensive training.

3.3 THE INTERNAL CONTEXT

3.3.1 FOSTERING A LEARNING CLIMATE

Organisational learning has gained increased attention in recent years from academics and practitioners alike. One explanation for this is offered by Maden (2011, p71), who identifies organisational learning as having the potential to offer organisations 'increased innovative capacity, increased productivity, and higher competitive advantage'.

One particular approach to organisational learning advocated by Senge (1990) is the concept of the learning organisation. Senge (1990) identified a series of specific criteria under which an organisation could be defined as a learning organisation. However, Senge's characterisation faced criticism in that he was accused of representing a utopian organisational state that would be virtually unachievable in its entirety (Harrison 2009); a series of ideals, criteria that could be strived for but seldom wholly achievable. For example, one of Senge's learning organisation characteristics is the creation of a learning culture where all members are committed to learning. Harrison argues that it would be highly unlikely in reality for any organisation to gain 'buy in' from all of its members in this regard.

However, the concept of the learning organisation and its characteristics have since been the focus of others' research. For example, Slater and Narver (1995) identify five characteristics of the learning organisation, two based on building a learning culture (eg creating a marketing and entrepreneurship focus) and the remaining three based on fostering a learning climate. Within their consideration of a learning climate, Slater and Narver include supportive leadership, open and adaptable organisation structure, and a shared, decentralised approach to planning. Extending these authors' attention to adaptability, Finger and Brand (1999, p132) refer to the learning organisation as 'one that is open to change or even more so, one that can change from within itself', in light of the continued focus on the learning organisation as a means of achieving greater organisational flexibility and adaptability to changing environmental conditions. More recently, Örtenblad (2004) has introduced a model that includes the following four cohesive characteristics:

- *learning climate* (the creation of conditions that support experimentation and risk (Garvin 1993) that do not always fit with originally accepted behaviours and routines)
- *organisational learning* (making reference to Argyris and Schön's (1978) single-, double- and deutero-loop learning, Örtenblad maintains that organisations develop their own memory and learning through rituals and routines and the production of documents that are accepted by organisational members)
- *learning at work* (or on-the-job learning that can be easily applied to real work situations)
- *learning structure* (a decentralised, flexible, flat organisation structure, supporting individual and collective decision-making that is in the organisation's best interests).

Consensus exists from all of these authors that the creation of a learning climate and culture that is open and flexible is likely to enable organisations to become more adaptable and much better prepared for facing changing environmental conditions.

3.3.2 COMPETENCY FRAMEWORKS

Garavan and McGuire (2001) observed that the world of work has seen an increase in the use of competency frameworks as a means of developing employee business responsiveness and flexibility. This trend began in the USA and more recently has become widespread within European and UK organisations. One of the factors identified by Garavan and McGuire that has made a significant contribution to organisational preoccupation with the competency to employee performance development links with the influence of national governments. Governments' support and development of nationally recognised competency standards (for example, the National Council for Vocational Qualifications (NCVQ)) have highlighted the benefits of the competency approach in terms of the recognisability of the standards and the expectations of attainment that can be placed upon them.

However, competency development has come under criticism for holding the assumption that employees should behave in specific predetermined ways if they are to optimise their own and organisational efficiency and productivity. This, Garavan and McGuire argue, stems from a Tayloristic (scientific management) philosophical perspective that takes a simplistic view that a perfect combination of employee skills, knowledge and attitudes can be found for each work role. Furthermore, this perspective argues that these perfect combinations of skills and knowledge should be strived for. Nevertheless, competency frameworks and competency development appeal to organisational leaders as they make possible the identification of development needs, the measurement of employee development against specified competency targets and the linking of development needs and organisational objectives.

EXERCISE 3.1

1 How and to what extent are competencies used within your organisation, or an organisation with which you are familiar?

2 What are the benefits of this approach within the context of this specific organisation?

3 What are the difficulties associated with a competency approach?

4 How does the competency approach to employee learning and development support or hinder considerations of the learning organisation?

3.3.3 WORKPLACE LEARNING

Organisations are faced with having to respond to an ever-increasing pace of technological change. As such, many leaders are focused on continuously developing their employees to equip them with the skills, knowledge and attitudes required for them to continue to positively impact upon their organisation's performance. However, the potential cost and relevance of learning and development interventions have come under increasing scrutiny from leaders intent on reducing overheads whilst optimising productivity. Workplace learning is described by Hicks et al (2007, p64) as 'a process whereby people, as a function of completing their organisational tasks and roles, acquire knowledge, skills, and attitudes that enhance individual and organisational performance'. An important feature of Hicks et al's quote is the linkage that is made between employee development and organisational performance. Doyle and Young (2007) agree that learning is associated with enabling individuals to adapt to environmental changes. Hence, it is argued that workplace learning is likely to remain a major concern for organisational leaders seeking to optimise the adaptability and performance of their employees.

3.3.4 WORK-BASED LEARNING STRATEGIES AND GOAL ORIENTATION

Work-based learning strategies are defined by Holman et al (2001) as cognitive and behavioural strategies that are adopted by individuals in order to develop their work-related knowledge. Warr and Allan (1998) identify the following two forms of work-based learning strategies:

- *Cognitive* – this approach involves considering existing understanding in light of information gained from new learning. Decisions are then based on new understandings.
- *Behavioural* – this involves learning from colleagues, written documentation or through the application of ideas to practice.

Holman et al (2011) found the extent to which employees enjoy control over their work has a positive influence on the learning strategies adopted and consequently their idea-generation. Additionally, the level of demands placed upon employees is also associated positively with the learning strategies adopted. Consequently, they argue that those in higher levels of employment with more control over their work and facing high work demands will demonstrate more positive learning strategies and generate better ideas. The implications here for organisational leaders are that by providing more senior-level employees with greater autonomy and an increased workload, their initiative and idea-creation could benefit. However, they do warn that higher work demands are not always associated with positive learning strategies and outcomes, and make reference to the work of Taris and Kompier (2005) relating to job demands, strain and learning behaviour to support this point.

Payne et al (2007) identify goal orientation as an important consideration in relation to the learning strategies adopted by individuals. They make the following distinction between approach and avoidance performance goals:

- *approach performance goal* – involving employees working towards higher achievement than their colleagues
- *avoidance performance goal* – concerned with avoiding the embarrassment of employees not achieving as much as their colleagues.

This is also argued to be an important factor in understanding employee motives for engaging in workplace learning. For example, an avoidance goal orientation could be more easily linked with the negativity often associated with organisations facing downsizing or other significant change. Whereas, if the organisation is fostering a more positive and progressive learning climate as detailed earlier, a more 'approach' performance goal orientation might be more evident.

3.3.5 FORMAL AND INFORMAL LEARNING

Marsick and Watkins (2001) differentiate formal learning from informal learning in terms of the former resulting from planned and structured learning interventions that are often 'off the job' or institutionally centred and facilitator driven; whereas the latter is more likely to be controlled by the learner, occurring 'on the job' and away from a formal classroom setting. Workplace learning is often considered a more cost-effective approach than traditional 'off the job' offerings as it usually requires fewer external resources and can be much more closely related to specific work roles and environments.

Crouse et al (2011) also pay particular attention to 'incidental learning', learning that occurs by chance and the learner may not even be aware that learning has taken place. However, Billet (1995) notes that under these completely unplanned and unregulated circumstances it is possible that learners may adopt behaviours or attitudes that are unwanted by organisational leaders. Matthews (1999) maintains that workplace learning strategies include a mix of formal and informal learning approaches. Crouse et al (2011) carried out an extensive literature review in order to identify the strategies adopted by people in work to develop themselves and acquire new knowledge. These workplace learning strategies include the following:

- taking up opportunities for attending taught courses that are often delivered off-site or away from their normal workplaces
- taking on new tasks and duties (this could be within existing work roles or as a result of taking on new job roles)
- working with and learning from other colleagues/co-workers
- learning from the observation of others at work
- learning by making mistakes – trial and error
- carrying out reading or research
- creating opportunities for reflection upon experience, either individually or collectively
- learning from feedback and the insights of others.

A more detailed overview of the literature reviewed regarding workplace learning strategies is available from Crouse et al's (2011) original paper.

Contextual issues also influence workplace learning strategies in that employees from larger organisations tend to participate in more formalised learning opportunities, as opposed to employees from smaller organisations, who are more likely to participate in more informal learning. In addition to the explicit goals leaders have regarding their learning interventions (ie agreed specified learning outcomes), Rowold (2007) also makes reference to implicit goals. These implicit goals are associated with creating more positive work-related attitudes and improved commitment etc.

3.3.6 ANALYSIS OF ORGANISATIONS' INTERNAL CONTEXTS

As discussed earlier in this chapter, the creation of an internal organisation context that is supportive of individual and collective learning and growth is a key contributor to the organisation's overall development. Therefore, it is crucial for organisation leaders to establish the extent to which the transfer of any learning intervention or experience has taken place. Tannenbaum and Yukl (1992, p240) define transfer as '... the extent to which trainees effectively apply the knowledge, skills and attitudes gained in a training context back to the job'. It is important, therefore, to identify individual and collective learning and development needs and establish the extent to which the interventions introduced to address these needs have been successful. The identification of learning needs will be discussed in more detail in Chapter 4. However, it is worth noting at this point that the creation of an organisational infrastructure (including leadership, supervision and support systems) that is conducive with supporting a learning climate will be critical to enabling effective learning needs analysis to take place.

3.3.7 THE PERSONAL DEVELOPMENT PLAN (PDP) – A STRATEGY FOR TRACKING, NURTURING AND EVALUATING EMPLOYEE PERSONAL DEVELOPMENT

Continuous employee learning and personal development are seen by organisations as crucial if their members are to be ready for and successfully adapt to technological developments and changes in their business environments. Creating internal organisational contexts that foster and nurture personal development are considered an important factor in achieving this. One means of encouraging employees to focus on their continuous development is by incorporating PDPs into their working lives. PDPs provide employees with an opportunity to document their personal development and make plans for future development. They are seen by some as an effective way to monitor and evaluate the relative benefits gained from training and development activities that have been undertaken. PDPs can, according to Beausaert et al (2011), be used in the following ways:

- to provide an overview of competency development, detailing those competencies that have been achieved and those that the employee is planning to develop
- developed by the employee in consultation with their supervisor(s)
- to form the content of personal development conversations that take place between the employee and their supervisor (for example within a structured developmental performance management process)
- to form the basis of employee, joint or management decision-making in determining the most suitable training upon which to embark or to consider the potential for advancement or promotion.

In addition to these uses it is also argued that the PDP can be used to evaluate the longer-term impact of learning interventions that have been undertaken by employees. In line with Kirkpatrick's (1994) four levels of evaluation this level of learning evaluation takes place at level 3 and possibly level 4. Level 3 is concerned with evaluating changes in behaviour and/or attitude as a result of knowledge or skills transfer. This evaluation would usually take place around three to six months after the learning intervention. Evaluation at level 4 is concerned with measuring results, ie the impact or effect the learner has had on the business as a result of the learning intervention. This is in contrast to the first two levels, which are more immediate and deal with evaluating learners' thoughts and reflections of the learning intervention (their reaction) and whether or not there is evidence of enhanced knowledge, skills or attitude (their learning). Evaluation of learning is discussed further in Chapter 7 of this book.

3.4 DEVELOPMENTS IN ICT

Returning to developments in ICT and their impact on L&D within organisations, this section will provide a broad overview of their nature and scope, then go on to discuss e-learning as a specific example. Finally the opportunities and limitations of ICTs will be discussed. ICT refers to information and communication technologies, although there is no general consensus on how ICTs are defined. This is probably because the nature of information, communication and technology is constantly and rapidly changing, as well as varying greatly within different organisational contexts. Nevertheless, the term ICT has been used to describe a myriad of communication and technological devices (or hardware) such as mobile telephones, televisions, radios, audio and video players, computers, tablets and satellite systems. However, the term also refers to the programs or applications (software) which run on these devices such as word processing, spreadsheets, databases, mobile apps, etc.

The use of ICTs to support and facilitate learning and development is not new, indeed the Open University has been utilising such methods since the late 1960s. However, in the succeeding 50 years, the application and scope of ICTs has transformed considerably, a most notable example of this being the emergence of the Internet, which has provided a platform enabling global, 24-hour access to, and sharing of, a range of information, products and services.

EXERCISE 3.2

How has the use of ICTs in the facilitation of learning changed and developed since you began employment?

3.4.1 E-LEARNING

The broad scope and widespread availability of ICTs has enabled flexibility and choice in terms of both the hardware and software available to support learning and development initiatives. However, the development of e-learning has revolutionised the way in which organisations design, deliver and evaluate workplace learning and development. Just as in the case of defining ICTs, there is no generally accepted definition of what constitutes e-learning. However, the CIPD (2013a) provides a definition of e-learning as 'learning that is delivered, enabled or mediated using electronic technology for the explicit purpose of training, learning or development in organisations' (www.cipd.co.uk/-resources/factsheets/e-learning.aspx). An alternative definition provided by DeRouin et al (2005) describes e-learning as an instructional strategy for imparting knowledge, skills and attitudes in organisations through the use of technology. What does seem generally accepted is that e-learning usually requires access to a device (whether this is a computer, laptop, tablet or mobile phone etc) in order to access learning materials.

E-learning as a training medium existed long before access to the Internet was widely available. In its early days (late 1970s to early 1980s) e-learning would have been accessed on computers, floppy discs and more recently via CD-Roms.

LEARNING LANGUAGE THROUGH E-LEARNING

Background to case

For the urban elite in India English is a main language. It is also regarded as the second language for much of the educated city-dwelling population. It has been suggested that this ability to communicate in English has given the country a competitive edge within a global market, which has in turn supported the economic growth and development of the nation. This has resulted in a rising demand for English language training from students wishing to improve employment prospects and those wishing to communicate in English on a regular basis.

Compulearn is a regional e-learning business employing approximately 150 people and is based in a suburb of Delhi. It produces tailor-made e-learning products for clients and has developed a range of both 'off-the-shelf' and bespoke tools designed to support English language training in India. In 2008 they released their latest product, 'Easy English', which incorporates a CD-ROM-based instructor-led language course, together with online learning activities and support. The product was based on similar packages developed for a UK market but it has been designed so that is flexible enough to be tailored to specific needs of particular countries. The product utilises a range of films and television programmes recorded in English as well as current affairs and news items. However, the issues involved in adapting the product for Indian users provide some useful insights on the attractions and problems in using e-learning.

Barriers to learning

There are several issues facing those who wish to achieve a high level of spoken English. These include: pronunciation; thinking in your own language when needing to speak in English; words or phrases that may be lost in translation; issues around grammar and tense. Furthermore, learners need to be able to distinguish between different English accents and dialects and regional variations of language. These potential barriers have to be considered when addressing learning needs and any product developed needs to be adaptable enough to cope with these variable contexts. Thought had to be given to how and when learning was accessed, and whether this was part of a specific college programme for students, for employees within organisations, or as training for any individual wishing to improve their spoken English.

The potentially wide market for the 'Easy English' product places emphasis on the need for a high level of learner support. Compulearn achieve this through a blended learning approach which incorporates trainer-led face-to-face learning, individual online learning and online group forums and discussions. This in itself has led to challenges as for some learners training in the use of ICTs has run alongside their English language training.

Future developments

Rapid advancements in technology have seen Compulearn develop an interactive app which can be accessed via smart phones and tablets, thus increasing flexibility of learning still further. Audio, video and voice recognition are also built in, enabling learners to fully engage in their own learning. The use of news and current affairs items in the delivery of the training also ensures that material is relevant and up to date.

Today, many e-learning packages are available to download from the Internet, or can be operated interactively online. Just as ICTs have developed at a phenomenal rate over the last 20 years, so too have the capabilities and scope of e-learning. The CIPD (2013a) identify three main types of e-learning: formal, informal and blended. Formal e-learning utilises technology in a fairly passive way to deliver training to individuals or groups, eg a PowerPoint presentation, or an instructional video. Informal e-learning, on the other hand, involves a more participatory approach and is aimed at supporting informal learning in the workplace and encouraging collaboration, eg online communities, chat rooms and social networking sites. The third type encompasses blended, or supported, e-learning. In this case, e-learning is combined with other forms of learning such as traditional classroom-based learning, one-to-one tutorials, coaching, group work and so on. However, the key aspect here is that information, materials and other learners are accessed online. Recent trends have seen expansion in social media such as Facebook, Twitter and LinkedIn; virtual learning environments and networked e-learning; web and videoconferencing; increased integration with mobile apps and games and the development of artificial intelligence and virtual assistants.

Questions

1   What were the challenges experienced when attempting to set up e-learning for language training?

2   How did these challenges influence the design of the learning programme?

3   What methods would you employ to evaluate the success of such an initiative?

EXERCISE 3.3

1   Think about the ways in which your organisation uses formal, informal and blended e-learning.

2   Which of these have you found to be most effective in supporting individual learning?

3   Why do you consider this to be the case?

3.4.2 OPPORTUNITIES AND LIMITATIONS OF ICT

Fink and Disterer (2006) suggest there is a common acceptance that ICT provides organisations with many benefits which enable them to become more effective, efficient and competitive. However, they go on to argue that much research in this area has been focused on ICT practices in large organisations and the impact within SMEs is largely under-researched. They found that while ICTs were used in micro and SMEs, their use is emerging and mainly focused on systems with the potential to facilitate interactions aimed at developing customer relationships. In terms of delivering learning, a great advantage of e-learning is its immediacy, coupled with 24-hour flexible access. There is also the potential to reach large numbers of employees in multiple locations across the globe. A knock-on benefit here is the relative cost-efficiency in reaching such big numbers of employees, as well as saving time and ensuring consistency of information. From an individual perspective, learners can work at their own pace and tailor learning to their own specific needs.

Yet, with all the acknowledged benefits and opportunities afforded by e-learning, it is important to recognise potential pitfalls. In order for e-learning to be effective at both an individual and organisational level, learners should be prepared and supported in its use. There is often the assumption that employees are IT-literate, with 24-hour access to computing facilities, but this may not necessarily be the case. Therefore, access to IT equipment and facilities also needs to be considered, and whether this is available on or off-site. Furthermore, organisations' IT infrastructures need to be capable of supporting e-learning systems both on-site and remotely. Although e-learning can be time-effective, management buy-in and time still needs to be made available in order for learners to engage with the technology, otherwise it can just become something that is squeezed in with other work demands. Just as with any other learning intervention, the quality of material must be relevant and fit for purpose and should be aligned with identified training needs. Individual learning preferences may mean that e-learning is not a one-size-fits-all and it should not, therefore, be used in isolation, but encompassed as part of a wider blended learning approach. Finally, individual motivations for learning require consideration. E-learning is often (but not exclusively) undertaken as a solitary activity which, for some, has the potential to cause isolation and detachment. In such instances a high degree of self-motivation is necessary. Making use of social networking to encourage team and collaborative working could be one strategy to overcome this.

EXERCISE 3.4

Listen to the CIPD (2011) podcast *Learning and development in a socially networked age – podcast 54*. Available at:

http://www.cipd.co.uk/podcasts/_articles/
_learninganddevelopmentinasociallynetworkedage.htm

How do the issues and topics discussed compare and contrast with your experiences of learning and development in a socially networked age?

3.5 BARRIERS, INHIBITORS AND FACILITATORS OF L&D

3.5.1 BARRIERS TO LEARNING

Whilst organisations are striving to develop a high-performing culture and remain competitive in their field and industry, they still feel the strain of investing in training unless they have a clear belief and can see a visible link to how training will impact the bottom line. One of the biggest barriers is the cost of training and translating this to the return on investment. From an external perspective, the cost will be a decider of the design of the training and whether it will be delivered in-house or externally by an approved supplier. The economic climate and competitive industry will also have a bearing on the extent of any training delivered. There is a growing shift from residential training to in-house work-based training. A major cause of this shift is the cost and also the time employees are away from the workplace.

EXERCISE 3.5

1   What do you consider to be the internal and external barriers to learning and development for your organisation?

2   How can you eliminate or minimise the impact of these barriers?

Hicks et al (2007) defined barriers to learning as 'those factors that prevent learning from starting, impede or interrupt learning or result in learning being terminated earlier than it might have been ordinarily' (p64). Different barriers to learning are often evident within different professions and organisational contexts.

As detailed earlier, Crouse et al (2011) conducted a comprehensive review of the literature associated with workplace learning. Particularly, their review highlighted the following barriers to learning that exist within the workplace.

The limited 'resources' available for learning and development:

- the financial restraints faced by organisations
- lack of time available for the arrangement of learning and development initiatives
- a shortage of people with the appropriate knowledge and expertise to provide direction on learning and development interventions
- the absence of appropriate accommodation for learning events to take place
- difficulties with ensuring the cost-effectiveness of learning interventions
- the absence of learning resources
- a shortage of the availability of relevant information sources
- the limited direction available for learning and development resources.

Difficulties with the accessibility:

- issues with access to learning and development opportunities
- lack of exposure to stimulating employment experiences
- limited access to resources for learning and development.

Technological issues:

- issues with the availability of appropriate information technology and technological constraints
- limited access to technologies for instruction.

Individual barriers:

- limited personal understanding of learning and development needs
- issues of a more personal nature that have an impact upon ability or capability for engaging in learning and development activities

- cautiousness about taking on new challenges
- avoidance of making mistakes and the anxiety of getting things wrong
- limited engagement relating to considerations of lack of relevance or importance
- negative associations made with past experiences of learning and development
- a reduction in enthusiasm and motivation
- cynicism relating to opportunities for learning
- where learning and development involvement is considered to be over and above acceptable requirements of the work role.

Difficulties with the interaction with others:

- low levels of communication and interpersonal skills
- issues associated with individuals showing reluctance to develop their knowledge and expertise
- difficulties with levels of leadership and management competence
- limited availability of appropriate coaches and mentors.

Issues associated with organisational context:

- limited strategic direction regarding the support of learning and development activity
- an organisation culture that is not conducive with the encouragement of learning
- limited opportunities created by the organisation for time away from normal duties for the participation in learning and development activities
- lack of legitimate acknowledgement or compensation for learning and development efforts
- difficulties with appreciating the role of HRD within learning interventions, employee and organisation development
- increased job enlargement within organisations, impacting on the potential for employees to find time to engage with planned learning opportunities.

Difficulties with learning intervention content:

- the inaccurate or unsuitable acquisition of information
- the transfer of unclear information
- a lack of authority from learning intervention facilitators
- the overload of information
- in-house learning and development interventions that fail to meet stakeholder expectations
- disappointment with and disapproval of the way in which learning interventions are developed and facilitated.

Issues associated with power and influence:

- differences of opinion regarding the ownership of learning and development
- a shortage of influence of those involved with learning and development in relation to wider organisational decision-making
- the exclusion of some members from the organisational community
- the potential for trade union or staff representative backlash or resistance where changes are being proposed or enforced.

Learning and development and change:

- the pace of organisational change being 'out of kilter' with the development and delivery of learning interventions.

3.5.2 NEGATIVE OUTCOMES OF BARRIERS TO WORKPLACE LEARNING

Sostrin (2011, p14) highlights the following three potential negative outcomes of barriers to workplace learning for organisations:

- *First-order impacts on workers* – resulting in employee lack of focus, motivation and disengagement; potentially causing work-related stress and a reduction in performance.
- *Second-order impacts on teams* – resulting in the eroding of communication processes, collaborative decision-making and morale, thus undermining the potential for effective teamwork.
- *Third-order impacts on the workplace* – resulting in a rise in employee turnover, absenteeism, and presenteeism; detracting employees from working towards strategic goals and objectives.

3.5.3 FACILITATORS OF WORKPLACE LEARNING

There are a number of external influences which facilitate the direction and approach of training. Some of these have been discussed earlier and include:

- customers (both internal and external)
- suppliers
- competitors
- government initiatives
- labour market.

Customers – Whether internal or external, customers are key players in supporting the design and development of training and can act as critical friends. Their requirements and expectations for customer service and quality would drive the agenda for training. From an external customer perspective, and to ensure the organisation is seen to offer customer excellence in what it offers, it needs to continuously develop and up-skill employees to develop new knowledge and competences to remain market leaders and competitive in their field. Standing still is not an option. Organisations need to stay ahead of their competitors.

Suppliers – Suppliers also support the facilitation of learning through maintaining an ongoing dialogue about new and differing products and services which an organisation needs to recognise. Suppliers, like customers, are a catalyst to learning and development, feeding the organisation with new market information such as emerging trends, keeping the organisation aware of its competitive arena, and enabling the organisation to prepare its workforce accordingly through training.

Competitors – Similar to customers, competitors drive organisations to continuously develop skills and knowledge to remain sustainable and keep their position in the marketplace. Whilst the irony is for competitors to stay ahead of all the market leaders, this push for success drives organisations to continue with training interventions so as to ensure they maintain their place as a market leader.

Government initiatives – Government-funded programmes and initiatives promote and set the agenda for learning and development by offering training incentives and funding for organisations who invest in their workforce. This enables organisations with limited funds to provide learning opportunities to their employees which may not otherwise have been possible. The Government is keen to ensure people are equipped with the right skills and are employable through the development of vocational qualifications and work-based learning. The driver for the Government is to ensure growth in the economy and that people remain employed, therefore investing in learning is essential.

 EXERCISE 3.6

1   What do you consider to be the internal and external facilitators of learning and development for your organisation?

2   How can these facilitators support your organisation to maximise the role of learning and development?

Crouse et al's (2011) review of relevant literature also offered an overview of the perspectives relating to the facilitation of workplace learning interventions. It is recognised that the majority of these learning facilitators are associated with the creation of a learning climate, as discussed earlier. The main learning facilitators as identified through this process include the following.

Contextual and strategic support – organisational culture, structure and leadership:

- the formulation of a working environment that is supportive of learning and development activity
- optimising management involvement, engagement and support in relation to employee learning and development
- creating changes to job design (for example – job enrichment, flexibility and adaptability) that are conducive with enabling employee involvement in learning and development to take place
- encouraging collaborative leadership that allows for the collective drive towards organisational learning
- supporting trial and error, ensuring that making and learning from mistakes are accepted cultural norms
- rewarding positive behaviours
- engaging employees with change
- the inclusion in performance management processes of targets based upon current work-related knowledge.

Facilitators of learning connected with work role:

- creating job design that involves challenge
- optimising opportunities for employment to include a variety of experiences
- the encouragement of learning from shadowing and observing of others
- building independence into work roles
- allowing for risk-taking and experimentation without fear of repercussion/punishment
- building adaptability and flexibility into work patterns.

The involvement of others:

- building in collaboration and interaction between organisation members
- engaging employee representatives in the development of learning interventions.

Supporting learning and development:

- ensuring that new employees receive induction training that places emphasis on the importance of workplace learning
- engaging the support of experienced organisation members to support, advise, counsel and mentor more junior members
- creating opportunities for employees to receive feedback on their performance (for example, within performance reviews)

- providing clarification in relation to the role of HRD employees in the support of organisational learning
- building HRD into organisational strategy, ensuring learning and development is at the centre of strategic decision-making
- providing access to a range of learning resources
- combining in-house and external learning and development opportunities
- ensuring that learning and development interventions can be directly related to work roles.

Individual characteristics that are conducive with the facilitation of workplace learning:

- employees that are happy to seek advice and support when required
- being able to reflect upon and learn from experiences
- a propensity to listen and learn from colleagues
- employees who can work using their own initiative
- individuals who have an understanding of their own potential, strengths and weaknesses – self-efficacy
- having an authentic passion for their area of work or profession
- an enthusiastic orientation to learning and development
- optimising the inquisitiveness of individuals.

Optimising the resources available for learning and development interventions:

- creating opportunities for access to information technology and learning materials and other resources.

EXERCISE 3.7

Reflect upon one of your own experiences of workplace learning and consider the following:

1   Which of the barriers or facilitators identified by Crouse et al featured within this experience?

2   What factors did you consider to be out of your control?

3   How could the organisation go about addressing the factors that you identified in answer to Question 2?

4   What did you learn from this experience?

5   What, if anything, might you do differently next time?

3.6 CONCLUSION

This chapter has considered the external and internal factors which influence the design and delivery of learning and development initiatives within organisations. A PESTLE analysis was used as a technique for identifying a range of external factors such as government policies and practices, the current economic climate, legislative constraints and developments in ICT. It is clear that any consideration of external influences has to be set within the prevailing political, social and economic context. Internal organisational influences were also considered in detail and a key element here is the need to foster an organisational learning climate. Developments in ICT were discussed and this is an area of rapid development and growth. There are many opportunities for organisations to embrace and incorporate this technology into their design, delivery and evaluation of learning. However, for this to be successful there is a need for effective technological infrastructure, access to facilities and equipment and buy-in from all levels of the organisation.

Finally, barriers, inhibitors and facilitators to learning were discussed. From these discussions it is clear that a range of complex factors, both from outside and within the organisation have a bearing on the design and facilitation of learning interventions within organisations, and indeed their level of success. As such it remains crucial for practitioners to have an understanding of these factors in relation to their own, and wider, organisational contexts.

CASE STUDY 3.2

BRAND VALUES AND RETAIL LEARNING AT MURRAYS

Background

Established over 100 years ago from a single store, Murrays is now a well-respected department store retailer of luxury goods. The company is a West Midlands-based enterprise with 12 stores located across the Midlands and the north of England, with a flagship store in Birmingham. In 2010 Murrays launched a major project across the business in order to embed a set of brand values that had been identified as defining business success. These three brand values were:

- We provide an excellent shopping experience for the customer.
- We are exclusive, but accessible.
- We provide retail leadership reflecting our approach to customer service.

A key challenge for Murrays was to determine how these values could be expressed in terms of visible behaviour on the shop floor. Therefore, they could not progress with individual skill development until this had been determined. In order to address this challenge a project team was set up to identify how these core values could be practically applied and embedded. The HR director was appointed to head up the project team and store managers nominated customer service champions within their own region to represent sales advisers. Representatives from the Learning and Development department were also involved as they would be key in the development and rolling-out of the subsequent development plan. From this initial project team, smaller project teams were set up at store level. This enabled open consultation and both top-down and bottom-up communication, as well as sharing of ideas and best practice across stores. From these discussions a set of values and associated behaviours were developed and these are presented in the following table.

Values Identified	Associated Behaviour
Visible desire to deliver excellent customer shopping experience	Welcoming and approachable – use of positive body language and maintaining eye contact
Willingness to go above and beyond what is required	Actively helping and assisting customers and staff
Positive and enthusiastic	Actively listening and responding to customers and staff
Excellent communicator	Sharing ideas and encouraging teamwork

As well as the behaviours outlined in the table, several scenarios illustrating customer experiences were developed in order to present specific examples of expectations, barriers, threats and opportunities.

Implementing the plan

During the spring of 2011, events were launched across all stores in order to present and disseminate the values identified and associated desirable staff behaviours. These events were driven by the store managers together with appointed customer service champions and involved question and answer sessions, quizzes and role-plays. Following the launch events, responsibility for the implementation of the values and behaviours was delegated to department managers across each store. All department managers attended a one-day 'train the trainer' course and were provided with strategies and practical tools to enable them to develop discussions and activities. At a company-wide level the identified behaviours were incorporated into job descriptions, person specifications and the performance management system. An on-going challenge for managers, the HR department and the Learning and Development department was to ensure that the desired behaviours become embedded into the culture of the business through continued reinforcement and recognition.

According to Murrays' Learning and Development Manager, adopting an 'off-the-shelf' learning package for sales advisers would not be appropriate for the type of learning and behaviours the company wishes to foster. She considers staff learning to be more effective when it is reinforced with immediate constructive feedback and ongoing support from managers and colleagues. Following on from this Murrays has set up a team of elite sales advisers made up of customer service champions. These sales champions receive extra recognition and potential financial compensation and part of their role is to act as mentors for less experienced staff. Any member of the sales team is eligible to become a sales champion and colleagues are responsible for identifying and nominating potential champions.

Adoption of the new values and behaviours has led to an increase in sales and customer satisfaction at Murrays. However, there is a challenge in creating learning opportunities for the less proficient. Again, the Learning and Development Manager believes this also needs to be based on immediate peer feedback and manager support. The new mentoring scheme put in place is one way to support this and there are plans to extend this scheme. Managers also need to develop skills which enable them to question and provide feedback in a positive way in order to support the on-going learning and performance management of staff.

Questions

1   What are the internal and external factors affecting the learning context at Murrays?

2   How did the organisation address the issues identified?

3   What are the potential barriers/inhibitors to the approach adopted by the organisation and how could these be overcome?

4   How would you recommend they meet the challenge of creating learning opportunities for the less proficient?

EXPLORE FURTHER

BEEVERS, K. and REA, A. (2013) *Learning and development practice*. London: CIPD.

Contains practical advice and theoretical perspectives on learning and development practice.

CIPD (2009) *Annual Survey Report 2009* [online]. London: Chartered Institute of Personnel and Development. Available at: http://www.cipd.co.uk/NR/rdonlyres/FFC9C11E-20A6-4E30-9F50-8E58BC9FFA1B/0/Learnanddevsur2009.pdf

CIPD (2010) *Factsheet: PESTLE Analysis*. Available at: http://www.cipd.co.uk/hr-resources/factsheets/pestle-analysis.aspx

CIPD (2010) Podcast: *Pushing the boundaries of learning and development – podcast 42*. Available at: http://www.cipd.co.uk/podcasts/_articles/_pushing-the-boundaries-of-learning-and-development.htm

CIPD (2011) Podcast: *Learning and development in a socially networked age – podcast 54*. Available at: http://www.cipd.co.uk/podcasts/_articles/_learninganddevelopmentinasociallynetworkedage.htm

CIPD (2013) *Factsheet: E-learning*. Available at: www.cipd.co.uk/hr-resources/factsheets/e-learning.aspx

GOLD, J., HOLDEN, R., ILES, P. and STEWART, J. (eds) (2013) *Human resource development: theory and practice*. 2nd ed. London: Palgrave Macmillan.

MAYO, A. (2004) *Creating a learning and development strategy: the HR partner's guide to developing people*. 2nd ed. London: CIPD.

This book explains how to plan, create and implement a learning and development strategy that is aligned with your business's goals and objectives.

CHAPTER 4

Establishing Learning Needs

DR TRICIA HARRISON AND DR RANDHIR AULUCK

LEARNING OUTCOMES

By the end of this chapter you will be able to:

- understand the concept of learning needs analysis
- describe the purpose and benefits of learning needs analysis
- explain where learning needs analysis fits within the wider learning and development process
- identify the variety of methods of learning needs analysis
- understand the implications of learning and development needs analysis on practice.

4.1 INTRODUCTION

Training interventions need to be built on a clear understanding of the specific learning needs of the target group, be it at the level of the individual, team or organisation. This chapter will begin by identifying the purpose and value of learning needs analysis within the employee development process. The strengths and limitations of approaches to and methods of identifying learning needs at organisational and individual levels will then be explored and critically evaluated. As part of this discussion, the role of information-gathering and analysis, the forms it takes in organisational settings, and its use in identifying learning needs, will be critically examined. The implications of the results and methods of building support among stakeholders will also be explored.

4.2 LEARNING NEEDS ANALYSIS AND EMPLOYEE DEVELOPMENT

4.2.1 LEARNING NEEDS ANALYSIS: PURPOSE AND VALUE

This section discusses the role and purpose of learning needs analysis (LNA) within the context of employee development and its value to human resource development (HRD) practice and the organisation more widely. It is also important to establish where assessing learning needs analysis specifically fits within the broader learning and development framework, and the role that HRD specialists and other stakeholders play in the process.

The value of employers investing in the development of their employees' skills and capabilities has been widely discussed and recognised over many decades (Bee and Bee 2004; Boydell and Leary 1999; Buckley and Caple 2009; Harrison 2009; Leitch 2006). Organisations invest in employee development in order that their staff gain and enhance the knowledge, skills and attitudes (KSAs) they need to do their jobs and to do them well (Buckley and Caple 2009; Goldstein and Ford 2002).

Bartlett and Kang (2004) suggest that employee development is positively related to employee commitment to the organisation. It is argued that employees are likely to view investment in their learning as an indication that their organisation is prepared to invest in them and cares about their development (Chaing and Jang 2008). In a study by Bulut and Culha (2010) the relationship between access to training and employee commitment suggests that HRD practitioners can have an important role in this process as they can proactively create learning opportunities, which in turn can act as a catalyst to enhancing employees' feelings of commitment to the organisation.

In addition, Bulut and Culha (2010) lend weight to the view that investment in employee development enhances workforce performance and organisational productivity, vital to an organisation's competiveness (Barney 1991; Bartel 1994). Investment in learning and development enhances employee and organisational performance because it builds on and improves employee knowledge, skills and attitudes, thereby increasing the quality of knowledge capital available within and to the organisation. Learning and development interventions are also seen as an integral tool for facilitating organisational change, as illustrated in the Spotlight on Practice concerning the experience of the Bangladesh Civil Service.

SPOTLIGHT ON PRACTICE 4.1: BANGLADESH

The Bangladesh Civil Service's Managing at the Top (MATT 2) is an initiative aimed at improving performance across the highest levels of the civil service. This includes an established, needs-based management development programme targeted at round 2,000 senior leaders, which its commissioners expect will promote individual, organisational and institutional change.

The management development programme has been informed by a detailed Development Needs Assessment (DNA). As part of this DNA process, approximately 10% of the target population participated in interactive, full-day workshops aimed at identifying learning needs. These were in seven groups covering all levels of top and senior management.

The DNA results showed a very high degree of consistency in identifying the key organisational and personal factors which give rise to staff development needs. In summary, the needs analysis identified a number of areas that needed learning support:

People management
People development
Client-focused service
Understanding organisations
Programme/process management

The DNA informed the strategy and design of MATT 2 development courses, including the management development programme, to ensure they were relevant to the specific areas of development of the target group. The DNA findings continue to be revisited, modified and developed.

Source: http://www.matt2.org/about_us.php?c_id=reform#ln

4.2.2 EMPLOYEE DEVELOPMENT AND COMPETITIVE ADVANTAGE

Advancements in technology have contributed to changes in the nature, processes and methods of work. Take, for example, the increased use of social media. The largest professional networking site LinkedIn, which started in 2003, now has 175 million members in 200 countries representing some 2 million companies. Employers and job-hunters use LinkedIn to make contact with each other (Bonet et al 2013). Such technology-based developments have created conditions giving rise to the need for a highly skilled and highly trained workforce able to take on more demanding roles and more sophisticated, skill-intensive practices. Various established business and management analysts have written about the global shift from an industrial-based workforce to a more knowledge-based workforce (Drucker 1995) and the fact that this brings with it the requirement for greater and continued investment in development and a commitment to continuous learning principles. It is worth noting Drucker's (1995, p69) observation, made nearly two decades ago:

> In the knowledge society the most probable assumption for organizations – and certainly the assumption on which they have to conduct their affairs – is that they need knowledge workers far more than the knowledge workers need them.

Employee development has been linked to organisational as well as to national competitiveness. It has been argued that investing in employee knowledge and skills development can be a source of competitive advantage (Goldstein and Ford 2002; Leitch 2006) and reputational value (specifically in terms of attracting high-calibre new recruits). The Leitch report (Leitch 2006) argued that UK employers fare less well in terms of the levels of investment in employee development compared with their European counterparts. According to the figures published by Cranet (2011), the situation remains unchanged; on average EU members spent 3.72% of the annual payroll on staff training against a UK spend of 3%. However, Rothwell and Kolb (1999) note there has been an increasing recognition of the value of learning and development as a means of dealing with anticipated but fast-moving market and organisational changes. Brewster et al (2011), in a discussion of international comparisons of the types and levels of investment in education and training, suggest that, in the main UK competitor countries, there is wide acceptance of the value of and investment in continuing education and training as a vehicle for advancement and adaptation.

It is widely accepted that in order to maximise the return on investment of employee development, it is essential that learning and development provision is business-led (Harrison 2009) and, specifically, connected to the business strategy and current and emerging business priorities (Beevers and Rea 2010). Identifying employee learning and development needs is a vital element of the design and delivery of learning provision. Effective learning design and delivery is based on understanding the specific needs of the organisation as well as the learner. An illustration of this is how the Government of India recommended the use of collaborative teams to identify needs, as outlined in Spotlight on Practice 4.2: India and Training Needs.

SPOTLIGHT ON PRACTICE 4.2: INDIA AND TRAINING NEEDS

The Government of India's 2007 analysis of the challenges facing the Bihar region of India recommended that small teams should be set up in each of its ministries as part of improving the performance of government departments in that region. The report recommended that these teams, reporting to the relevant minister, should consist of experts to work 'participatively' with the heads of departments and staff to identify key performance indicators, staffing needs and training requirements.

Source: http://planningcommission.nic.in/aboutus/taskforce/tsk_binnotv.pdf

Given that employee development does have associated costs, for example, according to the McKinsey Quarterly Report January 2014, US companies spend almost $14 billion annually on leadership development alone (Gurdjian et al 2014). Also, given the pressures employers are facing in terms of budgetary cutbacks, there is an even greater level of scrutiny about how money is being spent. The global financial crisis has placed pressure on organisations and human resources practitioners to make difficult decisions about how increasingly limited budgets are deployed, rendering it even more important to ensure that any learning provision offered adds value to the organisation by improving employee capability and performance (McCauley et al 1989). As Beevers and Rea (2010, p73) suggest:

> Few, if any, organisations have unlimited training budgets. Time spent clarifying learning needs and priorities help ensure limited resources are used to maximum effect.

It is hoped that the reader now has some understanding of the organisational significance of undertaking training needs analysis; the next part will begin with a discussion of the concept of LNA and then move on to critically analyse the different approaches to conducting LNAs in practice.

EXERCISE 4.1

TRAINING BUDGETS

Think about your organisation or one with which you are familiar, then consider the following questions:

- Does the organisation have a dedicated budget for learning and development?
- What is the level of the budget set aside for L&D?
- Has the level of spend on L&D in the organisation gone up, down or stayed about the same over the past five years?
- Has the budget been used in a different way, for example, less money has been spent on training courses but more on knowledge-sharing, work-based peer-to-peer or expert-to-new entrant coaching?

4.3 WHAT IS LEARNING AND DEVELOPMENT NEEDS ANALYSIS (LNA)?

Learning and development provision can be categorised into a variety of types. It can take the form of, for example, mandatory training related to organisational policies and legal requirements such as health and safety, ethics and equal opportunities. It may also include occupational-specific development interventions, for example, updates in professional practice or individualised development driven by an employee's specific interests, perhaps to acquire new skills or qualifications. As a starting point in order to explore the construct it is relevant to understand the various conceptual dimensions of learning needs analysis as well as some of its limitations.

In an organisational context, learning needs analysis can be described as the process of identifying and reviewing the work-related learning needs of employees. The concept refers to the process of critically examining employee knowledge, behaviour and skills gaps, and is used interchangeably with the related concept of training needs analysis. Harrison (2009, p191) defined it as:

> ...a generic term used to cover the processes of identifying what successful task, job or role performance looks like, and what is needed from individuals in order to achieve those results.

Iqbal and Khan (2011), in their detailed examination of studies and articles on learning needs analysis, discovered the use of different terms. These included such language as 'need', 'needs assessment', 'needs analysis', 'training requirements analysis' and 'performance analysis'. An illustration can be found in Spotlight on Practice 4.1: the 'MATT 2' programme cited earlier uses the term 'Development Needs Analysis'. Dingle (1995, p7) emphasises the limitations of terms like 'analysis' or 'assessment' and suggests that practitioners might find it helpful to avoid the use of what could be perceived as off-putting expressions like 'training needs analysis' and 'training needs assessment', in favour of the term 'competence requirements/enhancement analysis'. It is suggested that the term 'competence' defines outstanding performance and what employees require to achieve this. However, Simmonds (2003) disputes this assumption, owing to the method of development and implementation of the UK competency framework. In addition, with the primary emphasis on behaviours in the competence model, others may disagree with the use of the term.

Notwithstanding the varying author opinions on defining a learning need, the practicalities of identifying a learning need will be explored in the next section.

4.3.1 IDENTIFYING INDIVIDUAL LEARNING NEEDS

In any organisation people are frequently the greatest asset and more often than not one of the highest costs to the business, particularly with labour-intensive industries, such as call centres. Maximising the return on investment in employees must, therefore, be a key concern for all organisations. Everyone within an organisation has learning needs, although these may vary considerably. The extent of the learning needs of an apprentice, for example, will include both depth and breadth, compared with the specialist requirements of a chief executive. Nonetheless, both will require some form of development in order to develop and maintain their engagement and performance. Unfortunately, there is evidence that the identification of learning needs is not given enough attention nor is it conducted in the necessary manner (Clarke 2003). A further criticism noted in a comprehensive review of training needs assessment by Ferreira and Abbad (2013) is that there is relatively little theoretical and empirical research on the subject.

The practice of evaluating learning needs is often characterised by a 'diagnostic' element underpinned by a process of information-gathering and analysis (Iqbal and Khan 2011; Leat and Lovell 1997). This phase is characterised by seeking data and insights about the level and quality of employee capability and making some judgement about whether this fits the manager's/organisation's expectations. For example, in their article examining why, typically, leadership development programmes do not always deliver the value they could, Gurdjian et al (2014, p2) highlight the failure to really understand what is needed in terms of learning as one main reason:

> We have found that when a company cuts through the noise to identify a small number of leadership capabilities essential for success in its business—such as high-quality decision making or stronger coaching skills—it achieves far better outcomes.

The suggestion is that there must be a focus on the specific learning need. Therefore, the system should provide the information needed to make decisions about appropriate development activities which match and respond to the identified learning need (Brown 2002; Goldstein and Ford 2002).

EXERCISE 4.2

IDENTIFICATION OF LEARNING NEEDS

Describe what your organisation typically does when it comes to identifying learner needs as a prelude to a specific learning intervention or programme. How are the main stakeholders involved, if at all, in this process? What steps are taken to 'quality assure' the methods of identifying specific learner needs?

The process of identifying learning needs can suggest that the employee is subject to a degree of comparative analysis in which their existing skills, behaviours and actions are evaluated against some model of 'ideal performance' (Leat and Lovell 1997, p144) or even 'idealised performance'. This could bring with it some risks around the legitimacy, robustness and neutrality of the presented model of 'ideal performance' and the degree to which it is objectively defined and free from distortion based on assessor bias and hidden motives.

It will become evident when reading further into this chapter that some of the commonly used needs analysis methods can be time-consuming, resource-intensive and require some degree of technical or specialist expertise. This can sometimes, in practice, limit the extent to which a systematic and rigorous approach is used with the result that the methods identified are not fully utilised. According to theory, essentially a systematic, rather than ad hoc or intuitive approach, is needed to identify learning and development needs. However, Anderson (1994, p23) claims that a comprehensive approach is rare:

> ... most organizations follow their own less systematic procedures based on tradition, office politics and various internal and external pressures.

Anderson (1994) also suggests that despite the general recognition of the importance of employee development being underpinned by systematic learning needs analysis, in many instances the work done is little more than lip-service, and moreover, considerable amounts of investment are made in learning provision based on individual wants rather than objectively defined learning needs. Unfortunately, according to Cekada (2011), the limited scholarly literature available on TNA makes it difficult to know if the situation has changed dramatically since the findings of Anderson (1994). In addition, there is limited information and advice in the training needs literature about how the linking of organisational goals with training needs can be achieved at a practical level (Ofluoglu and Cakmak 2011). Notwithstanding these comments, there is some evidence from the systematic review undertaken by Ferreira and Abbad (2013, p92) that there has been some slight progress as TNA has moved 'from ad-hoc frameworks to a more professional and scientific basis'. Despite this, overall the authors suggest that issues remain with linking individual and organisational needs. In practice, data collection and analysis require a strategic, systematic approach that can be adopted throughout an organisation. Consequently, a process by which all stakeholders – such as line managers, senior managers and HRD specialists – can understand their role in achieving such an outcome is needed.

To illustrate some of the possible issues arising from a lack of systematic learning needs analysis, consider the potential impact on a new recruit. Organisations invest a significant amount in recruitment and selection processes; consider the growth in the use of assessment centres and their substantial cost. However, once an employee joins an organisation, if no individual training needs analysis is undertaken, it can be difficult for that individual to perform at their optimum. The selection process can typically identify the technical skills and competence required for a job; however, it is not until an individual is working in the organisation, with all its complexities, that a full review of the required behaviours/attitudes can be undertaken.

Figure 4.1 illustrates the impact of identifying learning and development needs for the new recruit. If an individual does not perform, most organisations have an option of exiting them using the probationary period process. However, this is not only a costly system but can have a psychological impact on other staff, for example, tapping into security needs (Maslow 1943). For some individuals, however, their successful performance, if not strategically planned, is achieved to a significant degree by chance. It is therefore critical, in order to maximise the potential performance gain to an organisation, that training needs analysis is undertaken in a systematic and horizontally aligned manner, for example, with the recruitment and selection process.

Figure 4.1 Impact of LNA on new recruit

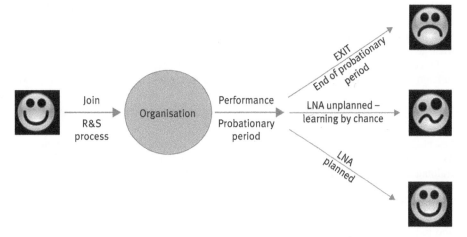

Source: developed by authors

4.3.2 KNOWLEDGE, SKILLS AND ATTITUDES

This section explores the techniques that can be used to identify individual learning needs. The most common theoretical approach is to use knowledge, skills and attitudes (KSA) as the basis for identifying specific learning, although, in practice some organisations categorise these as technical and behavioural skills. The framework of KSA originated from the work of educational psychologist Dr Benjamin Bloom (1956). Bloom's taxonomy comprises three domains of learning – cognitive (knowledge), affective (attitude) and psychomotor (skills) – in order to stimulate higher forms of thinking in education. These have been translated into KSA, as follows:

- **Knowledge:** All societies have both common and esoteric knowledge (Wheelahan 2007). Common knowledge can be understood by many; for example, employee contract law is generally recognised, but specific aspects that may be used in an industrial tribunal are less known. Esoteric knowledge is generally known by only a few, rather than many. The concept has received much attention with an array of different references to the knowledge economy, workers and sharing (Drucker 1995). Individual knowledge has provoked reaction in many disciplines and has increasingly been deemed a top priority for management (Davenport and Prusak 1998).

- **Skills:** Stewart and Rigg (2011) highlight three different types of skills including intellectual, physical and interpersonal. Intellectual refers to IQ skills such as spatial reasoning, mental arithmetic and judgement. Physical skills are also frequently referred to as manual skills. Examples of interpersonal skills include non-verbal skills.
- **Attitudes:** Attitudes are opinions which are evaluative and emotional, as held by individuals. In practice, particularly since the introduction of competency frameworks in the 1980s, organisations now tend to refer to attitudes as behaviours, for example, identifying how sales staff should communicate with customers.

In practice, the term 'technical', combining knowledge and skill, is utilised by some organisations. Generally speaking, it is easier to identify and test the knowledge and skills required for a role. This is because there is frequently quantifiable data available and it is possible to use a range of methods to confidently test for this type of knowledge. More difficult is the identification and development of attitudes (behavioural). For example, many organisations have comprehensive sickness absence systems in place. Managers attend training courses to learn the process and what they need to do to record and monitor absence, therefore, they gain knowledge. However, less attention is given to dealing with the frequently more challenging task of dealing with attitudes and behaviour, for example, with the poor attender. These can be difficult conversations. This type of training need is an individual need but one that is frequently challenging and difficult to manage.

Discussions of learning needs analysis, in the literature, also frequently refer to the different levels at which the analysis can be carried out. These different levels of LNA will be explored in the next section.

4.3.3 LEVELS OF LEARNING NEEDS ANALYSIS

Learning needs have been traditionally explored at different levels in the organisation. This section will analyse the most common three-tiered systems model of identification of training needs in the organisation as well as noting the Harrison (2009) and IiP model (IiP 2013).

One of the earliest and most utilised approaches is the three-tiered system, produced by McGehee and Thayer (1961), of analysing needs at the organisational, job/occupational and individual levels, as shown in Figure 4.2. The framework has been adapted, with the latest and most commonly known version being attributed to Boydell (1983).

Organisational-level learning needs are generally of two types: a synopsis of all needs, and those that are required by the vast majority or all members of the organisation (as illustrated by Case Study 4.1 towards the end of this chapter). In terms of the latter type of learning need these could be in relation to a specific organisational change or a compulsory business requirement. For instance, there may be a change in strategy, policy or business priorities that results in a training need for all or a significant section of staff. Likewise, certain quality or health and safety training can be compulsory for all staff. Essentially, it is necessary to conduct a type of organisational analysis to enable the organisation to maintain and meet future performance expectations.

All jobs have specific requirements and demands. As a result the job will require all staff to have an appropriate level of KSA. Consequently, in order to achieve high performance it is important that all staff have developed these to the needed level or proficiency. For example, call centre operators may require training in telephone techniques or computer literacy skills. An output of this analysis should be a specification that includes the training needs of all individuals involved in a particular role.

Figure 4.2 A basic framework for levels of LNA

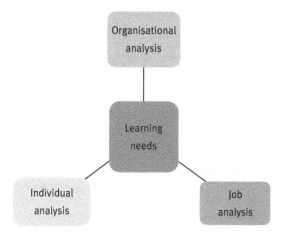

Source: adapted from the work of Boydell (1983)

Individuals are all different and, therefore, have a variety of personal development needs. This is not only the case for all new employees, but may also flow from those needs identified from a change in the job or role specification. All individuals will join an organisation with their own personal set of KSAs. However, in the vast majority of cases these will not be an exact fit to the KSAs identified for the job. Consequently, there will be a gap to be filled through training or other development intervention. Once the individual is established in the organisation their training needs are frequently identified through the performance management system. Some of the specific activities related to each of the three KSA areas, forming part of a comprehensive learning needs analysis, are summarised in Figure 4.3.

Despite criticisms that the three-tier approach does not include environmental analysis nor the impact of group work (Moore and Dutton 1978), overall, it has had and continues to have a major influence. Essentially, in practice, however, it is important to ensure that the levels are not considered solely as independent entities and to evaluate them in a continuous spiral with one another (CIPD 2013a).

Figure 4.3 Specific activities underpinning levels of LNA

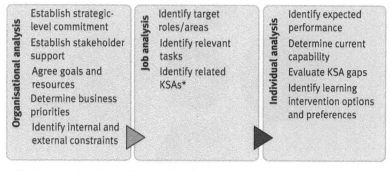

* KSAs: Knowledge, skills, attitudes

Source: developed by authors

EXERCISE 4.3

LEVELS OF LEARNING NEEDS ANALYSIS

Drawing on your experience, identify an example for each one of the three levels of learning needs analysis specified in this section:

1   Organisational

2   Job or professions

3   Individual

As an alternative way of thinking about learning needs analysis and with a focus on the job, Harrison (2009) presents four particular methods – comprehensive, key task, problem-centred and competency-based analysis – and discusses their relative advantages (see Figure 4.4). The author suggests that some of these methods can be mixed and cites the example of the combined use of problem-centred and key task analysis in situations where an employee takes up a new job but already has most of the competence needed to perform well (Harrison 2009). Comprehensive analysis refers to a detailed examination of the whole job. Owing to the process being extremely time-consuming, it is most appropriate for jobs that typically have a relatively straightforward, unchanging skill set. The outputs of a comprehensive analysis are commonly a job description and job training specification. Key task analysis is related to the essential elements of the job. Problem-centred output relates to major performance issues. For example, sickness absence for paramedics was attributed to a lack of de-briefing and support after their involvement in major incidents. This type of training need could have arisen through a problem-centred approach. Competency-based analysis relates to competency-based frameworks that are utilised in organisations to identify behaviours that are important to achieving success in a particular job. Competency-based analysis is time-consuming and expensive but, when used in combination with a framework, can be usefully deployed in many HR practices.

Figure 4.4 Four common methods of LNA

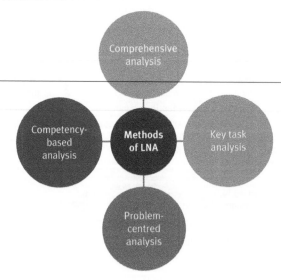

Source: Harrison (2009)

Another pragmatic but formal way to identify training needs, commonly used by employers, is the Investors in People (IiP) model. A range of forms can be downloaded for use by organisations to conduct training needs analysis. More information can be found on the Investors in People website (IiP 2013).

SPOTLIGHT ON PRACTICE 4.3 – CAPABILITY REVIEW

In terms of assessing organisational capability, the UK Government's Capability Reviews are an interesting example of a strategically led initiative aimed at assessing the capability of government departments on how well placed they were to meet the demands of the future (Cabinet Office 2006, 2009). The reviews provided, for the first time, a transparent set of assessments, reached with the help of independent experts, to judge the relative capabilities of departments going forward.

4.3.4 STRATEGIES TO IDENTIFY L&D NEEDS

The following model for analysing training needs has been adapted from the work of McClelland (1993). It also includes the practitioner perspective of Barbazette (2006), who suggested a three-phase process (points 8, 9 and 11 in this model):

1 Define assessment goals.

2 Determine assessment group.

3 Determine availability of qualified resources to conduct and oversee the project.

4 Gain senior management support and commitment.

5 Review/select assessment methods/instruments.

6 Determine critical time frames.

7 Schedule and implement.

8 Gather information – this stage is a formal or informal process to identify performance issues or areas for development.

9 Analyse information – analyse, interpret and conclude from the data gathered.

10 Draw conclusions.

11 Create a development plan by utilising the information that has been analysed to provide solutions to resolve the performance issue or development needed.

This process provides a straightforward way to analyse training needs. However, note the need to take a holistic view and ensure that in Step 1 the assessment goals fit with the organisational strategy.

Goldstein and Ford (2002) offer an alternative to our model with a focus on the process of learning needs analysis. They identify the various aspects of learning and development needs assessment as comprising the following:

- identifying organisational support
- conducting an organisational analysis
- conducting a requirements analysis
- undertaking a task and KSA analysis
- completing a person analysis.

The Goldstein and Ford (2002) approach has a focus on specific types of analytical methods that can be adopted to inform the practice, as opposed to providing the step-by-step approach of McClelland (1993). Another way to consider assessment goals is to identify possible indicators of training needs. Gold et al (2013) suggest a list of possible indicators:

- Output: Where individual or organisational productivity is below standard, this could be indicative of a training issue. Possible issues include poor communication, weak standards and procedures, job demarcation and so on.
- Varying standards: There may be a training issue where there is evidence of disparity in performance norms across similar groups of employees.
- Turnover and absenteeism: Staff turnover is the most utilised measurement tool by the HR department (Gates 2004). High staff turnover can indicate an issue that may relate to attitudes, weak recruitment and selection practice etc.
- Delays: Lack of knowledge and skills could be one of the reasons for operational issues.
- Complaints: Complaints from key stakeholders, and in particular customers, can provide valuable feedback for the organisation. As the feedback is deliberated on at a strategic level this can highlight both organisational and individual development needs.

This list is not intended to be exhaustive as, in the real world of practice, the factors causing a training issue may be extremely complex involving a mix or additional indicators.

EXERCISE 4.4
USING MCCLELLAND'S THREE-PHASE PROCESS

Identify a situation, from your personal experience or one with which you are familiar, where there is a potential training need. Using McClelland's (1993) three-phase process, explore and provide possible solutions.

4.4 SOURCES OF DATA

Various sources of data from within the organisation will provide information that can be utilised not only to identify specific learning needs, but also to enable HRD practitioners to produce an overall learning and talent development plan. However, much of the data may be sensitive, relating to the KSA issues of an individual employee. Consequently, any learning needs analysis system must accommodate the need for respect, confidentiality and ethical application. Also, some of the information supplied will need to remain confidential, for example, if the organisation is planning a business transformation change programme. Once potential sources of data have been identified, different techniques can be used to access the information. In their extensive reviewing and critique of training needs analysis, Moore and Dutton (1978) identify the most common methods utilised, most of which originated from the work of McGehee and Thayer (1961).

Figure 4.5 provides detail of the most commonly known and utilised sources of data available to organisations. In practice, organisations are likely to be selective about the sources they use. It is also rare that all the sources identified will be used by an organisation. The choice of method will depend on the following: depth/degree of information required; time available; experience of the human resource investigator; and financial implications (McClelland 1993).

Figure 4.5 Data source methods

Data source	Purpose	Key considerations
Organisational goals and objectives	Provide direction. Deviations from objectives can be identified.	TNA needs will support overall business goals; however, dependent upon hierarchy, an individual may not recognise the personal benefit.
Human resource plan	To understand demographic data and potential gaps in knowledge, eg effect of retirement.	Provides important demographic information that is difficult to obtain through other methods.
Organisational climate indices including: Labour turnover, grievances, absenteeism, suggestions, productivity, accidents, sickness, attitude surveys, customer complaints	These indices provide valuable information about the practical and emotional life of the organisation. Moreover, they can highlight if the psychological contract of individuals is being met. Frequently, behavioural training may be a remedy.	The indices are relatively easy to access and analyse. Nevertheless, care must be taken that issues may be attributed to an individual training need when, in reality, there is a flaw in the system.
Efficiency indices: Material costs, quality control, distribution costs, waste, down time, late deliveries, repairs	This information can provide information about the difference between actual and desired performance.	'Real-time' information can be valuable to understand issues, although the relationship to training needs may be more complex.
Exit interviews	Valuable personal insight can be gained.	Issues that may not be obvious or are difficult to uncover, such as attitude, may be found. However, sensitive issues may surface that need to be carefully handled.
Appraisal and performance management system	Appraisal schemes can highlight current and future development needs.	There is an opportunity for the employee to influence their development. Nevertheless, care in terms of possible bias needs to be taken if systems linked to pay.
Competency frameworks	To provide specific behavioural needs, including positive and negative ones.	Best-practice competency frameworks provide an integrated system for recruitment, selection and development. Owing to their behavioural nature, they can be valuable to helping poor performer understand frequently challenging issues.
Development centres	To identify development objectives and training needs.	Well-structured development centres can provide an opportunity for a thorough exploration of training needs. However, they are expensive and time-consuming.

Source: developed by authors

One of the most common sources of information for learning needs analysis is the performance appraisal (Gibb 2008). Most formal performance appraisals usually have a section on development needs, but the extent to which these are identified and documented in a systematic or rigorous way is unclear. The contribution of performance appraisals as mechanisms for determining workforce development needs at a strategic level is debated. There is evidence that systems can lack the level of analysis needed to match individual learning needs with organisational goals (Gibb 2008; Leat and Lovell 1997).

Another source of learning needs information is development centres, as opposed to assessment centres (BPS 2011). However, they can be costly to set up and administer and, if they are going to be utilised effectively in the training needs process, the data they provide will need to be analysed in detail in order for it to be useful. This is one of the issues found by Winter (1995, p17):

> We used development centre assessments to identify individuals' training and development needs. However, the ratings are based on observations of behaviour and, although they gave broad indications of development needs, they were not specific enough to target a training or development intervention ...

The concept of competence, derived from the work of Boyatzis (1982), was mentioned in relation to learning needs analysis earlier in the chapter. In practice, the idea of 'competence' has been translated into competency frameworks. The purpose of competency frameworks is not only to identify learning requirements but also to align these with business needs. The majority of frameworks identify what competencies employees need if they are to perform at superior levels, with some also defining poor performance. Although they can be usefully deployed, it is important to recognise their limitations. The prescriptive nature of competencies and belief that the possession of specific competencies will automatically lead to higher performance is disputed. The latter assumption does not take into account organisational factors and the overall notion of competency suggests that they are straightforward, linear and mechanistic (Simmonds 2003).

Finally, organisational and efficiency indices, including balanced scorecard assessments and knowledge from exit interviews, can provide valuable information that, when investigated, can lead to the identification of learning needs. However, especially in the case of exit interviews, it is important to maintain an open mind as the issues identified could be attributed to a variety of causes other than learning needs.

EXERCISE 4.5
SOURCES OF DATA

Identify the sources of data that are commonly used in your organisation, or one with which you are familiar. Choose two and in pairs critically evaluate their use in practice.

4.4.1 METHODS TO ACCESS SOURCES OF DATA

It is necessary to access the sources of data identified in the previous section. The way each method is explored will vary considerably but is dependent upon the situation, context and skills available. Figure 4.6 provides an overview of the primary methods available, including analysis of their strengths and weaknesses.

There may be an assumption that, as the most common method of data collection, the survey would automatically involve quantitative methods. However, from the systematic review of TNA undertaken by Ferreira and Abbad (2013), many of the questionnaires included open and closed data, thereby utilising qualitative and quantitative approaches.

Figure 4.6 Methods to access sources of data

Method	Purpose	Strengths	Weaknesses
Surveys/questionnaires	Traditionally in form of a survey of sample or whole population.	Surveys are relatively inexpensive, can reach large number of participants.	Lack of depth of information. Will not explain causes of issues.
Interviews with stakeholders, eg supervisor or employee	Can be informal or formal. Could interview whole sample or representative group. Flexible as could use telephone or face-to-face approach.	Rich data including opinions is gathered. Opportunity to probe individual, particularly if current job-holder.	Data collection and analysis is very time-consuming. It is not possible to generalise from the data.
Focus groups	Can be formal or informal. Can be focused on goal, task or theme.	Confidence of participants can be increased owing to group dynamics.	Data can be difficult to analyse. Experienced facilitator required to manage focus group.
Observations	Can yield qualitative or quantitative feedback.	Generate real-life data. Particularly useful to try and elicit tacit knowledge.	Highly skilled observer with subject knowledge needed. Time constraints as data can only be collected at operational level.
Tests	A variety of tests could be utilised to gather understanding.	Opportunity to understand deficiencies in terms of KSA. Easy to quantify and compare.	Development of tests requires specialist knowledge.
Social media, eg Twitter	Primarily useful to obtain informal information, eg personal view of tasks.	Good to capture attitudes.	Limited contral over data collected.

Source: developed by authors

Nevertheless, the authors criticised the fact that the methods were generally dealt with independently. In their view there should be greater use of mixed methods and the simultaneous use of qualitative and quantitative approaches. They also suggest that greater use should be made of 'heterogeneous and probabilistic sampling methods' in order to avoid gaining the views from one, possibly like-minded group such as middle management (Ferreira and Abbad 2013, p94).

Spotlight on Practice 4.4 provides detail of the line manager responsibilities in the development of professional practice for novice HR practitioners. In this case the novice HR practitioners are normally attending university on a part-time basis to learn and attain professional qualifications, termed PDS. The training needs were developed and analysed from a longitudinal piece of research that followed the careers of HR novice practitioners over a number of years.

SPOTLIGHT ON PRACTICE 4.4: HR PROFESSIONAL DEVELOPMENT

In small groups, using the information below, identify the training needs for a manager of a novice HR professional. Once identified, produce a training plan that will meet the suggested needs.

Line manager responsibilities	Overview
Regular meetings	One of the significant aspects is that time needs to be set aside for professional development. A commitment is required from both the individual and the line manager. Consequently, regular meetings initiated by both the manager and the individual, with the specific purpose of discussing professional development, are needed.
Proactive management support	The role of the line manager is to assume a proactive stance in the development of the novice. They should initiate meetings, create opportunities and be proactive in the career planning of the trainee.
Stakeholder perceptions	The line manager should be fully aware of their role in directly or indirectly affecting other stakeholder perceptions. In order for the individual to progress, they will need others to believe in them as a professional. This perception will not only be formed through the work and impression left by the novice HR professional, but also by the way the manager speaks of them; for example, the manager could ideally refrain from sharing criticisms to other managers of the novice during this development phase.

To enable the above, it is recommended that the line manager:

- Should initiate regular formal and informal meetings with the novice HR professional regarding their professional development.
- Must create development opportunities that match what the novice HR professional is learning on the PDS (Professional Development Scheme). If the novice HR professional has completed their PDS, opportunities could match development with business and individual needs, plus personal interests.
- Should encourage the building of professional and other relationships, perhaps through the manager's contacts, both internally and externally.
- Needs to create wider opportunities for the individual to use and share their knowledge, perhaps in the community.
- Must fully support risk-taking involving 'disorientating dilemmas'. Mistakes, whilst learning, need to be tolerated, with a primary focus on encouraging learning from these.

4.5 LEARNING NEEDS ANALYSIS: CURRENT PRACTICE, IMPLICATIONS AND LIMITATIONS

Having considered the various methods of learning needs analysis, this section explores some of the challenges of implementation in practice. For example, Goldstein and Ford (2002, p25) suggest that the potential value of some learning and development interventions can be hampered by '... trainers [who] are more interested in conducting the training program than in assessing the needs of their organizations'. Given the pressures for responsiveness and rapid turnarounds, and the limits on resources, it is possible to see how, in practice, those at the front end of learning and development provision might be tempted or persuaded to curtail the level and depth of the needs analysis phase. Instead, they may forge ahead with the more tangible and visible activity of learning delivery. Goldstein and Ford (2002, p25) also suggest it can be a case of HRD practitioners putting the proverbial 'cart before the horse' and being captivated by a particular delivery method or tool before properly understanding learner needs:

> ... [they] are sometimes sold a particular approach [such as technology-based learning provision] before they have determined the training needs of their organization and whether the techniques will be useful in meeting those needs.

What this suggests is that the process of needs analysis should not only consider the individual learner and organisational needs but that the HRD practitioner must have the knowledge and skill to objectively evaluate the best method(s) for meeting a need.

Another limitation is that there may well be a time-lag between a decision being taken to undertake a learning needs analysis, it actually being conducted and the subsequent learning intervention being designed and delivered. This, in turn, could result in a situation where the original needs may well have changed, thereby limiting the value of the time and energy put into carrying out the learning needs analysis. This may also limit the relevance and benefits of the actual learning provision (Anderson 1994). Also, Harrison (2009, p204) points out that HRD professionals and line managers '... often blame lack of time for their failure to carry out all their L&D tasks adequately', all of which can contribute to costly mistakes and poor use of training budgets.

It is also worth questioning the extent to which typical learning needs analysis practice takes account of the 'organic' nature of adult learning as well as the contribution of non-formalised, incidental and spontaneous workplace learning opportunities. Moreover, the extent to which learning needs analysis approaches, particularly those based on rigid behavioural objectives, place unnecessary and artificial boundaries on our understanding of employee competence is also questionable. Commenting on the specification of the behavioural objectives approach to identifying learning objectives, Mager (1984) suggests that often the identified learning objectives do not specify what the learner will be able to do, and to do differently, once they have fulfilled the specified learning objective and that this can limit the fit between specific learner needs and the learning provision.

4.5.1 IMPLICATIONS FOR HRD PRACTITIONERS

As discussed in this chapter, learning needs analysis, when conducted well, can make a positive contribution to the subsequent quality of learning provision. The needs analysis can inform the design and delivery of learning intervention and can help ensure that the related learning intervention is relevant and enhances capability, thereby ensuring that the investment in it is maximised. It can help organisations assess their internal capability, 'fitness' and readiness in terms of operating within a changing environment both internally (such as following a restructuring exercise) and externally (such as technological innovations affecting business practice). Furthermore, it can have an additional benefit of signalling to employees and the target of the needs analysis that the organisation is interested in and has invested in understanding their needs and helping them to prepare to adapt to the new working environment. This could leave employees feeling valued and, in turn, could lead to improved levels of motivation and engagement.

On the downside, the benefit of the learning needs analysis process is not always shared. For example, some might view it as a cosmetic exercise that will be of no or little direct benefit to them as individuals; others might treat it warily as a 'deficit oriented' approach and 'the management's' attempt to highlight the shortfalls in their skills and knowledge. What this suggests is that HRD professionals have an important role to play in terms of communicating not only the intentions and purpose of the needs analysis, but also how the information gathered will be used.

HRD professionals have a role to play in terms of building commitment and engagement with the needs analysis process. Specifically, it is incumbent on HRD practitioners to brief senior leaders and managers properly about the planned needs analysis process, especially in cases where it is targeted at a large number of employees or requires an organisation-wide analysis. They need to make a business case for why the organisation should invest in conducting the needs analysis, and to work with the senior leadership team, where possible, and especially where the needs analysis is organisation wide, to develop a well-thought-through communication strategy. The purpose of such a strategy is to inform employees about what is taking place, related time frames and what is expected from them. In certain cases, as well as disseminating information about the purpose and potential value of the needs analysis, it is useful for senior leaders to verbalise plus demonstrate their commitment to the process. Explicit management support for the learning needs analysis can affect the quality and level of engagement with its implementation.

Also, HRD professionals need to be familiar with the range of tools and techniques and possess the skills and abilities to carry out the needs analysis. For example, designing needs assessment questionnaires, particularly web-based ones, and data analysis, especially of quantitative data, might require specific technical expertise in areas such as statistical analysis. It is also important for those carrying out the needs analysis to have some competency in presenting the data and of prioritising which of the needs are of greater relevance to the organisation.

In terms of conducting an organisation-wide learning needs analysis, it is important that there is some flexibility in relation to the approach used so that it is responsive and appropriate to the variations in different parts of the organisation, such as different professional roles, cultures and priorities. In terms of culturally diverse teams or in international settings, it is critical, for those leading the needs analysis, to recognise the influence different cultural values might have on specific methods used. For example, when running focus groups comprising people with different levels of seniority from the same team or department, to identify skills gaps, it is worth being mindful of issues such as 'the pecking order' in high power distant cultures (Hofstede 1991; Trompenaars 1993). In such a situation, it might be that only the senior participants actually speak and the junior members remain silent or simply go along with whatever the senior people say. This could limit the amount or quality of the information that is elicited.

Realistic time frames also need to be set for planning and conducting the needs analysis. While it is accepted that this may not always be possible in practice, it is important for HRD professionals to help organisational leaders and decision-makers to recognise that an effective needs analysis, especially if it incorporates a large number of employees, will take time. Moreover, that a superficial approach to the needs analysis may be of limited value in the longer term. For example, an insurance telesales call centre might want to increase the number of policies their sales people sell and the HRD professional is told to get a motivational speaker to 'get the team energised'. However, this might be a case of jumping to a 'solution' without understanding the specific needs of individual sales advisers. For sales operatives it might be a case of needing to be energised, in which case the motivational speaker might have some positive benefit. For others it might be a case of understanding some of the specific techniques in terms of 'sealing a deal' or 'getting a customer to commit to a policy', and underpinning this could be the need to enhance their communication and negotiation skills. A motivational speaker might have little to offer in terms of helping develop such skills and they might be better developed by sending the sales staff on a training course or coaching with an experienced member of staff.

All in all, HRD practitioners have an invaluable contribution to make in terms of ensuring that the learning needs analysis is an effective and useful process.

4.6 CONCLUSION

Overall, an effective learning needs analysis ensures that the organisation implements learning provisions that are 'needed' by the individual, team and organisation. The chapter has conveyed the idea that learning needs analysis plays an important part in ensuring that the learning and development in which a company invests corresponds to and goes some way to meeting the specific development needs of the recipient of the learning provision, be it to an individual employee, team or organisation.

To achieve this, the chapter has emphasised the importance of the process of learning needs analysis being strategically led and aligned, identifying how the process is an essential part of the learning design and delivery process. An analysis of the methods and sources of data has been introduced; however, the use of these methods will be context-dependent and, in practice, much more complex to use than can be expressed in the chapter.

CASE STUDY 4.1

NATIONAL SCHOOL OF GOVERNMENT – SKILLS MAPPING AND ANALYSIS PROJECT

The National School of Government conducted an organisation-wide skills survey as part of its Change Programme. The project was tasked with reviewing staff capability and readiness for emerging business challenges. The process included identifying staff skills and expertise and skills gaps and development needs.

A tailor-made online skills survey was used to help identify the current skills and expertise together with the development needs of Corporate and Business Support staff. A similar survey was used with the Teaching and Consultancy staff.

It was anticipated that the information gathered would help identify specific areas of strength and weakness, inform the School's Learning and Development Plan, and be used to update HR databases.

All corporate and business support staff (179) and teaching staff (81) were asked to complete the skills survey during a two-week period, with a 73% response rate for the former and a 74% response rate for the latter.

Staff were asked to rate themselves in relation to a list of 58 skills that they are likely to use in their day-to-day work. This list was developed through a process of interviews with individual staff and through a series of focus groups with specific work teams.

The skills were grouped into three categories – Business, Management, and Personal Effectiveness. In terms of Technical and Professional skills, professional Heads of Finance, Library Services, Marketing and Communications, Human Resources, and IT were asked to assess themselves and their teams against existing professional standards.

Generally, Corporate and Business support staff reported a good breadth and level of skills and expertise. However, there are areas that need attention. Overall, of the 58 skills people were surveyed on, the top three where higher capability was reported were business skills including working across organisational and team boundaries and building customer relationships.

The overall top three reported management skills reported were managing fairly and inclusively, giving constructive feedback, and managing team dynamics. The overall top three reported personal effectiveness skills were listening attentively and responding appropriately, understanding own strengths & limitations, and joint third, managing stress at work and writing clearly in a way that others can understand.

There are many areas where weaker capability was reported, for example, in terms of management skills: assessing and managing risk, coaching, one-to-one development, and providing a vision for the team; and in terms of personal effectiveness skills: delivering convincing presentations, coping with aggressive behaviour and handling conflict at work constructively.

Additionally, there were some differences in the level of reported capability across the grades. In terms of the number of higher-level skills reported by each individual, these ranged from 0 to 52 out of the total of 58. Most people said they had between one and five higher-level skills. Thirteen people reported no higher-level skills, of which 10 were women, and of the 20 people that indicated none or only one higher-level skill, 16 were women. Staff on Grade C (lower grade) reported, as an average, the least number of higher-level skills.

The final section of the survey asked staff to identify their learning and development needs. There were a number of common responses and many of these are consistent with the skills gaps identified elsewhere in the survey.

Respondents also identified a variety of technical learning and development needs specific to their area of professional practice.

Twenty-five per cent of Corporate and Business staff reported having an academic (under-graduate or post-graduate) qualification and 64% of the teaching staff reported having a post-graduate qualification. Many others reported having a variety of professional qualifications.

The Skills Survey Process

The main stages of the skills survey process are outlined in Figure 4.7. In terms of specific actions, the survey design process included the following:

(a) discussions with internal experts
(b) initial discussions with potential participants
(c) draft survey design
(d) consultation with potential participants on the draft survey
(e) consultation with internal stakeholders including senior management and trade unions
(f) survey formatted into electronic version using Communigator (an electronic survey formatting tool).

Further, individual team leaders were consulted and three open sessions were held to discuss the design of the proposed survey.

Figure 4.7 Stages of the skills survey

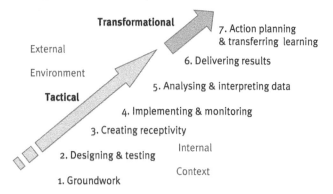

Transformational

7. Action planning & transferring learning

External

Environment

6. Delivering results

5. Analysing & interpreting data

Tactical

4. Implementing & monitoring

3. Creating receptivity

Internal

2. Designing & testing

Context

1. Groundwork

Questions

Having read the case example and the approach taken to identifying organisational learning needs, what do you think might be some of the possible:

1 Benefits of using this method of needs analysis?

2 Limitations of using this method?

EXPLORE FURTHER

CEKADA, T. L. (2011) Program development-peer-reviewed-need training? Conducting an effective needs assessment. *Professional Safety*, Vol 56, No 12, p28.

GOLD, J., HOLDEN, R., ILES, P., STEWART, J. and BEARDWELL, J. (2013) *Human resource development: theory and practice.* 2nd ed. London: Palgrave MacMillan.

HARRISON, R. (2009) *Learning and development.* 5th ed. London: CIPD.

McCLELLAND, S. (1993) Training needs assessment: An 'open-systems' application. *Journal of European Industrial Training*, 17(1).

McGEHEE, W. and THAYER, P. (1961) *Training in business and industry.* New York: Wiley.

SIMMONDS, D. (2003) *Designing and delivering training.* London: CIPD.

CHAPTER 5

Designing Learning Interventions

DR CRYSTAL ZHANG AND DR NIKI KYRIAKIDOU

LEARNING OUTCOMES

By the end of this chapter you will be able to:

- critically evaluate a range of learning and instructional design theories and principles
- apply them to select and justify appropriate learning and development methods and delivery channels with engagement and support of other professionals and managers
- design learning plans and interventions to meet identified needs in a timely, feasible and cost-effective way.

5.1 INTRODUCTION

This chapter is about designing learning interventions (DLIs), especially in the context of the modern diverse (for example, multicultural and multi-generational) workplace. Learning involves the organisation, the learner and the trainers. Each group brings their own perspectives on what constitutes an efficient learning intervention. Hence, it is important for us to explain what is learning, what are learning interventions, what do these involve in terms of design, and finally why the topic is important enough to warrant your attention and time. Sadler-Smith (2006, p2) argues that 'learning is at the heart of organization'.

This chapter will start with the definition of learning, training and education, then provide guidance to learning intervention designers (LID) as to what needs to be taken into consideration when designing a learning and development strategy. An LID or management development consultant will need to be aware of three aspects when designing learning interventions: the meaning of learning and learning intervention; the aspect of the organisation; and the learner and trainer himself/herself. Hence, this chapter will first examine the design of learning interventions from an organisational perspective, such as the culture and context of the organisation, the organisation's purpose and the objective of the training, the cost and resources available from the organisation, and finally, the stakeholders' expectation towards the organisation. Secondly, it is important for the trainers to know all relevant information from the learners' perspective. For example, it is important to have a full understanding of learners' current skills and knowledge, their attitudes towards learning and their individual learning styles. Finally, the chapter will apply the critical evaluation of the learning theories and organisational context to the design of appropriate learning and development methods and the delivery channels. Figure 5.1 summarises the structure of this chapter, ie the perspectives of the organisation, the learner and the learning intervention designer (LID). The ultimate goal is to produce a guide for LIDs to designing learning intervention based on the analysis of those three perspectives.

More often than not, learners are considered as a homogeneous target. The modern workplace is now markedly different from a decade ago, with changes in employment laws meaning that people of different generations now work next to each other. There is also more diversity at work with different cultures and backgrounds coming together. Thus a blanket fit-all learning intervention might not be the most suitable, and diverse learners' perspectives need to be considered.

At the onset of designing learning interventions, it is important to determine what the learning is created for. The aims are, generally:

- to raise awareness (of old or new techniques/issues)
- to facilitate consensus and teamwork
- to assist in formulating policy or strategy
- to implement plans or new approaches
- to enhance skills and foster networks.

During the learning intervention, both the trainer and the learner's perspective need to be aligned for optimum learning transfer.

This chapter reflects on research, theories and current practice in order to identify best practice in measuring the effectiveness of training delivered. For example, Kirkpatrick's four-level training evaluation model (reaction, learning, behaviour, results) or Kolb's experiential learning theory (which works on two levels: a four-stage cycle of learning and four separate learning styles), can help stakeholders involved in training programmes objectively analyse the effectiveness and impact of each stage of the process so they can evaluate the overall experience and provide strategies (action plans) for development in the future.

Figure 5.1 Factors affecting designing learning interventions (DLIs)

5.2 WHAT IS LEARNING?

It is important to understand the meaning of learning based on the distinction between 'education', 'training' and 'learning' even though these terms are often used interchangeably. According to Mayo and Lank (1994) and Rosenberg (2001):

- education: refers to a change in knowledge (Mayo and Lank 1994)
- training: refers to a change in skills (Mayo and Lank 1994)

- learning: refers to a process of acquiring new skills and/or knowledge for the purpose of enhancing performance (Rosenberg 2001).

According to the CIPD, training is defined as 'an instructor-led, content-based intervention, leading to desired changes in behaviour'. Whereas, learning is a self-directed, work-based process, leading to increased adaptive potential (Sloman 2005). One clear difference between these two terms is whether the intervention is instructor-led or learner-directed.

Figure 5.2 summarises these definitions, and the relationship between them.

Figure 5.2 Learning, development, training and education

5.3 THE ORGANISATIONAL PERSPECTIVE

This section will first examine the design of learning interventions from the organisational perspective, such as the culture and context of the organisation, the organisation's purpose and the objective of the training, the cost and resources available from the organisation, and finally, the stakeholders' expectation towards the organisation. (Detailed analysis on the objective and purpose of the training is already covered in Chapter 4.)

5.3.1 CULTURE AND CONTENT OF THE ORGANISATION

Culture is often explained as that which is taken for granted in a society or organisation. Although there is no standard definition of culture, at its most basic, it refers to the meaning (mental assumptions) that the people attribute to their actions (Ravasi and Schultz 2006). Within an organisational setting, culture is often related to the shared attitudes, beliefs, behaviours and assumptions about what the organisation is there to do, or the reasons for its success historically. Similarly, culture can also be thought of as the 'artefacts' of the organisation – such as organisational routines, working language, systems and structures. Organisational culture affects the way people and groups communicate and interact with each other, with clients, and with stakeholders (Modaff et al 2011). Personal experience is considered as a variable that impacts on organisational communication and sees culture in three different ways (originated by Putnam 1982, and Redding and Tompkins 1988):

- Traditionalism: views culture as an object that can be measured, labelled, classified related to other organisational paradigms such as stories, rituals, and symbols.
- Interpretivism: views culture subjectively through a network of shared meanings.
- Critical-interpretivism: critical scholars regard organisations as instruments of privilege or even outright oppression. This perspective views culture through a network of shared meanings and language which has been developed by the dominant thinking and acting of the 'privileged' classes (senior management, owners etc) during their relationships with disadvantaged or oppressed organisational groups (workers, women etc) working within the organisation.

Case Study 5.1 provides important evidence of a pattern of unlawful behaviour, attitudes and organisational paradigms. The evidence provided could show that the female employee has experienced direct sex discrimination (in access to training and being criticised where males are not) and mistreatment with regard to other colleagues' behaviour and work attitude.

CASE STUDY 5.1

DIVERSITY

According to the Equality and Human Rights Commission in the UK, it is against the law to subject employees or vocational trainees to harassment on grounds of their sex or gender reassignment. Harassment is a form of direct discrimination.

Sexual harassment is defined as unwanted behaviour that takes place simply because someone is a woman or a man. The behaviour is done with the purpose of, or has the effect of, violating the person's dignity, or it creates an intimidating, hostile, degrading, humiliating or offensive environment for her (or him).

I asked for the same training, which I need in order to complete my apprenticeship, but my boss called me a "stupid little girl" and said that if I couldn't do the job properly I should leave. My colleagues often play tricks on me such as putting my tools on a high shelf where they know I can't reach them. They do not behave this way towards one another. I am now keeping a diary to record all these incidents so that I can make a complaint.'

Source: http://www.equalityhumanrights.com/advice-and-guidance/your-rights/gender/sex-discrimination-your-rights-at-work/

Example

'I am a female apprentice electrician and all my colleagues are men. I feel like even though my work is of a high standard, my boss constantly criticises me and shouts at me whereas he does not bully the men in this way. A new male apprentice has started at work and he is receiving much more one-to-one training and assistance.

Question

Can you identify organisational practices/elements of organisational culture that impact on the formation of shared meaning, attitudes etc by taking into consideration the example on gender discrimination?

According to Johnson and Scholes (1999), it is possible to explore the organisational context and business environment, through an examination of an organisation's cultural web over a period of time (Simmonds 2003).

Figure 5.3 The cultural web

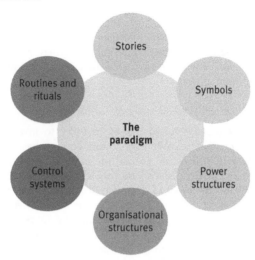

Source: adapted from Simmonds (2003)

The cultural web, as shown in Figure 5.3, is a representation of paradigms, of an organisation and its culture. It aims to help managers address the challenge of strategy-driven cultural change. Each of the components of the cultural web can be broken down further and they are also interrelated in order to obtain a fuller understanding of the organisational culture.

Rituals and routines: The routine behaviours that members of the organisation display both internally and towards those outside the organisation make up 'the way we do things around here' on a day-to-day basis. It may provide a distinctive organisational competence, but can also represent a taken-for-grantedness which can be difficult to change. The rituals of organisational life are particular activities or special events through which the organisation emphasises what is particularly important and reinforces particular organisational behaviours.

The stories told by members of the organisation to each other, to outsiders, etc, embed the present in its organisational history and also highlight important events and personalities. They tend to cover successes, disasters, heroes, villains and mavericks.

Symbols such as logos, offices, cars and titles can be a shorthand representation of the nature of the organisation.

Power structures are also likely to influence the key assumptions. The most powerful groupings are likely to be closely associated with the core assumptions and beliefs.

The *organisational structure* is likely to reflect power and show important roles and relationships. Formal, hierarchical, mechanistic structures may emphasise that strategy is the province of top managers and everyone else is 'working to orders'. Highly devolved structures may signify that collaboration is less important than competition, for example.

The *control systems* such as measurements and reward systems emphasise what is important to monitor in the organisation. Reward systems are important influences on behaviours, but can also prove to be a barrier to success of new strategies.

The *paradigm of the organisation* encapsulates and reinforces the behaviours observed in the other elements of the cultural web.

As we have seen in the definitions, and in the example about workplace harassment, there is a tendency for organisations' strategies to persist because they are taken-for-granted assumptions about the nature of the organisation, its environment and the way things are done in the organisation (shared meanings). Even when a strategy is formulated based on shared meanings and ground rules, organisations can often experience difficulties in making significant changes to current organisational strategy. One of the main problems organisations face in managing strategic change is effecting changes in organisational culture. By mapping aspects of organisational culture it may be possible to see where barriers to change exist and also what aspects of the existing culture are in line with the desired future strategy (Simmonds 2003).

5.3.2 INVESTMENT IN TRAINING AND DEVELOPMENT: VALUE FOR MONEY?

Many UK organisations spend a lot of money in order to invest in their employees' training and development activities. While economic recession has a significant impact on resources available, there is still debate around the importance of training as one of the most significant variables for sustainable employment (UKCES 2010).

Research conducted in this area has demonstrated that money allocated for training provision and career development of the employees has not been very well spent. Indeed, estimates suggest that between 15% and 20% of learning investments in organisations have a positive impact on employees' work performance (Leimbach 2010). This is more apparent within small and medium enterprise organisations. This is according to research from the Forum of Private Business (FPB), which found that cost was the main barrier to training in 61% of small businesses. The main concerns of SMEs in the successful implementation of their training provision are based on, first, their failure to identify needs effectively and, secondly, on their weakness/lack of expertise in designing appropriate training to meet the identified training needs.

EXERCISE 5.1

GLOBAL CHALLENGES ON SUSTAINABLE EMPLOYABILITY AND INNOVATIVE HRD PRACTICES

One of the most important challenges for contemporary leaders is to strive for engaged and productive employees for a long-term career within their organisations. However, current global trends (as identified by the G20 Training Strategy report in 2010) demonstrate that economic growth in the future will depend even more heavily than today on the productivity of the workforce, complemented by rising labour force participation rates, especially among women, graduates and older workers. In this context, the challenge of lifelong learning, particularly among unemployed graduates and/or ageing but economically active employees is very

intense. Similarly, the international flows of economic migrant qualified employees will continue to grow, raising challenges concerning fair access to employment opportunities and work training provision.

1   What particular challenges might a university lecturer face when teaching groups of international mature students with previous working experience undertaking an executive MBA programme?

2   Would a trainer/business consultant providing training for middle managers within a multinational organisation face similar challenges?

As we will see in the next sections, a careful consideration of learning needs within the organisation combines with a range of appropriate training strategies in order to design a systematic training intervention (framework) of organisational learning, education, training and development.

5.3.3 THE PURPOSE AND OBJECTIVE OF THE TRAINING

Training and development helps in optimising the utilisation of human resources, and in turn it helps the employee to achieve organisational goals as well as their individual goals. A structured approach to training and development helps to provide an opportunity and broad structure for the development of people's technical and behavioural skills in an organisation. It also helps the employee in attaining personal growth, increasing the job knowledge and set of transferable skills of employees at each level.

Therefore it is very important for the organisation in general and the trainer in particular to carefully identify the training needs and then design the principles for implementing training methods and good practices. Setting learning objectives will help the facilitator to provide direction and clear indication of what is to be achieved through running a training session.

A well-developed statement of intent in line with a set of learning objectives is the first and the most important step towards the design of a systematic training and development programme as it defines the purpose of the training activity and its outcomes. It also generates a set of learning principles/guidelines, such as the following, which will help to facilitate the design of internal and external training events:

1   Emphasise standards: One of the ultimate goals of training is to highlight the performance standards that attach to various jobs within the organisation and also provide the links between the training needs analysis and the design and delivery of training, enabling the trainer to consider which path to follow in order to achieve the end goal (Glaister et al 2013).

2   Provide consistency: A well-designed training programme should ensure that those attending training will be instructed, and there is consistency in terms of the information provided, throughout the section, department or company.

3   Develop objective outcomes: Clear learning objectives, which are based on a systematic review of training needs analysis of an individual, should develop outcomes that should be achievable, pragmatic and measurable during the performance appraisal reviews. In other words, learning objectives and the design of training methods should be geared to individuals, learning styles and training needs (Kolb 1984; Honey and Mumford 1992).

CASE STUDY 5.2

MEETING BUSINESS NEEDS THROUGH LEARNING AND DEVELOPMENT IN A LARGE SUPERMARKET RETAILER (NAMED ABC) IN THE UK

Since the economic recession in 2007, British supermarkets and retail industries have experienced a significantly turbulent time. However, ABC, a large British supermarket retailer, has managed to respond to the crisis through a long-term investment in learning and development of its employees. ABC has dedicated Stores of Learning (SOLs) across the company. These are stores which serve as centres for providing excellence through technical and behavioural training.

Julia, the Regional Operational Manager (ROM), shares her experience in learning and development in ABC.

'It's dynamic, fast-paced and challenging. I'm given all the space I need to do things my way, which I find really inspiring. Of course, we have a framework that we all work to which is based on a systematic training provision, but it is very flexible, so I never feel constrained at all. In fact, this is one of the reasons I joined ABC in the first place At ABC, if you put in the work and you are committed to learning and development programmes that are available to you based on your position, the reward and progression is definitely available.'

This example demonstrates that appropriate investment in learning and development increases retention of colleagues and leads to higher-performing and more productive teams, which in turn support ABC's growth and expansion plans.

The key benefits of ABC's training are seen in:

● increased productivity, improved quality of service provided, and thus enhanced customer satisfaction
● increased employee morale which leads to a more motivated team

● providing a pipeline for an internal talent pool.

Source: adapted from The Times 100, Business Case studies

http://businesscasestudies.co.uk/asda/meeting-business-needs-through-training-and-development/costs-and-benefits-of-training-and-development.html#axzz2kRCYqWxj)

Read more: http://businesscasestudies.co.uk/asda/meeting-business-needs-through-training-and-development/costs-and-benefits-of-training-and-development.html#ixzz2kRCnzoEx

Question

Reflecting on the principles of learning explored in the text, develop a framework of learning objectives for Julia that helps her develop effectively within the organisation.

5.4 THE LEARNERS' PERSPECTIVE

The illiterate of the 21st century will not be those who cannot read and write, but those who cannot learn, unlearn, and relearn.

Alvin Toffler

This often misquoted quotation from Alvin Toffler emphasises the learning, unlearning and relearning of the learner. Learning is mostly associated with the formative years of childhood and adolescence, when the child's mind, it has been argued, is akin to a blank slate and the learner is taught and expected to learn. Adult learning at the workplace, on the other hand, can be harder, as the learner has had years of life experience and has developed his/her own personality, learning and cognitive style. Furthermore, the modern workplace is now staffed with multigenerational and multicultural employees, each with their own personal life experience and culture. During the learning needs analysis, the learner analysis is performed to determine who needs training, what type of training is needed and whether training needs to be adapted for some learners. This section will consider the learning intervention from the learner's perspective. (Detailed analysis on learning theories is available in Chapter 2.)

5.4.1 ANDRAGOGY LEARNING THEORY

Until the mid-1920s, learning theory did not differentiate between children and adults, as learning was assumed to be unnecessary once adulthood had been reached (Knowles 1973). However, a series of studies from Lindeman in 1926, Thorndike in 1935 and Sorenson in 1938 (Knowles et al 2005) paved the way for andragogy (adult learning) as a separate theory from pedagogy (children learning). These were refined by Knowles (1973) into the basic components of a theory of adult learning.

1   Relevance and practicality
    Adult learners must first understand why they need to know something before they actually invest time in learning it. A study by Trueman and Hartley (1996) showed that 'mature students had better study habits than the younger students in that they engaged in more "deep" and less "surface" learning than did the younger students'. As such, it is preferable for learning interventions to have 'need to know' information rather than 'nice to know' information, and a clear learning outcome for what the knowledge/information will be useful for.

2   Self-image
    Adult learners use their experiences to build their self-identify, and tend to become resentful when these images are not valued in a learning situation.

3   Life experience
    Building on the previous theme, adult learners need to feel as if their life experience is important as it helps them make connections between old and new knowledge. Life experiences are wide and varied, but can be 'stereotyped' into generational experiences – the Baby Boomers, Generation X, Generation Y and Generation Z (see Table 5.1).

4   Preparation
    Adult learners will generally prepare more for a learning situation, and manage their learning time better. Trueman and Hartley (1996) showed that adult students reported the most use of time management strategies; however, this did not necessarily translate into better academic performance overall.

5   Motivation
    Adult learners want to learn to solve or address a particular problem, and are more satisfied with their learning if it relates to everyday experiences, is practical, or is current. They are in the learning situation by choice and do not require the extrinsic motivational rewards that children do.

5.4.1.1 Individual characteristics affecting learning outcome

Adult learners have individual characteristics, which may affect the learning outcome. Many motivation theories, such as Vroom's Expectancy Theory and Maslow's Hierarchy of Needs, place personality as an important factor in motivation (Ford and Weissbein 1997). We here can consider three individual attributes: self-efficacy, goal orientation and motivation to learn (Salas et al 2012), which are very closely related to the andragogy learning theory. Furthermore, they have also to be linked to the efficiency of the transfer of learning to the workplace (Burke and Hutchins 2007).

1   Self-efficacy
    The trainee with high self-efficacy is more likely to participate in learning, work harder and persist longer during learning activities (Phan 2011). This individual is more likely to be motivated to perform well in a training programme and to transfer newly learned skills to the workplace (Bandura 1997). A meta-analysis of the literature on training motivation found that self-efficacy has a strong correlation with motivation to learn and motivation to transfer (Colquitt et al 2000). Thus training should be designed to promote self-efficacy, such as ensuring early successful learning experiences during the training programme.

2   Goal orientation
    There are two types of goal orientation: performance-oriented or mastery-oriented. Mastery orientation and time on task were the strongest predictors of performance on

the learning outcomes (Fisher and Ford 1998). Trainees with high performance-orientation prefer to concentrate on training exercises where they can achieve better scores (to prove they are capable), and will avoid those where they may fail (so as not to show weakness). On the other hand, trainees with strong mastery-orientation will seek to acquire new skills. Performance outcomes may be poor, but this is compensated by acquisition of new skills and learning through experience and mistake. Thus, performance-oriented trainees prefer highly structured training programmes with successively more difficult tasks, while mastery-oriented trainees prefer the freedom to learn and explore.

3   Motivation to learn
    Motivation is a very individual characteristic and is dependent on numerous factors, including the previous two and also on individual circumstances and context. Cognitive abilities and learning styles affect motivation, as do age and culture.

5.4.1.2 The generational workforce

People resemble their times more than they resemble their parents.

Arabic proverb

It is dangerous to stereotype any group. However, members of each generation tend to be grouped according to shared experiences in their formative years such as music, values, education, communication styles, historical events and most importantly for this discussion: work ethics. While this holds true at the group level (hence the starting proverb), individual attitudes, preferences and characteristics can vary wildly. Nonetheless, understanding each generation from a broad perspective can make it easier to work more productively with members of each and offers a foothold for designing better training interventions aimed at each group.

Historically, the workplace consisted of mainly two groups: the old-timers and the know-it-all young hotshots (Johnson and Johnson 2010). However, the demographics in the workplace slowly evolved into three, then four generations working side by side: the Veteran generation (born pre-1945), Baby Boomers (born 1946–1964), Generation X (born 1965–1980), and Generation Y (born 1981–1995). As the Veteran generation retires, Generation Z (born after 1995) will soon be emerging into the labour market, so that by 2015, the workplace will stretch to potentially five generations in some instances (KPMG 2013). It is important to note that this construction of generations is preferentially applied to the West. In China, for example, the generations are grouped by decades, hence the post-80s (born after the introduction of the one-child policy in China) and the post-90s (born during the Chinese economic boom).

By 2020, 36% of the working population will be over the age of 50 (CIPD 2011). At the same time, older workers are increasingly looking to extend their working lives, with more than 50% of workers aged over 55 planning to work beyond the state retirement age (CIPD 2010). Furthermore, people are living longer, with a predicted 19 million people in the UK aged over 60 by 2030 (Urwin 2004). It is therefore important to understand the changing demographics in the workplace and what motivates the learners from the different generational groups. Table 5.1 summarises the attitudes to work of the four current generations (Adecco 2013). Importantly, a recent survey across workers from the UK, USA, China and India shows that Generations X and Y place greater emphasis on opportunities for learning when choosing a company (see Table 5.2; Johnson Controls 2010). While this was from a small sample group (around 5,000 respondents), it reveals the change in work perception as we grow older – a desire for learning when younger (most probably linked to an opportunity for promotion as a result of undergoing training) to a more content phase as approaching retirement.

Table 5.1 Attitudes to work from the generational workforce

	Veterans: 1922–1945	Baby Boomers: 1946–1964	Generation X: 1965–1980	Generation Y: 1981–1995
Work ethic/values	Hard work, respect authority, sacrifice, duty before fun, adhere to rules	Workaholics, work efficiently, crusading causes, personal fulfilment, desire quality, question authority	Eliminate the task, self-reliance, want structure and direction, sceptical	What's next, multitasking, tenacity, entrepreneurial, tolerant, goal-oriented
Work is	An obligation	An exciting adventure	A difficult challenge, a contract	A means to an end, fulfilment
Leadership style	Directive, command and control	Consensus, collegial	Everyone is the same, challenge others, ask why	The young leaders century
Interactive style	Individual	Team player, loves meetings	Entrepreneur	Participipative
Communications	Formal written	In person	Direct, immediate	Email, voice mail
Feedback and rewards	No news is good news, satisfaction of a job well done	Don't appreciate it; money, title recognition	Sorry to interrupt, but how am I doing? Freedom is best reward	Whenever I want it, at the push of a button, meaningful work
Messages that motivate	Your experience is respected	You are valued, you are needed	Do it your way, forget the rules	Working with other bright creative people
Work and family life	Family first	No balance, work to live	Balance	Balance

Source: adapted from Adecco (2013)

Table 5.2 Factors in choosing a company (per age group). Respondents from UK, USA, China and India (total = 5,375) were asked to rank their top three priorities in choosing a company to work for

	18–25 years	26–35 years	36–45 years	46–55 years	56–65 years
Top 1	Opportunities for learning	Opportunities for learning	Quality of life	Meaningful work	Meaningful work
Top 2	Quality of life	Work colleagues	Meaningful work	Compensation	Quality of life
Top 3	Work colleagues	Quality of life	Compensation	Corporate values	Corporate values

Source: adapted from Johnson Controls (2010)

Table 5.3 Percentage of workers receiving training, by gender and age

	16–24	25–34	35–44	45–54	55–59	60–64	65+
Male	34.6	31.1	27.5	26.8	20.7	11.9	6.9
Female	37.3	35.9	34.6	32.6	25.3	18.3	11.5
All cases	35.9	33.4	31.0	29.8	23.0	14.6	9.0

Source: adapted from Newton et al (2005)

5.4.1.3 Older vs younger employees

The later two generations, X and Y, are more tech-savvy, especially Generation Y (also called Generation N, for Net), for having grown up in the digital age. Thus, it is perhaps not too surprising that myths have grown up implying that earlier generations (Veterans and Baby Boomers) are less adaptable and less able to grasp new ideas and technologies, following the adage that 'you can't teach an old dog new tricks'. However, myths can be dispelled (Allen and Hart 1998; Newton et al 2005). Indeed, older employees are valuable assets to the company, especially with the experience gathered through years of service (CIPD 2012c). A review by Meadows (2003) concluded that there is no discernible deterioration in performance in the majority of different types of work, at least up until the age of 70. Nonetheless, it is normally the generations X and Y which are more likely to undergo training, at the expense and exclusion of the older generation (see Table 5.3; Newton et al 2005). This lack of training opportunities was found to be an important co-factor for the difference in performance between younger and older workers (Meadows 2003). However, older workers were also found to be reluctant to take up the training offered due to fear or lack of confidence (Guthrie and Shwoerer 1996; Allen and Hart 1998; CIPD 2012c). Thus it is important to bear in mind these generational differences when designing training interventions.

5.4.1.4 Cultural differences in attitudes to learning

Culture is, as Hofstede describes, the mental programming of the mind (Hofstede et al 2010). It provides the 'lens' through which we view the world, the 'logic' by which we order it, and the 'grammar' by which it makes sense. Different cultures have different attitudes to learning and training. For example, a recent survey of the attitudes to vocational education and training (VET) in the 28 member states of the European Union has revealed that most of the European countries view VET positively (71%), although this is much lower in some countries such as Latvia and Lithuania (about 30%), where a VET degree is perceived to hinder work opportunities (Eurobarometer 2011). A survey of Generation Y from different parts of the world found that Indian and Chinese members of Generation Y placed opportunities for learning as a top priority when choosing an employer. Generation Y participants from the USA preferred meaningful work, while those from the UK valued work colleagues (Johnsons Control 2010). Thus effectiveness of training can be maximised depending on cultural background.

5.4.1.5 Experiential learning

The transfer of the training material into a meaningful outcome such as behaviour or performance improvement relies on the trainee proceeding through what is termed experiential learning, or learning by experience. While many training programmes rely on didactic methods such as lectures, there is a strong emphasis on on-the-job training and practices to improve trainees' retention of training material and to help them transfer their training to the workplace.

The experiential learning theory from Kolb (1984) assumes that learning goes in a cycle, from concrete experience (obtaining new experience), reflective observation (reviewing and reflecting on the learning), abstract conceptualisation (gathering the thoughts and making conclusions from the experience) and active experimentation (testing the new knowledge). To help individuals to assess their approach to learning, Kolb (1984) developed the Learning Style Inventory (LSI), which provides information about the individual's relative emphasis on the four abilities in the learning cycle. Figure 5.4 summarises Kolb's learning cycle and the four different types of basic learning proposed.

Figure 5.4 Kolb's experiential learning cycle

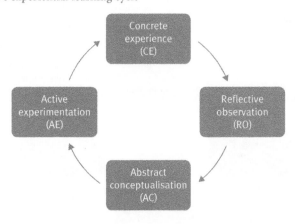

Source: adapted from Jenkins (1998, p43)

Table 5.4 The relationship between learning style and learning conditions

Learning style	Conditions under which learners learn better
Assimilators	When presented with sound logical theories to consider
Convergers	When provided with practical applications of concepts and theories
Accommodators	When allowed to gain 'hands on' experience
Divergers	When allowed to observe and gather a wide range of information

Source: Kolb (1984)

Each of these learning styles is suggested to have specific strengths and emphasis:

1   Assimilative style prefers building on theoretical models and is more on ideas and concepts than people.

2   Accommodative style prefers doing and risk-taking. More hands-on approach.

3   Convergent style prefers problem-solving and decision-making.

4   Divergent style prefers social interaction and brain-storming.

As such, it is believed that trainees with a specific learning style will benefit more from a training programme most suitable for their specific style. For the *assimilators*, learning is most effective when they are presented with sound logical theories to consider first. *Convergers,* on the other hand, learn more effectively when practical applications of concepts are provided. 'Hands on' experience is the preferred learning condition for *accommodators*. Last but not least, *divergers* prefer learn through observation and information-gathering (Kolb 1984).

Figure 5.5 Practical methods to implement the experiential learning cycle

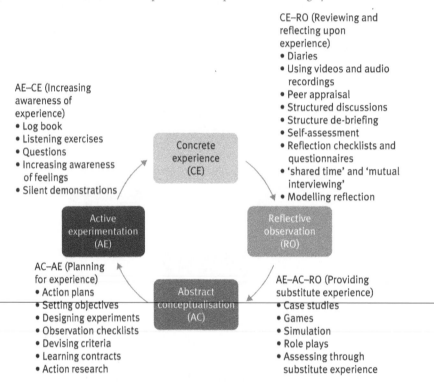

Source: adapted from Gibbs (1988, pp23–63)

5.5 THE DESIGNER'S PERSPECTIVE

The expansion of world trade, the globalisation of industry, finance, and the creation of more international roles and responsibilities of the work profile of many occupations, are creating a world in which cross-cultural interactions and national differences in business communications and negotiations occur more frequently than at any time in the past (Friedman 2005). Also, increasing specialisation and international roles within many professions have led to a widely dispersed audience for specialised professional education and training. International managers wishing to develop specialised skills that match the needs of a rapidly changing world, demand access to proper educational opportunities, even if this requires international travel or specialised knowledge in conducting business in different cross-cultural business settings (Berge 2007).

As a consequence, the growing multicultural nature of professional education and training environments makes it critical that training designers, especially those working in multicultural environments, develop skills to deliver culturally sensitive and culturally adaptive programmes. The following sections explore research, theory and current business practice relating to cultural differences to identify those dimensions of culture and business practices that are most likely to impact on behaviours, attitudes and certain types of learning interventions among a culturally diverse workforce.

5.5.1 CULTURAL CONSIDERATIONS

Culture and learning are intrinsically linked to each other. Just as a newborn learns culture through the mother (its teacher), a trainer (and a training programme) similarly imparts his culture to the learner, thus creating what Hofstede defines as the software of the mind (Hofstede et al 2010). A fundamental difference here lies in the fact that the newborn can be described as a blank slate for the cultural programming, while the (adult) learner has his own cultural baggage and needs to reconcile this cross-cultural educational experience and conflict. The modern workplace will generally include culturally diverse staff, with cultural predispositions to certain types of learning intervention. Thus it is necessary to consider whether attributes of the learning intervention can be tweaked to enhance a successful learning outcome. Studies with Chinese students showed that they had followership characteristics: reliance on rote learning, extrinsic motivation, high levels of achievement motivation, excellence in group projects, and willingness to invest in education (Pratt 1992; Kember 1999). They were also so accustomed to the teacher-centred class that once they were in the student-centred class, they complained that too much time was being wasted and insisted on more lectures from the teacher (Wen and Clement 2003). The opposite was also seen when Western students studied in an Asian setting (Chen 2014). Clearly learning outcomes could be improved by considering cultural differences in learning style. As a designer of learning intervention, it is important to consider learners' diverse background and learning style.

Congruent to this is the style of communicating the learning intervention. Studies from Kaplan (1966) show that different cultures use different ways of telling a story: ranging from a direct style seen in English and other Germanic languages, to a seemingly erratic and indirect style in Asian languages, appearing to circle round the theme before getting to the point. Judaic (and Semitic) language diverges from the main story before getting back to the point. Russian language style is found to be more fragmented. This sense of variety is further developed by Lewis (1996) in his study of cross-cultural business communication. Thus it is important to ensure trainers communicate their material in the most efficient way.

EXERCISE 5.2

What do you think of your communication style?

Go to http://www.crossculture.com/services/online-tools/ for more information on communication across cultures.

5.5.1.1 Caveats for a diverse trainee audience

Yet another area where cross-cultural differences should be considered is the validity of training material when applied to a different cultural market. A training programme which works for one culture might not work in another. This is most widely seen with learners from cultures different from Western culture, as most of the educational and training programmes originate from the West, and are based on Western philosophies and learning theories. For example, Hofstede's landmark work on culture, which is the basis of many cross-cultural training programmes, is based on his observation as a white European and builds on bodies of work from other Western researchers (Hofstede et al 2010). The original four dimensions of culture he proposed (power distance, individualism, masculinity and uncertainty-avoidance) did not adequately reflect the Asian perspective on culture. Based on the Chinese value survey by Michael Bond (Bond 1988), Hofstede added the dimension of long-term orientation, which looked at time-related attributes, such as persistence, perseverance and long-term/short-term gain (Hofstede et al 2010). With the rise of e-learning, learning interventions can be rapidly and efficiently deployed to a very diverse workforce and also to any units of an international organisation in the world. Furthermore, off-the-shelf training programmes can be purchased from training consultants. Thus there is a need for cultural considerations to maximise learning outcomes.

5.6 DESIGNING LEARNING INTERVENTIONS

A learning intervention is more likely to be successful if all the factors that have been analysed in the previous section such as clearly defined objectives, different learner types and the learning cycle as well as cultural differences of all stakeholders involved in the process have been taken into consideration. This section provides a structured approach to the design of learning interventions to ensure that the trainee's learning activities will achieve the outcomes s/he needs. This strategy includes the steps towards a systematic learning intervention strategy, followed by an analysis and critical evaluation of some of the most popular training methods.

5.6.1 DESIGN STRATEGY

Training interventions are not simply the training materials. To ensure an efficient learning outcome, it is important to consider and prepare for the steps happening before (planning and organising), during (conducting the training), and after the training (practice, learning transfer to workplace and feedback).

1   Steps before training
     A learning needs analysis (LNA) is conducted to determine what needs to be trained, who needs to be trained and what is the organisational system for training. This is necessary for clarifying the learning outcomes and preparing the next stages of training design and evaluation. During the LNA, an analysis of the job versus the task is performed to specify the requirements of the training and identify what the trainees need to know for the task. Thus the training provided specifically addresses real job

requirements and demands. A separate section will address the different types of training methods available (see Figure 5.6 on selecting training methods). At the organisational level, it is important to ensure that the organisation and work environment are able to support the training. There must also be consideration for the trainees: whether they need the training and whether the training needs to be adapted for some of the trainees. Finally, the learning climate needs to be addressed to maximise learning outcomes: these would be to schedule training (or refreshers) close to the time it is required, and to prepare the trainees and supervisors as to the expectations of the training.

2   Steps during training

The deployment of the training intervention is not without pitfalls. Following on from the andragogy learning theories discussed earlier, the trainer needs to increase motivation, greater learning, perseverance and encourage learning transfer to the workplace. These are enabled by tapping into the trainees' mind-set by building self-efficacy ('can do' and 'will do' attitude), promoting learning orientation and showing relevance and benefits of the training to their career and personal development. Transfer of learning to the workplace is the desired learning outcome and opportunities need to be created for the trainees to engage in activities that they may encounter during work (eg role play). This can also be enhanced by introducing error training strategy in the training material: the trainees are encouraged to make errors during training and are thus prepared to deal with unforeseen challenges on the job. Finally, not all learners learn at the same pace, and considerations need to be made to allow for individual self-paced learning and training experience.

3   After training

The learning outcomes of the training are generally determined at the TNA, before training has started. The popular model for measuring outcomes is the Kirkpatrick evaluation model with four levels (Kirkpatrick 1994). The evaluation criteria are to measure the trainee's: reactions (level 1: what they thought and felt about the training); learning (level 2: what skills, principles or facts the trainees learned); behaviour (level 3: resulting changes in behaviour and capability improvement and implementation/application to workplace); and results (level 4: the effects on the business or work environment, such as more profits or fewer errors).

To enhance learning outcomes, trainees should be given sufficient time and opportunities to use what they have learned and their supervisors should be given tools and advice on reinforcing learning outcomes (eg with on-the-job experience). Sometimes, debriefing and self-reflection (part of the Kolb's experiential learning cycle) can be used to reinforce and support what the trainees have learned.

5.6.1.1 Selecting training methods

From the LNA conducted before the training, the learning objectives and the learning strategy would have been identified and training methods can be selected (see Figure 5.6). Salas and Cannon-Bowers (2001) propose four characteristics of a thorough training programme:

1   Information (facts, skills, concepts) is conveyed to the trainee.

2   The desired behaviour and attitude to learning are present and encouraged.

3   There are opportunities for practising what is learned.

4   There is feedback to the training on how well the trainee is doing and advice on how to correct and improve the learning.

There are various forms of learning interventions linked with different sets of needs. These vary from *experiential* (which is learner-centred) to *didactic* (which is trainer-centred); from on-the-job to off-the-job training; and from individual to group learning needs. For example, Marchington and Wilkinson (2013) categorised training and learning methods according to two dimensions, namely pedagogical/andragogical and individually or group-based. Simmonds (2003) categorised learning interventions based on locations (that is, on-the job and off-the job training methods). In addition, Gudykunst and Hammer (1983) differentiate learning methods between didactic and experiential approaches.

Figure 5.6 Designing learning interventions

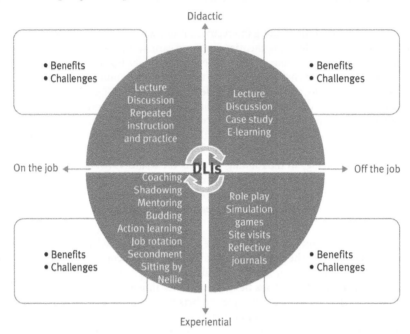

From Figure 5.6 and the information in Table 5.5 we can see that it is essential for the trainers to be familiar with a range of training methods.

Table 5.5 Benefits and challenges of learning interventions

Lecture	A structured presentation to convey required information, for example product knowledge, new policy/procedure.
Discussion	Free exchange of information and ideas, but working to a clear brief provided by the trainer, for example a discussion of barriers to effective internal communications.
Case study	Presentation of scenario (real or fictitious) describing organisational practice and behaviour. Trainees are asked to analyse the documented problem and/or reflect on described practice, for example an unfair dismissal case, a financial problem, departmental reorganisation.
Role play	Trainees enact a role they may have to play at work, for example interviewing a customer or negotiating an agreement. Other trainees, or actors, may be employed to play the role of significant others to enhance credibility.

Simulations	Realistic scenarios are provided for developing managerial skills in strategy decision-making and operations management in virtual reality (Stewart and Rigg 2011, p209).
Group dynamics	Trainees are put into groups to carry out a simulated exercise and behaviour is examined, for example group decision-making, intergroup conflict, intragroup communication.
E-learning	Learning is delivered through the Internet or an organisation's intranet.
Off-the-job skill instruction	A skill is taught by explanation, demonstration and practice, for example how to operate a computer.
On-the-job training	Sometimes referred to as 'sitting by Nellie'. Training is undertaken at the workplace, often involving demonstration followed by supervised practice. Often used for semi-skilled jobs but potential for developing individual skills in all types of work.
Coaching	Developing a person's skills and knowledge so that their job performance improves, hopefully leading to the achievement of organisational objectives. It targets high performance and improvement at work, although it may also have an impact on an individual's private life. It usually lasts for a short period and focuses on specific skills and goals (CIPD 2010).
Shadowing	Trainees observe a skilled, experienced practitioner at work, and discuss their perceptions with the practitioner. Process should require shadow to reflect on experience.
Mentoring	Relates primarily to the identification and nurturing of potential for the whole person. It can be a long-term relationship, where goals may change but are always set by the learner. The learner owns both the goals and the process (Clutterbuck and Megginson 2005, p4).
Exercise/project	Trainees are asked to undertake a particular work-related task leading to a required outcome, for example computerising client records or setting up a staff absence control system.
Action learning	Involves a small group of people meeting together at regular intervals to work on one or more issues that they can explore through questioning each other and they can take action to experiment with potential resolutions (Stewart and Rigg 2011, p192).
Job rotation	Moving around a number of jobs to build experience across job roles. Often a feature of graduate training programmes.
Secondment	Trainee spends a substantial period of time (typically 3–12 months) in a different job (sometimes in a different organisation) or with different responsibilities from normal. No special arrangements, just normal work.
E-learning	Learning is delivered, enabled or mediated using electronic technology for the explicit purpose of training in organisations (CIPD 2009).

Source: adapted from Glaister et al (2013, pp166–169) (in Gold, J., Holden, R., Iles, P., Stewart, J. and Beardwell, J. (eds) *Human Resource Development: Theory & Practice.* 2nd ed. Basingstoke: Palgrave Macmillan.

Every training method has its unique strengths and weaknesses (and for a comprehensive list of benefits and challenges, see Table 5.5).

Didactic learning has a strong focus on trainer-centred intervention, such as lectures for example. This provides benefits for the trainer to achieve a high level of control on content, structure and pace of delivery. However, there are limited opportunities for learner-led participation and interaction.

Experiential learning hands over the control to the learner. It focuses on learner-centred methods through action, learning by doing, learning through experience, and learning through discovery and exploration, such as shadowing and simulation games.

In order to decide which is the most appropriate learning intervention, it is essential to examine performance-related learning objectives, diverse learners' backgrounds, as well as the techniques, design and preparation involved.

It is much easier (and usually cheaper) to deploy lectures, videos and online learning to deliver the training material. However, these types of training methods lack adequate feedback and practice opportunities, and were shown to perform poorly in terms of behavioural and performance-related improvements (Smith-Jentsch et al 1996; Arthur et al 2003). More recently MOOCs (massive open online courses) have been much hyped in the higher educational sector as the modern way to reach out to millions on the Internet. For its ills, MOOCS can offer an alternative to e-learning, as it combines videos, lectures, coursework and online feedback and has been linked to corporate learning and development (Farrell 2012; Meister 2013).

CASE STUDY 5.3

THE RELEVANCE OF MOOCS FOR THE ORGANISATION

If you are a Chief Human Resource Officer or a Chief Learning Officer, here are five questions to consider as you think about how MOOCs can provide you with the impetus to re-think and re-imagine your employer brand and corporate learning department.

1   How can MOOCs build the employer brand by offering consumer education? Rather than limiting the innovation to the learning department, bring your Chief Marketing Officer in on the project and create branding opportunities, similar to the partnership between Khan Academy and Bank of America to create a series of self-paced courses for Bank of America customers on how to develop better money habits. One can imagine how this partnership could start a trend of company-sponsored consumer education using the MOOC model of free self-paced courses.

2   What's more important in learning: content or context? MOOCs' universal nature is central to their existence. Bringing them into the company's learning department inevitably means considering the context of training as well as the content. Chief Learning Officers should consider incorporating an opportunity to add a global dialogue to formal learning programmes by partnering with internal corporate social networks like Yammer and Jive Software or even external consumer sites such as Meetup.com.

3   How can data analytics help you improve your learning programmes? MOOCs offer real-time analytics that reveal each learner's progress and what formats work best for your learners. As big data sweeps the HR and corporate learning functions, more Chief Learning Officers need to be prepared to use data analytics to enhance the overall learning experience.

4   Can your company re-imagine the role of the learner? With MOOCs, the

learner takes on a role more expansive than ever before, acting as teacher, learner, and peer reviewer. Companies adopting MOOCs have to trust the learner to do this, by incorporating more opportunities for peer reviews and peer-to-peer dialogues into the course.

5   Could verified certificates mean huge reductions to your executive education budget? Millennials, who are projected to be 50% of the global workforce by 2020, are demanding more opportunities for learning and development credentials. MOOCs offer that – at a price point of under $100 for each certificate. Based on Yahoo! and Coursera's partnership to train and credential Yahoo!'s software engineers for a fee, this could become the 'new normal' for employees pursuing continuing education. That in turn would lead to budget re-allocations regarding how companies spend their continuing executive education budgets.

Source: adapted from Meister (2013) accessed Dec 20, 2013.

5.7 CONCLUSION

As organisations strive to compete in the global economic environment, differentiation and competence on the basis of the skills, specialised knowledge and motivation of the workforce take on increasing importance. To remain competitive, organisations operating in different national environments must ensure that their employees continually learn and develop through a well-structured design of learning and training interventions. In addition, modern organisations need to address the challenges of learning interventions based on increasing diverse workforce and multicultural working environments.

The chapter reflects on research, theories and current practice in order to analyse what constitutes learning interventions and also identify key terms; it has discussed key learning theories and also identified elements of best practice such as how a trainer can successfully design learning interventions that have a positive impact on both individuals and organisations involved in the process.

As such, one of the learning objectives of the chapter was to focus on the design of learning interventions from an organisational perspective, such as the culture and context of the organisation, the organisation's purpose and objective of the learning interventions.

Another learning objective was to identify methods of measuring the effectiveness of training delivered. This can help stakeholders involved in training programmes objectively analyse the effectiveness and impact of each stage of the process so they can evaluate the overall experience and provide strategies (actions plans) for development in the future.

Reflecting on the case studies, activities and information provided in this chapter, it is clear that a careful consideration of learning needs within the organisation requires a range of appropriate training strategies in order to design a systematic training approach (framework) of organisational learning, education, training and development. As such, a successful learning intervention is more likely if all the factors that have been analysed in the previous sections such as clearly defined objectives, different learner types and the learning cycle as well as cultural differences of all stakeholders involved in the process have been taken into consideration.

To conclude, the design of learning interventions provides a structured approach to training development to ensure that the trainee's learning activities will achieve the outcomes s/he needs and enhance on-the-job performance. As such, HRD professionals need to consider training as a system that includes the steps towards a systematic learning intervention strategy; followed by an analysis and critical evaluation of some of the training methods that are appropriate to a diverse workforce involved in, and benefitting from, this process.

EXPLORE FURTHER

CLUTTERBUCK, D. and MEGGINSON, D. (2005) *Techniques for coaching and mentoring*. Oxford: Elsevier Butterworth-Heinemann.

GOLD, J., THOPRE, R. and MUMFORD, A. (2010) *Leadership and management development*. London: CIPD.

ILES, P. and ZHANG, C. (2013) *International human resource management*. London: CIPD.

SIMMONDS, D. (2004) *Designing and delivering training*. London: CIPD.

STEWART, J. and GIGG, C. (2011) *Learning and talent development*. London: CIPD.

STEWART, J., GOLD, J., HOLDEN, R., ILES, P. and BEARDWELL, J. (2013) 'Encountering HRD', in GOLD, J., HOLDEN, R., ILES, P, STEWART, J. and BEARDWELL, J (eds) *Human Resource Development: Theory & Practice*, 2nd ed. Basingstoke: Palgrave Macmillan.

CHAPTER 6

Delivering and Facilitating Learning

MICHELLE MCLARDY AND NIGEL O'SULLIVAN

LEARNING OUTCOMES

By the end of this chapter you will be able to:

- examine the skills associated with facilitating learning of groups and individuals
- evaluate the approaches to and techniques of giving and receiving feedback
- examine the role of coaching and mentoring within organisations
- evaluate how to support learning of groups and individuals through blended learning and use of technology.

6.1 INTRODUCTION

Delivering and facilitating learning examines the roles and approaches in practice. It examines the skills associated with facilitating learning of groups and individuals and explores how these can be applied to create appropriate and effective learning climates. In addition to theory and practice of learning, it also considers the organisational context and the economic aspect an organisation needs to consider when trying to develop its workforce. This chapter is aimed at helping students to understand the concepts around learning and how individuals can learn effectively. It focuses on the development of individual development plans and also on the considerations that need to be taken into account when developing development plans for an organisation. It will help facilitate students' understanding of learning and also promote the concept that individuals need to develop their own learning framework that suits their learning styles and environment.

Chapter 2 has explored the leading theories of individual and collective learning including cognitive, behavioural, social and constructivist models and this chapter seeks to apply these in the work environment. The delivery and facilitation of learning is constantly evolving and the use and application of one-to-one coaching and mentoring will be discussed in an organisational context, as will the use of a range of presentational and instructional skills. Coaching and mentoring occur both internally and externally and each has a role in the performance and productivity of employees in organisations. Coaching and mentoring is an important development opportunity for any organisation and the link to the concept of high-performance organisations will be explored. For organisations to tap into their talent effectively, it is suggested that they should coach and mentor their teams. Coaching draws on a range of different fields such as psychology, leadership and organisational development and has been widely recognised in the fields of engineering, business and academia for its wide-ranging applications and support of both individuals and groups. A range of approaches and frameworks for coaching and mentoring will be explored.

The chapter continues with a section related to giving and receiving feedback. There are a wide range of approaches to and techniques of giving and receiving feedback and these will be explored through both theory and practice. This section supplements the section on coaching and mentoring by considering how the effectiveness of coaching and mentoring can be measured. The section on feedback discusses the individual approaches and the importance of communication within each one. The section explores how to give feedback effectively, directly and provides a framework for structuring effective feedback.

The final section of the chapter explores the ways in which learning can be delivered and received. This section complements the section on learning and looks at the methods used to facilitate learning. It is recognised that different forms of knowledge are best delivered by different methods, and that multiple methods of delivering knowledge and facilitating learning are becoming more important. The chapter will in addition provide guidance on supporting the learning of groups and individuals through blended learning and the use of technology.

6.2 DEFINING AND UNDERSTANDING WAYS OF FACILITATING LEARNING

6.2.1 LEARNING CONCEPTS

The concept of learning is a critical element of HRD and is often used interchangeably with other concepts, such as training and education. Although it is important to be more precise, this can, however, be troublesome. There are many definitions of learning and the debate about its precise meaning has been the focus of much discussion. From an educational point of view, a purist definition could be explored. From a psychological point of view perhaps another perspective might be appropriate. However, there is also an organisational perspective to be considered. This section will build on Chapter 2, and is based on six theories of learning. These are then developed into a practical concept of learning that can be transferred into an organisational context.

6.2.2 THEORIES

There are six key theories of learning:

- reinforcement theory
- cybernetic and information theories
- cognitive theories and problem-solving
- experiential learning theories
- learning to learn and self-development
- mental process.

These are briefly outlined in the following section.

6.2.2.1 Reinforcement theory

This theory is often associated with the work of Skinner (1965), who conducted numerous experiments to explore the factors that motivate individuals. This learning theory is often associated with behavioural learning; examples often centre on how children learn through positive reinforcement when their behaviour pleases their parents (reward), and negative behaviour that contradicts the expectations of their parents (punishment).

6.2.2.2 Cybernetic and information theories

This is often associated with the learning of skills. For example, when learning to drive a motor car, this often needs to be done slowly to start with so the impact of steering can be controlled effectively. As the driver turns the steering wheel, the effect this has allows the driver to adjust their actions to correct any over- or under-steering that may have occurred. This monitoring and information feedback to the driver is important and becomes part of the learning. As the driver gains experience, she/he begins to steer more accurately and can increase the speed of the car and drive more effectively. As the driver becomes more proficient, the driver can make judgements on the road about her/his speed and make sure that she/he is not driving too fast or too slowly when negotiating bends and corners (Reid et al 2007). In an organisational context many skill-based apprenticeships rely heavily on this type of learning to ensure employees learn these skills. The manufacturing sector would lend examples for this type of learning, such as the skills necessary to learn machining or hand craft skills.

6.2.2.3 Cognitive theories and problem-solving

Cognitive theory (Stammers and Patrick 1975) is seen as a contrasting approach to cybernetic and information theories of learning. It can be considered as the approach people take to problem-solving. People can learn from trial and error; by reasoning from first principles; or by seeking information and help to solve the problem. In reality, a combination of all three often happens when people are learning. This learning approach has also been witnessed in animals throughout the world. Those that are more advanced have learned to develop tools to help solve problems.

A typical example of this approach is where craft apprentices are given a wiring diagram and through trial and error they learn the principles of how electricity works and how to put them into practice (Reid et al 2007). Perhaps a more current example is the tool set many organisations develop for their improvement teams. The work organisations put into training staff in the skills of Six Sigma and Lean improvement initiatives is important. Many organisations are now recognising the benefits of developing staff with specific improvement skill sets so they can lead improvement initiatives and also help people within their organisations become Green Belt and Black Belt lean practitioners. These investments are seen by many organisations (eg GE and Unipart) as key investments in skills development, aimed specifically at improving the organisation's performance and profitability. Much of this work is built on the work of the quality gurus (eg Deming 1986) and the Toyota Motor Company.

6.2.2.4 Experiential learning theories

This theory is often explained through a model developed by Kolb et al (1974). It is based on an individual learning from their experience and reflection on specific activities to learn how the world around them works. Kolb conceived the learning in four stages: concrete experience; observation and reflection; formation of abstract concepts and generalisations; and finally testing implications of concepts in new situations. This approach to learning offers a framework so that individuals can adopt a structured approach to their learning in a real-life context. One example of this approach is where individuals in organisations are required to use learning logs to reflect on their experiences and what they have learned. The work of Honey and Mumford is also relevant here and their work builds on that of Kolb. They developed their theory and created a learning styles questionnaire in 1986, and this has become popular in learning and academic circles.

Within an organisational context there are a couple of examples and contexts where the reflection element can be seen to be in use. Organisations that run apprenticeship schemes will need their apprentices to keep learning logs. They will also need to complete assessments which require them to reflect on what they have learned, and give examples of this learning within the context of the subject area of the apprenticeship scheme. Also many professional institutes now insist on their members keeping learning logs and developing continuous improvement plans.

6.2.2.5 Learning to learn and self-development

As far back as 1979, Kenney, Donnelly and Reid were promoting the concept of learning to learn. The trigger for this work and view came from the observation that we are in a world of ever-faster change and it could be argued that this is more evident today than ever. Much of the management literature (eg Peter Drucker) and many of the professional institutes (eg the CIPD and the IMechE) promote the concept that people will need to continue to learn throughout their careers. One example of where organisations are promoting this concept is in the promotion of individual development plans and continuous learning concepts.

Many organisations are now creating their own organisational universities (eg McDonald's) and also online learning solutions for a wide range of learning courses (eg Rolls-Royce). These organisational infrastructures have been under development for many years and different organisations are at different stages of their own level of development. What can be said is that they will continue to develop and mature in future years.

6.2.2.6 Mental processes

For some time scholars have explored the concept of how the brain works and the idea that certain parts of the brain have specific functions and control how we undertake processing thoughts. Arguably an important theory with respect to learning is the concept of left-brain and right-brain activities (Ahn 2012). The concept goes on to allocate certain processing capabilities of both the left- and right-hand side of the brain – logic is associated with the left brain, and creative abilities with the right brain. It is argued that people often have preferences for one side or the other, ie an emphasis on the analytical or creative capabilities. However, there are also a growing number of academics and practitioners who are challenging this theory.

In Chapter 2 there is a comprehensive assessment of the different perspectives on learning, including analysis of the different ways in which individuals and groups learn. These concepts and models are important for the HR/HRD professional to understand, in order to develop appropriate learning solutions for themselves and for the people and teams within their organisation. It is now necessary to take this to the next stage, the actual application of these concepts, and consider the practitioner's perspective. Chapter 2 covers Bloom's taxonomy of cognitive capabilities (adapted from Gibb 2002, p66), the work of Kolb (1984), the work of the traditionalist learning theorists (eg Harrison 2005 etc) and also the behaviourist theorists (Pavlov 1849–1936). These different perspectives should be considered when developing an individual learning plan.

EXERCISE 6.1

Select three aspects of your personal learning requirements and develop an appropriate learning plan for the next two years. Include the following in your development plan:

- The learning required, eg inter-personal skills development.
- The method of learning, eg on the job, off the job, formal or informal learning.

- Identify the 'traditional learning theory' associated with the training need, eg cybernetic, cognitive etc.
- Assess how well this is likely to match your personal learning style, eg consider Kolb's or Honey and Mumford's theory.

With reference to Bloom's theory, which type of cognitive capability has your plan developed?

Once you have completed Exercise 6.1, it is necessary to reflect on it. It should be recognised that activity is not an easy one to undertake and there will be a number of factors to consider. Matching the learning requirements with the method of learning is an important step in the development of a learning and development plan and of learning effectively. Whilst on the surface it seems a fairly simple and straightforward step, once the aspects of individual learning styles start to be considered, this proves to be more challenging. This identifies an important point that needs to be considered in the section on organisational context. To effectively develop the people within the organisation, the HR/HRD team need to consider not only what needs to be learned, but how this is best facilitated. There are, however, organisational constraints and these will be explored in the following section.

6.2.3 ORGANISATIONAL CONTEXT

In the previous section we have explored the theory of learning and more precisely the theory behind how various academics believe people learn (both in this chapter and Chapter 2). But there is also an organisational context to consider. In order for an effective learning process to be developed, it is important to understand how people learn and, more importantly for individuals, to learn how effectively they learn. It also has to be recognised that each individual in an ideal world would create a unique learning and development solution to meet their specific needs. Each individual will have different preferences as to how they learn best and therefore to maximise the learning from an individual's point of view, it would be beneficial to that individual to have a tailored learning solution. However, in the world of learning (either academic or organisational) it is not always feasible or economic to tailor the learning solutions to meet each individual's preferred learning style. Individuals and organisations will thus need to recognise that a compromise in matching learning styles and the delivery of learning may be necessary.

As an economic entity, the organisation has to consider its customers and how best to serve them. Therefore, whilst it needs to train and develop its staff, it also has to deliver products and services to its customers in an economic manner. There is inevitably going to be a level of compromise between effective individually focused training (and as a consequence the individual learning) and delivering products and services economically. Therefore, from an organisation's perspective it will want to develop learning solutions that have the most economic benefits for the money spent. This is likely to compromise certain individuals' learning preferences because the training solution will not necessarily suit everyone's learning style.

There is much research (for example, Taggart and Sheppard 2010) suggesting that organisations that invest in training achieve better business performance. However, the specific of what training and how that contributes to the business bottom line is less easy to match. Taggart and Sheppard (2010) have attempted to link the training equation with the profitability of organisations. Their work suggests that it is possible to measure the return on investment of training, which is important in a competitive economic environment.

Chapter 2 also identified two more important areas for consideration. One is the issue of adult learning and the challenges this brings. The other is the context of learning in terms of individuals, groups and teams. The importance of individual learning, it can be argued, is self-evident. However, the perspective of group and team learning may be less obvious. Group learning still has much of an emphasis on the individual (Argote et al 2001) whilst team learning has more of an emphasis on performance. Group learning may happen as part of a formal course that members of staff participate in. This is a consideration the organisation needs to bear in mind when developing training courses: should the individual be sent on a course with people from other departments (or even organisations) and therefore gain the benefits of fresh and alternative insights, or should a specific course be organised specifically for the members of a department? If the course is designed to address individual learning, in reality some degree of group learning will also be encountered through the transfer of experience and deeper understanding of the topic being explored. However, the course may also need to be organised to address a learning requirement of the whole departmental team. In this instance the learning may address multiple requirements and have learning being undertaken on an individual, group and team level.

Many organisations have performance management systems and use this as an opportunity to integrate their performance management and personal development reviews. The competencies that are part of an organisation's performance management system can be useful in helping identify individuals' personal development needs and ensuring that they have the necessary competencies to undertake their role. In this context the perspective of learning and development is very much aligned to the organisation's goals and ensuring the personnel within the organisation have the necessary skills and competency for their existing roles and future career aspirations. When considering learning from an organisational perspective, it is important to link these to organisational objectives. This links with the area of performance management and aligning objectives with the overall business goals. Whilst in academic terms the emphasis is on understanding what learning and development is and how this is best achieved, from an organisational perspective it is most often viewed as the process of giving individuals the skills, knowledge and competencies necessary to be effective in their job. From this perspective the individual learning needs must be put into the context of how does learning take place effectively to deliver organisational goals. The work on group and team learning links to this in an important way. Exercise 6.2 now encourages you to consider learning from an organisational perspective.

EXERCISE 6.2

In the context of your organisation's requirements (it may be appropriate to consider a departmental perspective), develop an appropriate learning plan for the next two years (consider approximately five or six pieces of training and development for this exercise). Include the following in your development plan:

- The learning required, eg health and safety training for all staff members.
- The method of learning, eg on the job, off the job, formal or informal learning.

- Identify the 'traditional learning theory' associated with the training need, eg cybernetic, cognitive etc.
- Assess how well this is likely to match your personal learning style, eg consider Kolb's or Honey and Mumford's theory.
- Assess whether the training addresses individual, group and/or team learning.

How do these contribute to achieving the organisation's overall business objectives?

6.2.4 SUMMARY

This section has reviewed the different ways in which people learn. The research suggests that people need to find their own framework for learning that suits their learning styles and development aspirations. However, individuals will need to recognise that there are also organisational requirements that may mean their preferred style of learning cannot always be catered for and therefore they may have to be adaptable to achieve their personal development aspirations and needs.

6.3 COACHING AND MENTORING

According to the latest CIPD surveys (2011), coaching and mentoring have developed, expanded and evolved at a phenomenal rate. For many 'coaching' and 'mentoring' are one and the same and have become quite interchangeable. Both are aimed at supporting individuals' learning and development needs in their current role, but both can also be used to address future career developments. Hall et al (2013) make the point that the coach usually comes from outside the organisation, which implies that external expertise is required. Mentoring, on the other hand, is usually undertaken by an experienced manager or person of senior position within the organisation. Therefore mentoring is linked with personal guidance within an organisational context. There are many definitions of each and they differ if a person is a coaching or mentoring practitioner or if they are an academic researcher.

6.3.1 MENTORING

Mentoring has been defined in many ways, but Kram's definition (1983, p608) is perhaps the most widely used:

> a relationship between a young adult and an older, more experienced adult that helps the younger individual learn to navigate in the adult world and the world of work. A mentor supports, guides and counsels the young adult as he or she accomplishes this important task.

Whilst the mentor role as defined here still exists today, it is becoming more common and accepted for a mentor to be a peer taking on the role, not necessarily someone older. Peer mentoring provides benefits for both participants as it offers the opportunity for both individuals to become the giver and receiver. The role of a mentor itself has been divided by Kram (1983) into two functions: career functions and psychosocial functions. Career functions can include the mentor putting forward their mentee (also known as protégé) for desirable projects or jobs; exposing them to senior people in the organisation with a view to giving opportunities for promotion and increased visibility; sharing ideas; protecting them from risks to their reputation and therefore facilitating career progression. The psychosocial function includes: behaving as a role model; providing acceptance; discussing anxieties and fears and also acting as a friend. According to Arnold et al (2010) psychologists have been keen to undertake research into mentoring, in particular focusing on the impact on the mentee. The rationale behind this is that it could be considered an effective way to introduce and socialise new employees into the organisation's culture and to pass on the knowledge and wisdom of more senior or long-serving employees. It is also considered to be a motivational tool for employees, who may be in mid- or even late career, as they take on the role of the mentor. Studies have been undertaken to analyse whether mentoring has had an impact on the mentee's salary and promotion rates (Whitley et al 1991; Aryee and Chay 1994); however, they have only shown a small increase. It is therefore unclear whether it is mentoring that has had the impact and benefits to the mentee. It is also important to note that mentoring is not aimed purely at financial benefits.

HRD has three domains – career development, organisational development and training and development – of which mentoring is one tool. The benefits of mentoring are reported according to Ghosh (2012) 'to be pervasive in multiple fields as diverse as business, nursing, education, accounting, law, engineering and others'. Crucial to mentoring success is the development of the relationship between mentor and mentee as this is often considered to be more connected to 'friendship' – this is not necessarily so in coaching. However, Kram (1983) has undertaken research to assess the role of personality traits and mismatches in mentoring that have a serious impact on the relationship and therefore the outcome on individuals. Whilst there is not space to discuss this in detail in this chapter, it is important to note that although the aim of mentoring is to support learning and development, it can become nothing more than a superficial alliance, not a friendship. Merriam (1983 cited in Ghosh 2012) identified that mentoring represents different things to different fields:

> developmental psychologists viewed it as an 'intense emotional relationship contributing to adult development in all aspects of life', the business world primarily focused on how the mentor can guide the protégé's career, and the world of academia viewed the mentor's role to be similar to that of a teacher. (Ghosh 2012, p145)

In 2011, the CIPD, in conjunction with the Department for Work and Pensions and JobCentrePlus, introduced their own mentoring scheme for young adults looking for work. The aim is to assist young adults aged 18 to 24 into the work environment. The CIPD Coventry and Warwickshire branch piloted the scheme as the area has a particularly high youth unemployment rate and invited local CIPD members to use their skills in one-to-one mentoring sessions to assist the mentees with support, pathways into the labour market, to build up their confidence levels and develop employability skills.

EXERCISE 6.3

Proctor and Gamble (P&G), the world's leading consumer goods company, is determined to keep a balanced approach in these tough times and wanted to celebrate the power of its people. On 27 January 2009, they held an event to encourage employees to focus on their personal development. 'All About Me' also featured an information fair, where employees were encouraged to take advantage of the services and opportunities offered, including a mentoring and coaching programme (Business In The Community, **www.bitc .org.uk**)

How effective do you think information fairs and activities such as these are in promoting the benefits of coaching and mentoring?

6.3.2 COACHING

Coaching has always been seen as dominant in sport and business. It is perhaps more widely associated with sports such as football, tennis and rugby amongst others, due to the focus being primarily on performance and attainment. However, from a wider perspective it is often linked to life skills, team building and executive coaching. As with the definition and role of a mentor, a coach is still seen as a more experienced and more knowledgeable person. Rosinski (2003, p21) defined the difference between the two techniques as:

> Coaches act as facilitators. Mentors give advice and expert recommendations. Coaches listen, ask questions, and enable coachees to discover for themselves what is right for them. Mentors talk about their own personal experience, assuming this is relevant for the mentees.

The 2004 CIPD *Training and Development* Survey identified that coaching had the overall largest increase as a training technique in organisations (51%), followed by e-learning (47%) and then mentoring or buddy systems (42%). However, the 2011 CIPD *Coaching Climate* Survey Report stated that the number of respondents using coaching had fallen from 90% to 77%; but 84% of those respondents stated that they were using coaching far more than ever before. This is somewhat contradictory in nature based on a range of coaching case studies given in the Report, for example: PricewaterhouseCoopers, who have a strong commitment to coaching to support individualised personal development; and career coaching at Orange to support people on the job and within leadership and personal development. It is therefore not clear whether coaching is an ever expanding area of significance to organisations or has decreased in popularity as per the CIPD's findings. Garvey et al (2010) argue for a multi-methodological approach, in that it is not possible to use one or the other technique in isolation, but rather a combination of the two, as they are not always easy to differentiate between and in many ways complement each other. They further argue that there can be no 'one best way' in mentoring and coaching and therefore no one preferred or agreed definition. Coaching and mentoring, although different, are used for a variety of similar activities.

Figure 6.1 Applications for coaching and mentoring practice

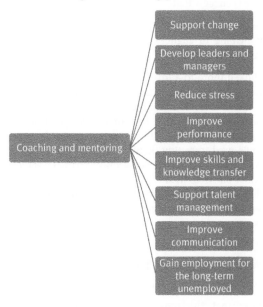

REFLECTIVE ACTIVITY 6.1

1   What do you consider to be the main differences in coaching and mentoring in your organisation?

2   Do you consider the coaching and mentoring activities in your organisation to be effective? How are they measured?

There is a debate regarding the best person to take on the role of coach in any organisation and whilst large organisations such as banks and the NHS can seek to bring in accredited professional external coaches, this is not always an option for small- to medium-sized organisations. Due to the cost involved of external coaching, a form of informal coaching is undertaken whereby senior members of the business help to develop, lead and support their junior colleagues. This is not the same as an internal coach as they tend to be outside the line management chain to differentiate them from the role of the direct manager in order to avoid any conflict of interest, particularly if there are sensitive issues that need addressing. However, coaching bodies, such as the Association for Professional Executive Coaching and Supervision (APECS), the British Psychological Society (BPS) and the European Mentoring and Coaching Council (EMCC), are seeking to increase demand for accredited and trained coaches who can handle the more complex organisational objectives required and adhere to professional codes and standards. However, the professionalisation of coaching does not mean that there is no room for internal coaches who can offer a service that provides coaching experience to talent and succession pools.

6.3.2.1 Coaching and the achievement of organisational goals

The impact that coaching or mentoring has on organisational goals has created a lot of discussion and debate, particularly in terms of how it is perceived and measured both from an individual's perspective and from that of the organisation itself. Willis and Britnor Guest (2003, p1) suggest that:

> Coaching can be one of the most effective interventions for development at all levels – and crucially for helping to align or balance personal employee development and organisational goals.

Coaching has been linked more to a formal process whereby specific goals are set and the pathway to achieving them has been agreed between the coach and coachee. It can be difficult to measure the success of coaching due to the focus of evaluation of coaching schemes and initiatives being primarily that of stories and testimony, according to the CIPD Coaching Climate Report 2011. However, it is generally considered to be a useful technique to get people used to setting themselves goals and objectives. Organisations are only just starting to consider coaching evaluation in terms of achieving key performance indicators (KPI), return on investment (ROI) and return on expectation (ROE) as forms of measurement. There are therefore three key evaluation questions identified by Garvey et al (2010) that need to be asked when considering the effectiveness of coaching practices within organisations:

1   How will I know whether the scheme has been successful or not?

2   What criteria will I use to make these judgements?

3   What measures will I use to assess the scheme against these criteria?

They further propose that the most appropriate method of evaluation is to use Kirkpatrick's model (1996) as it is considered to be useful in the context of coaching and mentoring evaluation. The model recognises that effectiveness is multi-layered and not just a measure of whether participants thought the coaching was useful or enjoyable; it acknowledges that participants are not the only source of data for judging the success of a training intervention. It recognises that, as with the case of formal mentoring and coaching schemes, the ultimate aim of a development intervention is to improve organisational results in some way. Finally, it recognises the importance of time as a key element in the process as the effectiveness of the coaching outcomes may be viewed in the short term rather than considering the long-term impact on the individual and the organisation, particularly as there is a real lack of longitundinal studies. However, a major drawback of using Kirkpatrick's model is that it doesn't allow ongoing evaluation and feedback, which is a key element of the coaching and mentoring process. Neither coaching nor mentoring are straightforward to evaluate as there are many factors that impact on their effectiveness, ranging from the selection of mentors or coaches, the personality traits of each participant and the expectations and perceptions of the process from each party.

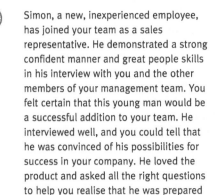

EXERCISE 6.4

Simon, a new, inexperienced employee, has joined your team as a sales representative. He demonstrated a strong confident manner and great people skills in his interview with you and the other members of your management team. You felt certain that this young man would be a successful addition to your team. He interviewed well, and you could tell that he was convinced of his possibilities for success in your company. He loved the product and asked all the right questions to help you realise that he was prepared to work hard for you.

When Simon started, he was partnered with another more experienced sales representative and was given the chance to step up and work on his own after just a short while. He exceeded expectations. His determination to find leads and get the close on clients was far beyond the company goals. His goals and accomplishments were independent of the rest of the sales team. He became well recognised for his efforts and was soon invited to relocate and gather new clients on another side of the country.

You are based at Head Office and have been assigned to manage his performance remotely. He reports to you via telephone and email, and you note that he continues to perform as expected.

Soon, however, you notice a drop in his productivity. He begins to lose steam and is not sending as many new clients to Head Office. When you are in contact with him you can sense that he is making many excuses for his failing performance. He avoids responsibility and attempts to convince you that he is still as determined as ever. Your concern for your employee is well placed. You have seen what an amazing employee he can be, and you don't want to lose him.

1   What do you do to help Simon without hurting his confidence in himself?

2   Taking into account the discussion of Simon's case, how would you evaluate the effectiveness of your intervention? How would you focus on his performance and the company's goals?

6.4 PRESENTATION AND INSTRUCTIONAL SKILLS

A presentation has been compared to a poster in that it has to communicate either a single message or a variety of messages clearly, and it has to get that message across the first time. Presentations are also considered to be a fast, effective and easy form of communication with most presenters using a version of PowerPoint to deliver that message. The traditional business presentation in front of a live audience is certainly not obsolete, according to Nelling (2013), but there are a range of alternatives available which are becoming more popular in their application. Business professionals and university students alike are identifying the need to deliver an effective presentation in a virtual setting and these are skills that are being developed in and outside the classroom or training workshops. Whilst there is a variety of research and literature regarding the techniques and tips for delivering an effective presentation, there appears to be little agreement on what is considered to be an effective presentation or how this is measured.

Firstly it is important to identify the message, the core concept or story that you wish to tell. Anderson and Anderson (2010) define a presentation, whether it is written, oral or visual, in essence as a performance. They consider it to be a form of acting out or communicating oneself, and can also be seen as the art of persuasion. However, all of this may be considered worthless if the presenter uses old, tired, uninteresting material, be that in the classroom, in a training room, a conference, or a workshop. Effective presentations are there to educate, entertain and act as a forum for questions. They should aim to motivate the audience into action by encouraging their interaction in the presentation itself. Gareis (2007) points out some of the pitfalls of the overuse or inappropriate use of presentation graphics. Presentation slides can go from one extreme of highly structured and filled with too much text, to graphics that alienate the audience and detract from the message being conveyed. However, DiSanza and Legge (2005) identify that graphics can be a great advantage as they can 'improve clarity, making logical structures more transparent, and illustrating complicated conceptual material' (quoted in Gareis 2007, p462).

Presentation formats appear to be an area of debate due to managerial and IT literature concentrating mainly on the 'cognitive efficacy of presentations for task performance and decision making' (Tractinksy and Meyer 1999, p397). Presentation software makes use of graphics as a means of communicating ideas and perspectives to persuade the audience. Bartsch and Cobern (2003) have examined the usefulness of presentations to deliver learning. The emphasis has been placed on students' preference for PowerPoint slides; however, there is no definitive evidence that these improve student performance. One factor that has already been mentioned is the complexity of the multimedia presentations used, for example from being simple text only to complex tables, graphs, sound effects, and video clips embedded into the slides.

Another aspect that needs to be addressed is the audience mix, particularly when faced with a multicultural audience. Trying to deliver a standard presentation is not appropriate as quite often materials can have a more Western focus or approach. An effective presentation is careful with the use of body language and humour – too little or too much of either can have an impact on the message being conveyed. However, whether the presentation is in a classroom, a workshop or conference, it is important to note that most people have a limited attention span, so presentations need to contain variety and interaction to sustain the audience's attention. The CIPD report (2012a) highlights the work of Baddeley (1966), who conducted research on short-term memory and identified that after 20 minutes the test subjects had difficulty recalling a collection of words that were similar in meaning. Therefore it is important to break down a presentation into stages and include different activities at key intervals to keep the audience engaged.

EXERCISE 6.5

Imagine you have been asked to deliver a presentation to a multinational audience but have been advised that a standard 40-minute presentation is not the best option. What would you include in order to make it more appealing to the mixed audience? What visual aids would you use? A DVD, a YouTube clip, a role play etc? Is it always better to use a mixture of methods in presentations in order to address all learning styles and to include interaction with the audience so that they have a participative role?

Quality presentations display a set of favourable characteristics which include a balance between text and graphics, displaying advanced preparation, clarity in thought and creativity of all documents and support materials, and demonstrate respect for the audience's time. These factors greatly contribute to the passion, enthusiasm and credibility of the presenter, which are then transferred to the receiver. Communication connectivity occurs when a sender successfully communicates his/her message in such a manner that the receiver is inspired or challenged to follow up on the message. Information presentations according to Tractinsky and Meyer (1999, p416) are 'communication means, used by both the presenter and the viewer'. They use a variety of criteria to assess the effectiveness or adequacy of the presentation itself based on their own criteria and expectations.

REFLECTIVE ACTIVITY 6.2

Think back on the last presentation you delivered and reflect on the following questions:

1   How do you know if your audience received the message contained within your presentation?

2   What do you use as your success criteria?

6.4.1 VIRTUAL PRESENTATIONS

Whilst presentations have moved on from the days of using handwritten or even typed OHP sheets, instructional aids may still include flipcharts, handouts and pointers. Today the virtual presentation is catching on rapidly in small, medium and large businesses alike, according to Flatley (2007). A virtual presentation is one delivered from a desktop or laptop computer to an audience anywhere in the world where there is Internet access and which can be available either for a set period of time, or readily accessible at any time of the day. A major change from the face-to-face presentation is that the virtual presenter does not usually see the audience, and often the audience does not see the presenter; however, this often depends on the sophistication of the organisations, the users and their equipment.

Although some early video-conferencing and distance learning used telecommunications technology where presenters could see the audience at remote sites, and audiences could see the presenter, today's most widely used technologies for delivering virtual presentations are web-based technologies that currently either don't use video or use it in very limited ways, for example podcasts, webinars and Skype. These new web-based technologies are easy to use and inexpensive, making them readily accessible for SMEs as well as large corporations. The traditional classroom lecture can now be recorded and posted online for students to access at any time, using podcasts whereby both the lecturer and the slides can be seen, paused, rewound and replayed as often as required by the student. Body language, as previously mentioned, and verbal communication skills are required to be clear and appropriate in order to achieve the desired outcome. Clearly this has more wide-ranging possibilities and applications, as will be seen in the process and methods of blended learning and use of technology section (6.6).

6.5 GIVING AND RECEIVING FEEDBACK

6.5.1 THE IMPORTANCE OF GIVING AND RECEIVING FEEDBACK

Feedback is an important part of helping employees develop. It is important to help individuals to identify their strengths and also their personal areas for further development. The importance of this is captured by Gratton: one of the most crucial organisational levers in the creation of cooperative working environments and collaborative teams is managers who coach and mentor others (Gratton 2008, cited in Harms et al 2010). This is core to the philosophy of performance management and, more importantly, embracing a high-performance culture. It also links closely to the section in this chapter on coaching and mentoring.

But it must be recognised that giving and receiving feedback is not only important, but also difficult. Harms and Roebuck (2010) highlight this difficulty and their conclusions are built upon their research with other key academics (including Cleveland et al 2007 and Krug 1998, amongst others). Whilst many organisations have performance management systems and annual appraisals, it is important that feedback is given frequently and in a timely manner. The impact and opportunity for improvement is lost if the feedback is not timely. It can be ineffective and frustrating when someone gives feedback with respect to an event that happened a week, a month or several months previously.

? REFLECTIVE ACTIVITY 6.3

1 Think of a time when you have given someone feedback. How did you undertake the task?

2 Think of a time when you have received feedback. How did you feel during the session?

3 How do your experiences of giving and receiving feedback compare with those identified above?

6.5.2 THE ART AND CRAFT OF GIVING AND RECEIVING FEEDBACK

It is important to consider the system used for feedback. There are systems such as 360-degree appraisals and personal development reviews. However, here we will concentrate on the one-to-one feedback forum. This can be done as part of a formal or informal review. Formal reviews often use a quantitative mechanism to score people's performance (behaviours or objectives). Whether formal or informal, it can be argued that qualitative feedback is the most important. This gives people the opportunity to recognise their strengths and look for opportunities to address their weaknesses.

6.5.2.1 Communication

Leaders are required to have many skills and arguably communications skills are the most important. With respect to giving and receiving feedback, Kline (2012) makes the point that communication is a vital part of this process and sometimes what is said can be misinterpreted. It is therefore as important to consider how the message is communicated as what the message is. When planning to give feedback, consider how the message will be received, but also, as pointed out later, make sure the message is clear (ie direct or indirect feedback). Put yourself in the other person's place and consider how the message may be received. Kline (2012) stresses the point that good leaders consider dual leadership when they communicate. The mission needs to be accomplished, but it can only be accomplished through motivated people. The sense of community through consensus is the most effective way of achieving this, although it is realistic to recognise that this is often difficult to achieve in certain circumstances.

6.5.2.2 Feedback about feedback

Nickols (1995) points out that goals within an organisation are a moving target and therefore feedback is also a moving target. Feedback is not just about the behaviour of individuals, but putting them into context so they are directed at achieving the organisation's objectives. Therefore, it is necessary to make sure that when feedback is given the context is also taken into consideration. We would like to think the world we live in is predictable, consistent and standardised; however, the reality is it is not – it is unpredictable, inconsistent and definitely not standardised. Within this context it is important to have principles around which we can make decisions, but recognise that the context in which we operate will influence the feedback and its effectiveness.

There are a number of considerations to take on board when giving feedback. It is not a one-off exercise or even an annual event. It is an ongoing commitment and investment that leaders need to take into consideration (which is one of the areas where it aligns with coaching). This means making time to have regular sessions with the team, but on top of that taking advantage of opportunities to give feedback when they arise. These often arise at unexpected and maybe inconvenient times. However, it is important to follow up on these opportunities as soon as possible and not store up the feedback for some weekly, monthly or even annual session.

We all have personal principles and standards, and so do the people we work with. This inevitably affects behaviours and leaders need to consider that other people's behaviours are just that, their behaviours. Many organisations are implementing codes of conduct and behavioural competencies which have the benefits of levelling the playing field within the organisation. This sets principles, values and beliefs for which the organisation stands and which it expects its employees to live up to. This approach should help leaders set their feedback within an organisational context and not just as a set of personal principles, values and beliefs, because personal principles vary from leader to leader. Although it would be naïve to think that leaders do not have a mix of personal and organisational behaviours, this approach should be to set the feedback within the context of the organisation's principles, values and beliefs. This makes the challenge of giving feedback even more difficult, but a critical challenge that needs to be taken on as part of being an effective leader.

Nickols (1995) makes a valid distinction between performance and behaviours. Often these two merge into one another, but it is vital to be clear on the differences between the two. People can achieve their objective by any means, but if this leaves destruction in its path, this can have harmful long-term effects for the organisation. So when dealing with feedback, it is important to be clear about the two (performance and behaviours) and also clear about where improvements need to be made. Addressing behavioural issues can be more difficult, as this can make people feel more vulnerable. However, done effectively, it can be very powerful and effective.

6.5.3 MODELS FOR GIVING FEEDBACK

According to Asmuß (2008) feedback can be given in four ways: positively, negatively, directly and indirectly (see section 6.5.1). An important point to consider here is that giving indirect feedback can be difficult for the recipient, because they often have to try and interpret the messages they are receiving. Therefore whether the feedback is positive or negative, where possible it is most effective when done directly and with examples. However, before giving the feedback, it is best to give the individual receiving the feedback an opportunity to reflect on their own performance and identify their own areas of strength and opportunities. This makes the feedback discussion more constructive and the individual is likely to identify their own areas for improvement, which can then be built upon.

It is often useful to have some structure to the discussion – this can help with the consistency of the feedback. The key elements of the feedback discussion should (Foster 2002):

- describe behaviour, performance, and results the evaluator has observed
- explain, illustrate, and support the evaluator's conclusions
- tell employees clearly what they are doing well and describe what they need to improve.

To help facilitate this approach and put structure behind the feedback session, a model identified by Foster (2002) is detailed in Box 6.1. The BET and BEAR model gives structure to the feedback session.

BOX 6.1

BET FEEDBACK MODEL (THE POSITIVE ASPECT OF THE MODEL):

B (Behaviour) ~ This should cover the behaviours the individual is exhibiting that are positive and beneficial. It is important to consider the context of the example.

E (Effect) ~ The effect the behaviour is having on other individuals (and team).

T (Thank you) ~ It is important to recognise and appreciate the good work people have done. A thank you.

BEAR FEEDBACK MODEL (THE AREAS FOR IMPROVEMENT):

B (Behaviour) ~ This should cover the behaviour that the individual is exhibiting that is having a negative effect on other individuals or the team. It is also important to also consider that there may be some behaviour that is absent and that the individual should be exhibiting.

E (Effect) ~ The effect the behaviour is having on other individuals (and team).

A (Alternative) ~ A two-way discussion to identify alternative behaviour that would have a positive effect on individuals (and teams).

R (Result) ~ This should identify the results expected and benefits of the change in behaviour. The results should be beneficial for the individual being fed back to, individuals they work with and the team.

EXERCISE 6.6

In groups of three (one receiving, one feeding back and one observing):

1   Give a piece of positive feedback (BET model).

2   Give a piece of improvement feedback (BEAR model).

3   Discuss how you found the process.

6.5.3.1 A two-way process

Up to this point the discussion has centred on feedback being given to praise or improve someone's behaviour or performance. Implicitly this has been a superior/subordinate relationship in concept. However, as argued by Richardson (2013), the most effective feedback is a two-way process. Richardson reinforces the point that it is often not given well and as a result not received well, therefore developing these skills is important. In addition to this Richardson also makes the point that the most difficult feedback, 'the feedback we find difficult to accept and would rather assign to the bottom drawer', is often the most important feedback. It is important to help us develop and address our biggest challenges.

EXERCISE 6.7

To help with two-way feedback: in groups of three (one receiving, one feeding back and one observing) undertake a feedback session as before. Now ask the following questions:

1   What worked well for you in that session?

2   What would you like more of, less of, or done differently?

What have you learned about yourself as a person by giving feedback?

CASE STUDY 6.1

COACHING AND FEEDBACK CASE STUDY

Jack's Perspective

Jack is a junior executive and passionate leader with a strong track record. He has recently been given new responsibilities on a number of important projects; he liaises with two other departments and has clear targets for keeping them on track. This usually goes well and he feels he is being quite successful. There have been a couple of recent setbacks with one of the departments, but these have been minor. On each occasion Jack has spoken to his opposite number, explaining clearly his expectations. This seems to have cleared the air and moved things on.

His manager, Brian, has largely left Jack to get on with the job, which Jack has appreciated. However, Jack sometimes feels his manager could show him more support when dealing with his staff and providing a 'united front' with some of his decisions. For example, Jack had an argument recently with one of his staff and he has asked to see Brian about it. The argument concerned lateness of a report and the staff member, Nick, was quite insolent when Jack chased him about it. Nick was subsequently told by Brian that a draft copy would suffice, and this seemed to undermine Jack's decision to press for it to be finished on time. Jack has asked for a meeting with Brian and his aim is to get Brian to support his

decisions in future, particularly when addressing Jack's staff.

Brian's Perspective

Brian oversees the running of several departments, with four departments reporting directly to him. He has had a complaint from a neighbouring department about Jack's attitude recently towards staff. It is claimed that Jack is always rude and arrogant with them, making unreasonable demands and running them down. Although Brian knows that Jack can be a little impatient and blunt, he suspects there has been some exaggeration. Jack has been in his present position for six months and is doing well and has a strong track record to date. Jack's role does require him to liaise frequently with the other department to ensure deadlines are met on a number of projects and there has been considerable progress. Conflict between the two areas could be very damaging. Brian would prefer not to become too involved, as this may be an awkward precedent and undermine Jack's confidence.

Fortuitously, Jack has asked to see Brian about a problem. He does not know if it is connected, but has decided to raise the issue. Brian wants to provide Jack with the opportunity to give his side of the story and see if the situation can be resolved by Jack himself, rather than interceding and potentially causing any further issues.

This case study can be used in class or can be delivered as a role-play exercise to provide learners with a more practitioner-based application of theory.

Questions

1   Based on your reading of this chapter, what relationship do you think Brian and Jack have? Which is the most appropriate approach to progress this relationship so

that confidence is not affected in the future? Coaching or mentoring? Or should this approach be carried out by a third party?

2   Considering the relationship Jack and Brian have, what type of approach should Brian take when giving feedback to Jack? Use the models discussed in this chapter to help formulate the best and most appropriate approach that Brian should take.

6.5.4 SUMMARY

In this section we have looked at the importance of feedback and how it is beneficial for both the giver and receiver and their own personal development. We have also covered some useful approaches and models to help structure your feedback sessions. The important thing now is to start putting it into practice and learning from your own experiences and those of your colleagues.

6.6 PROCESS AND METHODS OF BLENDED LEARNING AND USE OF TECHNOLOGY

ICT has become more and more important in educational development and within learning systems. It has provided opportunities for learning to support a variable demand from students. Whilst traditional face-to-face classrooms still exist these are, in essence, being changed into hybrid learning environments which are supported via ICT to increase activities and learning. Blended learning has been defined by Rees et al as 'a method of using a range of learning interventions based on different modes of delivery, for example web-based resources and work-based learning or classroom training' (2013, p159). Learning has moved away from the traditional face-to-face contact towards a more blended approach with a variety of lectures and workshops being delivered interactively online with supporting materials accessible at any time and forums held to support understanding and learning. There have been a number of factors that have contributed to the growth in both quantity and type of online learning resources which are now readily available to learners. The most obvious has been the improvements in the speed of Internet connections; and the second being the major advances in web technology. According to CIPD research 'From e-learning to "gameful" employment', April 2012 (citing research conducted by Overton in 2011), e-learning has gone from a fringe activity pushed by enthusiasts to a more encompassing activity. Technology is now rapidly becoming the focus of learning with more and more organisations believing that it will help them to respond faster to the changing business climate. Technology now offers learners a model of education and training, which has been developed based on adult learning principles and experiential learning theory, delivered entirely over the Internet.

Training spend by organisations has fallen, according to the CIPD report *Innovative Learning and Talent Development* (2009). Budgets for the private and voluntary sectors have risen per employee since 2008, with the public sector being worst off, with £127 spent per employee. The report identified that items most likely to be covered by training budgets are external courses and conferences (64%) and hiring of external consultants and trainers (60%). Therefore with less money to spend organisations are looking for alternatives to sending their employees to external learning and training events. They are looking at internal opportunities such as coaching and mentoring, which if delivered in a sustainable way can help underpin learning and talent development. In addition organisations are increasingly incorporating synchronous computer-based web-conferencing (sometimes referred to as webinars, desktop conferencing or net meetings) into distance learning education due to its affordability, scalability and ease of use (Senecal and Gazda 2010).

As previously mentioned, the 2004 CIPD *Training and Development* Survey showed that coaching had had the overall largest increase (51%), swiftly followed by e-learning (47%) and mentoring and buddy systems (42%). It is clear that organisations are beginning to understand the power and possibilities of e-learning and may already have the capacity to change; however, there appears to be a level of reluctance to embrace these new technologies. There is an element of stereotyping still involved within organisations, perhaps underestimating the usage of technology by all ages and backgrounds. The CIPD report *From Steady State to Ready State*: *A need for fresh thinking in learning and talent development?* (2012b) identified that learning and age is a growing agenda and that we have a tendency to generalise or characterise young people as 'digital natives' and older age groups as 'digital laggards'. However, this lack of understanding of the end user means that organisations could fail to identify and adapt to the reality of diverse engagement and capabilities. Flatley (2007) reviewed the role of virtual presentations with adult learners and identified that the main benefits of e-learning or online learning and their receptiveness to business people were 'because it saves them time getting to campus and the struggle of parking on campus'.

The Internet has become a major player in everyone's lives; we are living in the 'age of Google' where information is readily accessible at the touch of a button. We can network to our heart's content and people can now relate to the information that is provided to them. Whereas in the past information was 'pushed' onto employees via email and e-bulletins, employees can now decide what information they need to complete their role and 'pull' the content they require, at a time suitable for them.

Social media has a huge following with more and more academic institutions and businesses making use of it to deliver business information and development activities for employees and students alike. It provides an attractive opportunity for businesses now and in the future. Practitioners need to learn and make sense of the wave of new technologies available in order to make their application a reality. The introduction of smartphones and other tablet devices means that employees and all users can learn new skills and acquire knowledge more readily. There has been a massive increase in the number of apps to address learning needs from learning to speak a new language, to costs and budgeting and even universities collaborating with health professionals to produce real-time applications for midwives. Technology has evolved to address the needs of a more mobile, knowledge-driven workforce.

However, whilst employees may have access to the latest technology and gadgets, organisations are still falling behind and need to introduce the new connected devices in the workplace. E-learning is only as good as its implementation and application and the CIPD E-learning Survey 2011 showed that there is still a low level of completion of e-learning programmes and initiatives, or that user experience has been poor and therefore has resulted in poor learning effectiveness. Without both learners and instructors internalising the new approach and its practices and attitudes, this change might fail to take effect.

In 2011 Johnson et al discovered what they termed as the 'adjacent possible'. It is a readily reachable improvement made possible through a combination of technologies or ideas. These include wikis, social media, mobile learning etc. However, the rate of usage, as detailed in Figure 6.2, is still very low.

Figure 6.2 The rate of usage of various 'adjacent possibles'

36%   • blended learning programmes

20%   • webinars and virtual classrooms

17%   • use of learning libraries and wikis

14%   • audio learning and podcasts

13%   • rapid authoring software

11%   • e-books

5%   • learning through social media, ie Facebook

3%   • mobile learning using smartphones

Source: adapted from 'From e-learning to "gameful" employment' (CIPD 2012a)

 EXERCISE 6.8

1   How many of the 'adjacent possibles' listed in Figure 6.2 does your organisation make use of for learning and development activities?

2   What experience have you had of these as:

   (a)   the facilitator?

   (b)   the end user?

6.6.1 VIRTUAL LEARNING ENVIRONMENTS AND WEBINARS

As Corbridge et al (2013) identified, learning has been seen to be a flow of information from the teacher to the learner with the time, pace and location determined by the teacher. Virtual learning environments (VLE) and webinars are sophisticated platforms of information. They provide a multifaceted approach allowing information to flow from the teacher to the learner in the traditional sense, but also from learner to learner with additional materials such as discussion forums, online tutorials and media available directly. Possibly the most well known, within the context of universities and colleges, is Moodle, which provides a platform through which academics can deliver a variety of information both in the classroom environment and externally. It assists in the integration of both online and face-to-face interactions of learners both with their tutor and with other members of their group or class. According to the CIPD, approximately one-third of organisations use blended learning activities to improve the learning experience, including the use of face-to-face, Action Learning Sets (ALS) and project-based learning as well as coaching and mentoring (see previous section on coaching and mentoring). However, when teaching, and indeed learning, at a distance all participants need to work harder to have the same positive impact as that experienced within the classroom.

6.6.1.1 Monitoring and control

All virtual learning environments, whether as part of a class or external networking sites such as LinkedIn, Facebook, Twitter, or Yammer (and an ever-expanding number of others) encourage a sense of collaboration, knowledge-sharing and networking skills, for example in recruitment activities. However, there is still the possibility of inappropriate use and postings of unacceptable materials. Whilst organisations want to encourage innovation and creativity, there is still a level of control and monitoring needed to be exercised in order to ensure that no legal obligations are abused; that behaviours such as bullying and harassment either internally or externally are not carried out by employees. Reputation and competitive advantage are obstacles to the use of the online materials for some organisations and may be the reason behind organisations' reluctance to fully integrate technology and blended learning techniques into their daily working practices.

Whilst abuse and misuse is one issue that needs consideration, social media relies on learners adopting a more active and participatory role. Facilitators and instructors need to monitor the lack of participation of 'lurkers' or 'social loafers' (Leino et al 2012). Not everyone wants to contribute, or do so to the same extent as other users, and this can lead to rising levels of frustration which impact on the users' experience of both learning and social media.

REFLECTIVE ACTIVITY 6.4

Are you aware of your organisation's policy on monitoring and surveillance? Do you consider any activities that you carry out whether at work or from home are in breach of your organisation's policies?

6.6.1.2 Microblogging

Social media tools offer supportive social interactive environments as they encourage sharing, collaboration and communication across a broad range of users. They integrate social learning and e-learning in both the constructivist and collaborative sense. Twitter has become a worldwide phenomenon in a very short space of time. It has increased from 27 million posts in 2009 to 250 million in 2011 (CIPD 2012b). Short postings on sites such as Twitter or Yammer are used to stimulate debate and support learning, for example Yammer, or an equivalent, is used within many organisations including the Civil Service in order to keep employees up to date with the latest news and political debates and employees are encouraged to join. Indeed Derntl and Motschnig-Pitrik (2005) state that:

> knowledge that is not used tends to be forgotten very quickly. Rather, a form of learning that takes into account individual needs, interests and styles, and that encourages social learning, is preferred. (Wenger 1998, cited in Derntl and Motschnig-Pitrik 2005, p112)

If we view lectures as having the sole purpose of transmitting information rather than encouraging participation and interaction, the argument for the use of blended learning techniques is clear. Due to a variety of psychological and pedagogical theories, which are explored in this book, the traditional lecture will fail to be effective in the long term, whereas blended learning provides the basis for integrating the traditional lecture with more innovative, engaging, knowledge-sharing and collaborative techniques.

BLENDED LEARNING CASE STUDY

CASE STUDY 6.2

The Challenge

With the aim of creating a business-focused learning curriculum Bennetts Associates has consulted with internal clients and stakeholders to find out their views on what areas of improvement their training and development programmes need to address in order to meet the needs of the business. It came up with a shortlist to equip all new employees (mainly graduates) joining the company with the necessary business skills through a programme of management training. This programme should cover areas such as leadership and management skills, working in a team, communication, project management, and health and safety awareness: all agreed by the Senior Management team as the key skills required by new employees starting work with no previous business experience.

In the past this type of training was run through residentials; however, it took the employees away from the office and their appointed projects on a regular basis and this is considered too costly and time-consuming for the business. The Senior Management team want to deliver the training cost-effectively and minimise the amount of time employees spend away from their projects by reducing the residential training element without compromising the content or quality of the training.

The Proposal

Based on the above parameters it has been decided that a blended learning approach would be the most appropriate. The first step will be to look at the required learning outcomes of the training programme and break these down into two main areas:

1   Employees will need content that evokes discussion or that is best learned and embedded through group activities, experiential learning, feedback and interaction with the trainers and other employees.

2   Content that is primarily about giving information and where understanding can be checked online using interactive exercises and short assessments.

The e-learning modules will need to be designed to be engaging and entertaining and to fully immerse the employee in the learning process using animation, sound, pictures, video, quizzes and interactive exercises. However, the learning portal is required to be more than just a gateway for e-learning. It should also provide access to a range of additional resources, including the following:

- A forum that allows employees to network and chat online either with the whole employee community or with other members of their own cohort. They can also start discussion threads related to specific subject areas, issues or projects.
- A full suite of support materials for new employees who are undertaking other optional qualifications. This material is published online and includes resources such as study guides, help with assignments and a permanent reference source for every topic covered during the residential and e-learning modules.

- Access to news forums, video feeds, case studies and other material.
- Links to other websites that are relevant to the programme content and their projects ensuring that they do not violate Internet access of the company and policies.

The expected result through the blended learning solution is to have employees who are equipped with the right skill set early in the project life cycle and who spend as little time as possible away from the project. As well as relevant training and permanent access to online resources, it is hoped that the employees will build a strong network of like-minded individuals who will support each other both now and in the future.

Questions

1   Based on the information in the case study, do you think that Bennetts Associates has made the right decision choosing a blended learning approach?

2   How would you evaluate the success of the new portal? Is feedback from attendees sufficient or should you be considering the return on investment? Who else should be involved in the overall evaluation?

3   Considering the different factors discussed regarding blended learning, are there any aspects of the proposal that need to be reconsidered or improved?

6.7 CONCLUSION

In this chapter we have explored the concepts of learning from a practitioner perspective in order to develop individual frameworks for learners. We have discussed the importance of feedback and how it is beneficial for both the giver and receiver and their own personal development. We have also covered some useful approaches and models to help structure your feedback sessions. The important thing now is to start putting it into practice and learning from your own experiences and those of your colleagues. The focus of the chapter has been on the delivery and facilitation of learning and its evolution both in terms of usage and application. Coaching and mentoring has increased in popularity as organisations seek to encourage development and retain their employees during these difficult economic times. It is recognised that different forms of knowledge are best delivered by different methods and multiple methods of delivering knowledge and facilitating learning are becoming more important.

CASE STUDY 6.3

COACHING PROGRAMME AT CARTER MANUFACTURING

Carter Manufacturing produces high-tech products. The company has been operating successfully for the past nine years, but has faced increased competition. Like many others, it has had to resort to austerity measures, including making a reduction in its workforce in 2009. Since 2010 the company has been in crisis. Its staff are divided, there is little or no communication between

departments and no inter-departmental support. A strong blame culture has taken hold and this is impacting on their business. There are 6 departments, each has a total of 30 employees, some of whom are part-time members of staff. Staff are managed by four Team Leaders, two of whom have poor interpersonal skills and fail to communicate effectively with their teams and colleagues, resulting in a demotivated workforce, high levels of sickness absence, poor levels of customer service and minimum co-operation with management.

Training is ad hoc and employees are leaving at an alarming rate – often immediately after they finish their training. A recent employee survey has revealed that employee engagement is quite low at the present time when compared to previous years and the introduction of a recent pay freeze has not been well received.

The CEO has decided it is time to try something different as none of their current training initiatives seem to be working and it is costing the company well over the predicted training budget with little or no return on investment. You have been called in to facilitate a change in culture that it is hoped will lead Carter Manufacturing to become an 'employer of choice' where it not only retains its current staff but is attractive to external candidates.

The key aims of the coaching programme include:

- to change the current blame culture
- to look to assist employees who are in difficulty and improve working relationships across departments
- to reduce staff vacancy rates from 19.7% to around 15% to keep in line with or fall below the regional average
- to reduce turnover rates by 3% over the next two years (in the hope of creating an approximate £175,000 return on investment)
- to improve the results of the annual staff opinion survey
- to improve managers' communication skills and assist in the planning of their own continuous development

Questions

1   Based on your knowledge and the discussion on coaching, do you consider the above aims achievable?

2   What additional training and involvement by senior management is needed?

EXPLORE FURTHER

ARNOLD, J., RANDALL, R., PATTERSON, F., SILVESTER, J., ROBERTSON, I., COOPER, C., BURNES, B., HARRIS, D., AXTELL, C. and DEN HARTOG, D (2010) *Work psychology: understanding human behaviour in the workplace.* 5th ed. Harlow: Pearson Education Limited.

CIPD (2011) *The Coaching Climate Survey Report.* London: CIPD. Online version also available at: cipd.co.uk/surveys [accessed 1 March 2013]

CLEVELAND, J.N., LIM, A.S. and MURPHY, K.R. (2007) Feedback phobia? Why employees do not want to give or receive performance feedback. In: LANGAN-FOX, J., COOPER, C.L. and KLIMOSKI, R.J. (eds). *Research companion to the dysfunctional workplace: management challenges and symptoms.* Northampton, MA: Edward Elgar. pp168–186.

DERNTL, M. and MOTSCHNIG-PITRIK, R. (2005) The role of structure, patterns, and people in blended learning. *The Internet and Higher Education.* Vol 8. pp111–130.

GARVEY, R., STOKES, P. and MEGGINSON, D. (2010) *Coaching and mentoring: theory and practice.* London: Sage.

HARMS, P.L. and ROEBUCK, D.B. (2010) Teaching the art and craft of giving and receiving feedback. *Business Communication Conference Quarterly.* Vol 73, No 4. p413.

CHAPTER 7

Evaluating Learning and Development

MARIAN O'SULLIVAN AND MICHAEL McFADDEN

LEARNING OUTCOMES

By the end of this chapter you will be able to:

- understand the purpose of training evaluation
- appreciate various models of evaluation
- consider various methods of evaluation such as quantitative and qualitative approaches
- identify barriers to successful training evaluation
- appreciate issues in the design of evaluation tools.

7.1 INTRODUCTION

A quick look at academic journals or a selection of training providers on the Internet will reveal the abundance of training which takes place in the modern company today. This is also clearly demonstrated by a consideration of the vast sums of money that are spent each year on this activity. For example, the amount spent on training in 2012 in the US was $62 billion, with estimates of $135 billion globally (www.bersin.com/blog/post/Explosive-Growth-in-the-Corporate-Training-Market.aspx – accessed 27 September 13). It is not unusual also for national governments to prescribe in legislation the amount that its nation should spend on training. Hashim makes exactly this point with regard to Malaysia, where the government has passed the Human Resources Development Act 1992, requiring companies 'to contribute a 1 per cent equivalent of its monthly payroll to a fund which would then be used to promote training' (Hashim 2001, p374). Arguably then training is considered an important investment with regard to company success. But what types of training do companies usually invest in?

Griffin makes an interesting distinction between two types of training: general training and specific training. General training consists of skill acquisitions 'which workers may transfer to other firms' (Griffin 2011, p842). This might be, for example, an apprenticeship or the completion of the national qualification in say leadership and management. In both cases the individual could take this qualification and move on to another company. The company that provided the training may then consider this as a loss of its investment. This may in some instances explain why some companies are reluctant to offer training intervention which provides individuals with national qualifications. The second example Griffin mentions is specific training. This is training which is usually unique and particular to that company. For example, a retail company may wish to train employees to sell its latest product or its managers may need specific training relating to issues which have arisen in the retail sector.

According to Griffin, companies are less 'willing to pay for general training' (Griffin 2011, p844). The assumption here is that if you provide general training it might not directly benefit the company and might increase the possibility of individuals using the qualification to further their career with another company. Arguably then the benefits, or return on investment, of specific training are to the company and not necessarily to the individual. Nevertheless, once it was decided which type of training was required, the company would then commission the training either internally through its own training department, or externally by procuring a training provider such as a college of further education or a private training provider. Because of the investment by the company it would seem natural then to evaluate the training intervention to consider if the investment was worthy of the expense.

In summary, this chapter examines the purpose of training evaluation through developing an appreciation of the influence of various models that have emerged over time, for example Kirkpatrick (1996), Easterby-Smith (1986) and Holton et al (2000). Various methods of evaluation, both quantitative and qualitative, are explored which enable training providers to identify those that best fit their learning and development needs. No chapter on evaluating learning and development will be complete without identifying and understanding potential barriers that may exist.

7.2 THE 'IDEAL' VIEW OF TRAINING EVALUATION

We can perhaps identify what we might call an 'ideal' view of training evaluation. This would suggest that a training programme is devised by a training practitioner to meet a company's particular needs. As mentioned in the previous section, this may be an external training provider or the company's own training department. Examples of the intervention may be the need to provide training in customer service to selected members of staff or initial management training to newly promoted managers. In both instances the training practitioner would outline a suitable training programme. Appropriate trainees are then selected to attend the programme. Once the programme starts, the trainees are introduced to new knowledge and skills which are learned during the training programme. Upon completion of the programme trainees are able to transfer their new knowledge and skills to the work situation, which results in performance improvement for the individual, possibly their teams, and ultimately the company. Also, on completion of the programme, the training practitioner conducts a programme evaluation to ascertain if the intervention has been effective. If the company is able to measure performance improvement (either in the individual, teams or company), the programme is deemed a success. If, however, there is no performance improvement experienced, the training programme is questioned and may be considered a failure. We can perhaps suggest a causal relation here.

Training programme → performance improvement

The problem with this 'ideal' formulation though is that it assumes that the variable 'training programme' will result in performance improvement, and if this is not achieved then the 'training programme' has failed in its aims and objectives. In reality, though, the 'training programme' is not the only variable in this causal relation. Several other variables must also be considered in any evaluation if we are to fully understand the relationship between a training intervention and its desired consequence of performance improvement. Many models then have been proposed to capture the possible variables which may impact on the successful evaluation of a training intervention. This is what this chapter will go on to explore. But before discussing these it might be useful to first consider the purpose of a training evaluation, as discussed by one of the leading commentators on this subject – Easterby-Smith.

For Easterby-Smith there is 'some logic to the idea of being clear' about why we should engage in evaluation (1986, p11). As already mentioned, training is costly and if a company is to invest in this activity then it is prudent that it has an understanding of the purpose of evaluation. Easterby-Smith points out that although there are, for practitioners, differences in approaches and styles to evaluation, there is still a 'high degree of consistency' about what they consider to be its purposes (Easterby-Smith 1986, p12). He then goes on to identify and outline four purposes: proving, improving, learning and control. Let's look at each of these in turn.

7.3.1 PROVING

This aims to provide evidence of the value of the training intervention by demonstrating 'that something has happened as a result of training or development activity' (Easterby-Smith 1986, p14). He provides the example of a training intervention commissioned by the Training Within Industry service during the Second World War, which recorded production increases of over 25%. He accepts that other variables may have influenced the increase but nevertheless an improvement had been evidenced. Something had happened as a result of the training.

7.3.2 IMPROVING

The second purpose of evaluation identified by Easterby-Smith is concerned with attempting to provide feedback from the evaluation for the purpose of improving that particular training programme or future training programmes. So you have delivered your training session and you want to know how well it went and what you could do to improve it. The evaluation will hopefully provide this.

7.3.3 LEARNING

The third purpose of evaluation is to establish and measure that learning has taken place following the intervention. For Easterby-Smith, evaluation is 'an integral part of the learning and development process itself' (Easterby-Smith 1986, p14). The purpose of the training after all was to provide a learning experience to the trainees and thus we would want to ensure that this has in fact taken place. Challenges exist with regard to assessing the extent to which learning has taken place. When assessing the learning outcomes within a classroom situation, the environment is likely to be somewhat different from that of the trainee's place of work. The place of work is likely to be more complex and subject to many environmental variables, such as time constraints, limited resources, interruptions, etc.

7.3.4 CONTROLLING

This aspect focuses more on training managers or practitioners and to ascertain if they are 'performing to standard'. Are they for example doing 'a good job'? Likewise, if the training intervention is outsourced, the evaluation serves as a way of establishing if 'subsidiary training establishments are meeting targets according to some centrally determined plan' (Easterby-Smith 1986, p14).

These then were the purposes identified by Easterby-Smith. We need now to consider some of the models proposed with regard to training evaluation and establish also what variables impact on its successful outcome.

EXERCISE 7.1

Identify and discuss purposes of learning and development evaluation, other than those proposed by Easterby-Smith.

With reference to your organisation, or one that you are familiar with, consider the purpose of learning and development evaluation. If your organisation does not carry out learning and development evaluation, why do you think this is the case?

7.4 KIRKPATRICK'S FOUR LEVELS MODEL

The classic evaluation model is arguably that presented by Donald Kirkpatrick in 1959 following his dissertation on 'evaluating a supervisory training programme'. The model has gone through a number of modifications but still retains essentially four levels of evaluation.

7.4.1 LEVEL 1 – REACTION

This level is 'basically a measure of customer satisfaction' Kirkpatrick (1996, p55). Trainees engage in a training intervention and on completion of this are asked their reaction to the intervention by the completion of an evaluation sheet. Questions included might be: Did you enjoy the intervention? Was the venue suitable? Did the trainer start the programme at the correct time? These are all questions which attempt to measure the trainee's reaction to the intervention. Practitioners often refer to these as the 'happy sheets'. For Kirkpatrick, this is an important variable as 'the more favourable the reactions to the programme, the more likely trainees are to pay attention and learn the principles, facts and techniques discussed' (Kirkpatrick 1996, p56). At this level, though, it is important to point out that the practitioner is not 'measuring' whether trainees have achieved any learning. It is only a measure of their 'feelings' about the training intervention.

7.4.2 LEVEL 2 – LEARNING

The second level identified by Kirkpatrick is concerned with learning. It is 'a measure of the knowledge acquired, skills improved, or attitudes changed due to training' (Kirkpatrick 1996, p56). It is assumed therefore that when trainees engage in a training intervention they will have achieved some learning. So for example, if the training intervention is centred on improving customer service, you would expect that trainees will have learned new knowledge and skills about how to deal with customers. This might be, for example, techniques to deal with difficult customers or how to be more responsive to customer needs. It may be the case, though, that trainees have acquired the knowledge and skills but may not actually transfer this into behaviour. Someone may be perfectly aware of good customer service but when approached by a customer is particularly rude and not very helpful. In this example they know what good customer service is but have not transferred the learning into actual behaviour.

7.4.3 LEVEL 3 – BEHAVIOUR

From what we have already said it is clear that once trainees complete a training intervention the expectation is that the knowledge and skills learned by trainees are used at the place of work. This is often referred to as the 'transfer of learning'. It is a 'measure of the extent to which participants change their on-the-job behaviour because of training'

(Kirkpatrick 1996, p56). The third level of the Kirkpatrick model aims to measure the success of this.

7.4.4 LEVEL 4 – RESULTS

The final level in the model is arguably the most important and perhaps the reason why the training was commissioned in the first place. It is to evaluate the consequences of the intervention in terms of measuring impact for the company. As Kirkpatrick states, it is a 'measure of the final results that occur due to training, including increased sales, higher productivity, bigger profits, reduced costs, less employee turnover, and improved quality' (Kirkpatrick 1996, p56).

EXERCISE 7.2

To what extent is Kirkpatrick's model relevant to training evaluation in the twenty-first century?

The model is still extensively used, but there are questions raised about its effectiveness and indeed its application. It would appear that the model, even if it is adopted, is not extensively used at all four stages. Giangreco et al, for example, mention the 'poor usage of the full model' with take-up at level 4 varying from 15% to 31% (Giangreco et al 2010). Many reasons have been identified to explain the poor usage of the full model, varying from the cost to implement all four stages (Wang and Wilcox 2006) to a perception that the model is incomplete (Bates 2004), meaning that it does not capture all the necessary variables required for a successful evaluation. Others suggest that practitioners themselves are reluctant to adopt the full module for fear of receiving 'bad news'. In other words, the trainer has completed the training intervention but transfer has not occurred. This would be particularly worrying to an external provider who may be looking for further business from the commissioning company.

Estimates of transferability vary with some estimating that only 10% of all training results in participants transferring new skills and knowledge to the work situation (Baldwin and Ford 1988; Griffin 2011, p841)). Wexley and Latham (2002) suggest figures of 40% immediately following training but that this figure drops to 25% after six months and 15% after one year. From this we can perhaps appreciate Hashim's point that 'participants attend training, enjoy it, forget it, and carry on working exactly as before' (Hashim 2001, p375).

To encourage practitioners and companies then to engage in more effective evaluation we arguably need a fresh look at the whole process. In speaking of Kirkpatrick's model, Giangreco et al (2010) suggest that the model was developed for an industrial society and that perhaps it is not applicable in its full form to a post-industrial society. A revised examination would need to identify and consider other possible variables which may also impact on the successful outcome of a training intervention which have not been identified in Kirkpatrick's model.

7.5 GAGNÉ'S THEORY OF INSTRUCTION

Several academics have attempted to identify other possible variables by looking specifically at how we learn. What is being emphasised here is that if performance improvement is one of the main objectives and this is achieved through the transfer of learning from the training intervention to the work situation, we need to be confident that learning is actually taking place within the intervention. Learning becomes a pre-requisite of transfer. Thus, first we need to examine how it is that individuals learn. In this regard Kraiger et al (1993) and Driscoll (2000) have drawn upon the work of Gagné. He proposed a set of categories of 'learning outcomes' which impact on whether or not learning takes place. In other words, it would be inaccurate to judge the evaluation of the learning of trainees engaged in a training intervention without some consideration of these outcomes. The first three outcomes are referred to as cognitive outcomes and have three sub-categories. The remaining two outcomes are motor skills and attitudes. We can summarise the five outcomes as:

- intellectual skills
- verbal information
- cognitive strategies
- motor skills
- attitudes.

7.5.1 INTELLECTUAL SKILLS

Gagné (1984) uses the term procedural knowledge when referring to intellectual skills. Procedural knowledge is knowledge where the individual engages with the external environment and acquires concepts which are organised by a system of rules. So for example, Gagné mentions activities such as 'driving an automobile, using a lawnmower, making a telephone call, or shopping in a supermarket' (1984, p79). In each of these you can see the acquisition of concepts which are enacted through a set of rules or procedures. You fetch the shopping trolley; you walk down the supermarket rows; you place your desired groceries in your trolley. Once you have finished you take the trolley for scanning and pay for the products. In all of this there is knowledge of supermarkets (the concept) and the process which you tend to follow (procedure).

7.5.2 VERBAL INFORMATION

This Gagné acknowledges is better referred to as 'declarative knowledge' and 'its presence is shown by the ability of a person to "declare" or "state" something' (1984, p380). We might describe it as some of the knowledge an individual acquires through formal education. For example, a child can recite the five times table or can list the kings and queens of England. The child, though, does not just passively absorb this type of information. The information is organised into 'themes or schema'. For Gagné, a schema 'is a representation of a situation or an event' (Gagné 1984, p380). Success in problem-solving 'depends upon the learner being able to apply relevant information to the problem' (Driscoll 2000, p349). In other words, the ability to develop schemas will impact on the ability to solve problems.

7.5.3 COGNITIVE STRATEGIES

So far Gagné has identified two forms of learning, intellectual and verbal. These describe processes by which individuals acquire or learn information. These 'processes of learning' are, however, 'modified and regulated by some internal processes of executive control' (Gagné 1984, p138). By executive control Gagné means the thinking individual. So the thinking individual, as the executive, is able to modify and regulate their acquired learning. In modifying and regulating their acquired learning, individuals would employ various strategies and it is these strategies which Gagné refers to as cognitive strategies. An example of a cognitive strategy might be the use of mnemonics to store and retrieve information.

7.5.4 MOTOR SKILLS

The term motor skills refers to learning 'when gradual improvements in the quality of its movement (smoothness, timing) can be attained only by repetition of the movement' (Gagné 1984, p382). Examples of motor skills include 'serving a tennis ball, executing a triple jump in ice skating, dribbling a basketball, and lifting a barbell with weights' (Driscoll 2000, p357).

7.5.5 ATTITUDES

An attitude is defined as an 'internal state that influences (moderates) the choices of personal action made by the individual' (Gagné 1984, p63). The view here is that what is learned may be modified by the attitude of the individual. A positive attitude may result in a positive outcome whereas a negative attitude often results in a poor outcome.

The significance of Gagné's theory is that trainees, when engaging in a training intervention, are not necessarily of the same cognitive ability. Thus, it is perhaps not possible to judge if a training intervention was unsuccessful until you also have information of the cognitive capabilities of the trainees. Kraiger et al (1993), for example, point out that individuals have 'mental models' of different complexity when confronted with problem definition and problem-solving. More capable individuals are able to draw on more complex mental models using more complex 'cognitive strategies' in problem-solving situations. Thus, to ascertain if learning is achieved by trainees, any evaluation should consider the cognitive abilities of trainees which were present prior to the intervention. Likewise, a trainee may lack the appropriate attitude either before or after the training intervention. If the trainee has very little interest in the work they do, we might expect their attitude to the job to be low. They may well participate in a training intervention but not really engage and as a result achieve little or any new skills or knowledge. Equally, they may really enjoy the training intervention but make a clear separation of this activity from the work situation. Indeed, the trainee could possibly learn a great deal but consciously refuse to transfer this to their job because of their low levels of motivation and poor attitude. Reflecting on how individuals learn, more recent evaluation models have attempted to capture these and other variables. One of the most comprehensive models is that developed by Holton, Bates and Ruona.

7.6 HOLTON, BATES, RUONA – LEARNING TRANSFER SYSTEM INVENTORY

The Learning Transfer System Inventory developed from a conceptual evaluation model in a paper by Holton in which he is critical of Kirkpatrick's four-level model. The conceptual model proposed three 'primary outcome measures' of evaluation, which in turn contain a number of secondary outcome measures or 'influences'. The three primary outcome measures are:

- learning
- individual performance
- organisational results.

As mentioned each of these has a number of secondary outcomes or influences on learning. So let's now consider the influences on each of these primary outcomes.

7.6.1 INFLUENCES ON LEARNING

Trainee reaction – Holton (1996) discusses the potential link between trainee reaction and learning. He points out that some academics such as Warr and Bunce (1995) found 'no significant correlation' (Holton 1996, p10) between these two variables. Holton, however, feels that a reaction measure should be included in the model, but that it ought not to be a primary outcome of training. The point here is that trainees may well have enjoyed the training intervention but this in no way indicates that they have learned anything and thus it should not, as in the Kirkpatrick model, be a primary outcome measure. It is, though, still a variable to consider as a secondary outcome measure. Focus on trainee reaction has for Holton 'diverted the field's attention away from the truly important outcomes' such as performance (Holton 1996, p11).

Motivation to learn – This outcome in turn has four categories. These are: readiness for the intervention; job attitudes; personality characteristics; and motivation to transfer learning (Holton 1996).

- Readiness for the intervention – This refers to the fact that the degree 'to which a trainee is involved in the needs assessment process and given choices about training would be expected to influence motivation to learn' (Holton 1996, p11).
- Job attitudes – The view here is that a trainee's attitude to their job will impact on the learning which may take place in a training programme. A positive attitude will correlate with high levels of learning and a negative attitude with a low level of learning.
- Personality characteristics – For Holton 'certain personality characteristics would be expected to influence' the level of learning. These may include extroversion, openness to new experiences or self-efficacy.
- Motivation to transfer learning – This refers to the levels of motivation that the trainee has to transfer the learning to the work situation and is discussed by Holton in more detail in the influence on individual performance.

7.6.2 ABILITY

As previously mentioned from Gagné, for learning to take place we cannot assume that all the trainees come in to the training programme with the same cognitive abilities. Some will have more complex and specific cognitive abilities and thus it is likely that these variances 'will influence training outcomes' (Holton 1996, p12). For example, in a customer service training course, some trainees may have five years' experience, whereas others may be just starting in this particular role. Thus the first trainee is likely to have a more developed cognitive appreciation of the task than the second trainee.

7.6.3 INFLUENCES ON INDIVIDUAL PERFORMANCE

Motivation to transfer – The view here is that once trainees have completed a training programme they will have some degree of motivation to transfer that learning to the job situation. Holton suggests in turn that four factors will influence the motivation to transfer. These are:

- intervention fulfilment – the degree to which the trainee's expectations are met from the training intervention
- learning outcome – if the trainee feels they have experienced a positive outcome (ie they have performed well) from the training intervention, this increases the motivation to transfer learning
- job attitudes – trainees with high levels of commitment and job satisfaction are 'more likely to transfer' learning (Holton 1996, p13)
- expected utility – this refers to an awareness of and a measure of the expected utility of the training intervention.

Transfer conditions – This refers to the conditions which the trainee experiences at the place of work, and can be both positive and negative to learning transfer. Positive conditions can be simple supervisory support and negative conditions may include poor team dynamics. For example, an employee may come into work in the morning and their manager might ask them how they are and whether they need any support for the task to be completed that day. In contrast, a manager may not engage with employees and expect them to work with minimal input regardless of their capabilities. In the first instance this would be a supportive condition and the second instance a negative condition.

Transfer design – This is where the design of the training intervention 'does not provide the ability to transfer the learning' (Holton 1996, p13). Learning may be taking place within the training intervention but trainees may not have been shown how to apply that learning to the work situation and thus transfer of learning does not take place.

7.6.4 INFLUENCES ON ORGANISATIONAL RESULTS

Link to organisational goals – It is claimed by Holton that failure to link training to organisational goals is 'unlikely to produce results' (Holton 1996, p15). Thus any training intervention should start with identifying organisational goals and linking these to the intervention.

Expected utility of payoff – Before the intervention takes place practitioners ought to be able to calculate the financial benefits. It is argued that 'results are more likely to be achieved if the benefits are calculated and known to persons involved in the intervention, including both organisational sponsors and participants' (Holton 1996, p16).

External factors – It is acknowledged that a wide variety of factors can impact on the successful outcome of a training intervention and that these may be outside the control of the practitioner and the company. These could include, for example, changes to the economy, or a new product which has come to market from a leading competitor.

After having outlined the conceptual model, Holton with Bates and Ruona developed the Learning Transfer System Inventory. This consists of an 'instrument' of 16 factors divided into 'two construct domains' (Holton 2003, p64). The first contains 11 constructs affecting the training intervention and the second contains 5 constructs which are not 'programme specific' (Holton 2003, p64). The 16 constructs are listed below. The programme-specific constructs consist of 75 items (questions) and the non-programme-specific constructs consist of a further 36 items. In other words, a questionnaire formal consisting of 75 items which ask specific questions in relation to training evaluation questions. The model was finalised following its testing on 1,616 subjects. The programme-specific constructs and the non-programme-specific constructs are listed as follows.

Programme-specific constructs:

- learner readiness
- motivation to transfer
- positive personal outcomes
- negative personal outcomes
- personal capacity for transfer
- peer support
- supervisor support
- supervisor sanctions
- perceived content validity
- transfer design
- opportunity to use.

Non-programme-specific constructs:

- transfer effort – performance expectations
- performance – outcomes expectations
- resistance of openness to change
- performance self-efficacy
- performance coaching.

The reason for providing this level of detail is not only to provide a reasonable account of the model but to illustrate the comprehensiveness of the model. It seeks to measure variables way beyond that of Kirkpatrick. However, a criticism of the model might be the same as levelled against Kirkpatrick in that it is too complex and costly, and for that reason, practitioners and employers will not bother to use it. According to Holton, though, the inventory is 'quick and easy to complete, usually taking only fifteen to twenty minutes to administer' (Holton 2003, p65). Nevertheless, for some commentators, it is suggested that rather than design evaluation models which are comprehensive but rarely understood, practitioners should consider new and creative models which are simple, inexpensive and useable. Giangreco et al point out that practitioners and employers more often only engage in Level 1 evaluation, therefore it would be sensible to 'elaborate models that stop at (an enhanced) Level 1, or that have only one level but ensure that that level is relevant, feasible and economically sound (Giangreco et al 2010, p172). Alternatively, a way forward suggested by Anderson (2007) is to convince both practitioners and employers of the value of 'organisation learning' to organisations and, in turn, its evaluation. Perhaps then employers will be more willing to embrace evaluation models.

EXERCISE 7.3

Identify and discuss the advantages and disadvantages of the Holton et al model.

How could this model be applied in evaluating learning and development activities in your organisation?

7.7 ANDERSON – THE VALUE OF LEARNING

In discussing training and development, Anderson refers to several studies which highlight the challenges for evaluation. These include the view that practitioners find 'serious' evaluation to be too time-consuming. Also, she suggests that only 36% of organisations seek to capture the effects of learning on the 'bottom line'. Finally, she points out that line managers only rarely show interest in evaluation (Anderson 2007, p3). In response, she suggests that practitioners need to demonstrate the 'value contribution' that training and development make to their organisation. In other words, what attitude of value does the organisation have towards training and development? If it has a positive attitude to training and development, this would suggest that it has a high value of this function. Likewise a negative attitude would suggest a low value. It would be the role of practitioners to evaluate and provide evidence from the organisation of a high value contribution.

While Anderson acknowledges that practitioners still need to reflect on the learning of individuals through evaluation, she also suggests the need for them to focus more on developing 'metrics' that measure and align to organisation priorities. It is these metrics then which need to become the function of evaluation. These metrics suggested by Anderson are:

- return on investment
- benchmark and capacity of HR processes and performances
- return on expectation
- learning function (ie the efficiency and effectiveness of the learning function).

We can perhaps now appreciate the difficulty in attempting to evaluate a training intervention. We could have a relatively simple evaluation model such as a 'happy sheet' but not really fully ascertain the effectiveness of that intervention. Equally we could propose more comprehensive models but run the risk that both practitioners and companies do not adopt them for the reason that they are too difficult to understand or too costly to implement. Perhaps reflecting on Anderson's comments, the first step in evaluation though is to ensure that those commissioning training intervention have a good appreciation of the value of learning to their company.

EXERCISE 7.4

With reference to your organisation, or one that you are familiar with, what steps can be taken to raise appreciation of the value of learning and development?

7.7.1 SELF-EFFICACY

Once we have achieved an appreciation of learning and development, we could propose an alternative approach to evaluation which is relatively simple to understand and potentially low in terms of its administration. Many commentators are now suggesting this sort of approach and particularly looking at the concept of self-efficacy as a solution. The concept appears to have its origins in the work of Bandura (1977a), where he describes the individuals forming personal judgements of their own capabilities to enable them to achieve personal objectives or goals. Emphasising capabilities, Zimmermann (2000, p83), tells us that it should be a measure of 'performance capabilities rather than personal qualities' and Gist et al (1991) see it as 'a belief in one's capability to mobilize the cognitive resources, motivation, and courses of action needed to meet task demands'. So, when you are given a specific task or goal to achieve, if you feel confident in your ability to complete this task then you would be demonstrating high self-efficacy.

Commentators have then suggested that if an individual is introduced to new skills within a training programme and demonstrates high levels of self-efficacy toward these skills, then this is a strong indicator that the individual will transfer these new skills to the workplace (Gist et al 1991; Torkzadeh and Van Dyke 2002; Chiaburu and Marinova 2005; Velada et al 2007). Therefore, if a training programme can demonstrate increased levels of self-efficacy as an outcome, we would have evidence of the effectiveness of the intervention and a strong indicator that these skills will be transferred to the workplace. As such, a proposed solution with regard to training evaluation is to measure trainees' level of self-efficacy before the start of the training programme and then again at the end of the training programme.

7.8 DESIGNING EVALUATION TOOLS

Trainers have a choice of evaluation tools on which they can draw. For example, Perskill and Russ-Eft (2009) identify a number of tools which could be useful to practitioners. For our purposes here we have just identified three of these tools as an illustration of their approach. These are:

- behavioural objectives approach
- responsive evaluation
- goal-free evaluation.

7.8.1 BEHAVIOURAL OBJECTIVES APPROACH

This approach is concerned with identifying the extent to which the goals and objectives of the training programme have been achieved and works on the assumption that goals and objectives can be accurately articulated and measured. The results of achievement tests and other measures of performance are compared with the stated objectives of the training programme to establish if they have been met. The potential difficulties associated with this approach include the setting of objectives that lend themselves to measurement, and the design and accuracy of any summative tests.

7.8.2 RESPONSIVE EVALUATION

This approach draws on the work of Stake (1967), who argued that when evaluating a training programme it was important to represent the experiences of the participants and adopted a qualitative method using case studies and vignettes. This method of evaluation adopts a stakeholder approach, as they are the intended users of the evaluation. The process of conducting a responsive evaluation includes:

- talking with clients, programme staff and other audiences
- identifying the programme's scope and activities
- discovering individuals' concerns
- conceptualising the issues or problems
- identifying data needs and instruments
- collecting data
- developing case studies
- validating the data
- writing reports for different audiences
- assembling any required formal reports.

This approach is labour-intensive and requires a considerable amount of investment in resources to conduct; for example it may not be feasible to talk to all stakeholders, and the time available to conduct this type of evaluation may be insufficient.

7.8.3 GOAL-FREE EVALUATION

Goal-free evaluation adopts a broader approach to more traditional types of evaluation and focuses on actual outcomes rather than intended outcomes. In contrast to the foregoing, goal-free evaluation adopts the position that the stated goals and objectives are unknown to the evaluator. The purpose of this type of evaluation is to deduce the outcome of the programme from the activities carried out. Undertaking observations, interviews and document reviews, the evaluator examines the programme materials, activities and procedures and attempts to discover what the goals and objectives may be.

7.9 SOURCES OF DATA

An essential element in the design, development and delivery of learning and development interventions is concerned with evaluating whether or not training programmes have met their learning objectives. Trainers have a number of methods at their disposal to enable the gathering of evaluation data, for example, testing, questionnaires, observations, and so on. However, the selection of evaluation method will be influenced by the depth of evaluation required by the organisation, which is quite often determined by the importance attached to the learning and development intervention and the resources expended in its execution.

Therefore, in order to attempt to evaluate training at any of these levels, trainers can utilise a number of evaluation methods, as discussed in the following section.

7.9.1 QUESTIONNAIRES

Participants attending a training course are often asked to complete a course evaluation sheet immediately after the course has finished. The purpose of this evaluation is to examine the extent to which learners liked the learning and development intervention as identified by Hamblin (1974) and Kirkpatrick (1979), as previously discussed. This form of evaluation is commonly known as a 'happy sheet', where participants are asked to tick a number of boxes indicating their level of satisfaction with regard to such things as the quality of training delivery, the relevance of the materials and activities, the duration, the venue, whether the programme met its objectives, and so on. Whilst this method of evaluation can provide immediate feedback and can be used to make future adjustments to the training programme, caution must be exercised to ensure that there is not an overemphasis on its value. For example, the completion of this feedback may be influenced by the timing of its distribution; this is especially so if given at the end of the training session when participants are quite often anxious to get away. Other reasons as to why these sheets may not offer a great deal of value to either the trainer or the organisation is that participants may not want to upset the trainers, especially if they are from within the organisation; the questions may be ambiguous or inappropriate for the training intervention; a five-point rating scale may be used where participants may be inclined to opt for the middle point. Also, the performance of the trainer can be assessed by this form of evaluation and they will want to ensure that they receive the best possible rating as possible. To overcome some of these challenges, trainers can use anonymous online evaluation or participants can complete the evaluation sheet back at their workplace once they have had time to reflect on their learning experience. Online evaluation provides a confidential method of obtaining feedback; however, not all participants may have regular access to IT facilities, which may impact on completion rates. Equally, by allowing a period of reflection, this may result in participants not completing evaluation questionnaires and thus again lowering the completion rate and the opportunity to obtain valuable data.

This form of evaluation offers no insight as to how much knowledge the participant has acquired, whether they will be able to transfer their learning back to the workplace, the impact on their performance in the longer term and ultimately the potential long-term impact on the organisation.

EXERCISE 7.5

Is it feasible for organisations to use one standard questionnaire for all training and development interventions?

7.9.2 TESTS/ASSESSMENTS AND OBSERVATIONS

At the learning stage the aim will be to have specific and measureable learning objectives to evaluate the extent to which new knowledge or skills have been acquired by participants. This may be relatively easy for quantifiable skills but can be very difficult for complex learning and more investment and thought may be required. It may also be difficult to control other factors so that you can be sure that it was the training that made the difference. The types of methods available to trainers to evaluate learning and skill acquisition include tests/assessments and observations.

Testing provides one particular method of evaluating learning. Tests can be applied both prior to and following completion of learning and development interventions to assess the extent to which knowledge and/or skills have been acquired by participants. However, interpretation of results is dependent upon having clear and measureable objectives and competent assessors. Tests can be administered either in hard copy or online, and using online testing can provide quick feedback. It is also possible to use interviews or observations, though these can be time-consuming.

7.9.3 FEEDBACK ON TRANSFER OF LEARNING

This aspect of evaluation focuses on identifying the extent to which participants have been able to transfer their learning to the workplace. An important challenge for organisations is to examine whether it was the learning and development intervention that influenced behaviour upon return to the workplace or some other influences. Therefore, the establishment of a control group may be necessary to address this challenge; however, the resource implications associated with this particular approach may be prohibitive to many organisations. Also, it raises potential ethical issues as to how this exercise is managed.

In order to evaluate change in behaviour and possibly the need for further learning and development, it is possible to broaden the scope of feedback to include not only participants, but also their supervisors and/or line managers. Whilst feedback from participants is relevant, it is recognised that it can also be subjective and unreliable. Feedback can be obtained from line managers through their interviews with employees, observing their behaviour, or completing questionnaires. In order to effectively observe change and sustainability of behaviour and conduct interviews, time is required and as such feedback may be delayed, thereby reducing the impact and value of evaluation. In order to reduce potential subjectivity and bias on the part of the observer or interviewer, it is suggested that they are trained and developed in this aspect of evaluation, thereby attempting to improve reliability and consistency.

There is scope to further expand behaviour evaluation by the adoption of 360-degree feedback. 360-degree feedback involves collating data from a range of parties with whom the participant interacts as part of their role. However, it is noted that many of these parties may only have limited insight into the full role of the participant and lack understanding of the training received. Even so, respondents can make a judgement as to change after training, and this can be analysed for groups of respondents and trainees.

7.9.4 RETURN ON INVESTMENT (ROI)

How confident are organisations that their investment in learning and development programmes is resulting in improved organisational performance? A number of definitions of return on investment are presented that provide a useful platform from which to examine the rationale and challenges associated in answering this question. Mankin (2009, p264) offers this definition: 'return on investment measures the rate of return, expressed as a percentage, on an investment in training. It is based on an assumption that the benefits resulting from training can be quantified...'. A second definition provided by Noe (2008, p205) refers to return on investment as 'comparing the training's monetary benefits with the cost of the training'. It is suggested that benefits resulting from training can be quantified and therefore training evaluation requires a quantitative approach.

The costs associated with training can be identified as being direct and indirect costs. Direct costs can in most cases be easily identified, such as consultancy fees in the design of training programme, salaries of trainers, travel/accommodation, training materials, equipment, room hire, etc. Indirect costs, on the other hand, may be less easily identified as they are not usually related to the design, development and delivery of the programme (Noe 2008) and tend to be associated with the costs of general support functions necessary to enable the programme to take place, for example general administrative, accounting, financial support, etc.

7.10 THE EVALUATION PROCESS

The work of Reid and Barrington (1999) provides a useful framework for determining and evaluating training interventions. This comprises four stages.

The first stage is concerned with the determination of training objectives. Training objectives should express the desired change in behaviour as a result of the training intervention, ie what the participant is able to do following the training intervention. Changes in behaviour may refer to such things as tasks and procedures, standards of performance and the context within which the work will be carried out.

The second stage looks to identify the appropriate strategy to achieve the learning objectives. Choices can be made from such interventions as on-the-job training, planned organisational experience; in-house programmes; planned experience outside the organisation, external courses and self-managed learning.

The third stage involves the planning and implementation of the training and revolves around reviewing training objectives; determination of appropriate learning activities, assessment of training times, timetabling, briefing of trainers and preparation of materials and equipment.

The final stage of the process looks at the evaluation of the programme and raises four important questions that need to be answered:

- Why is evaluation required?
  The answer to this question has been addressed in part earlier in this chapter, but essentially looks to justify expenditure, especially when training budgets are closely scrutinised. Evaluation feedback to the trainers, opportunities to make improvements to the programme, and an indication that objectives have been met.
- Who should carry out the evaluation?
  It makes perfect sense for those receiving training to contribute to the evaluation process; however, to reduce the potential for bias and gain a wider perspective, it is also necessary to involve other stakeholders, such as the trainer, HRD managers and line managers.
- What aspects of training should be evaluated and when?
  Drawing on the work of Donald Kirkpatrick as discussed earlier, it is suggested that evaluation can be considered in a number of stages ranging from the initial reaction of participants to the training programme to the possible longer-term and ultimate stage of its impact on organisational performance.
- What kind of measurement will be used?
  These can comprise questionnaires, interviews, tests, projects, case studies, etc. However, it is more difficult to measure the impact on overall organisational performance 'because departmental and organisational results depend upon many people, and it is difficult to apportion improvements to the efforts of specific individuals' (Reid and Barrington 2000).

7.10.1 QUANTITATIVE VERSUS QUALITATIVE

In order to evaluate the effectiveness of training programmes, trainers can utilise a range of both quantitative and qualitative data. Quantitative data can include a calculation of ROI, results of tests, assessment of performance ratings, performance measures such as increase/decrease in sales, quality, etc.

According to Noe (2008, p198), qualitative data 'includes opinions, beliefs and feelings about the program'. For example, a range of stakeholders, customers, employees and managers may be asked for their opinions about the content, objectives, design and scope of programme design.

7.11 STAKEHOLDER SATISFACTION

Decisions concerned with the formulation of learning and development interventions will not be taken in isolation and will invariably require the need for consultation (Stewart 1999). Identifying and consulting with significant stakeholders may provide a platform from which to commence this decision-making process. The term stakeholders refers to all those parties who have a vested interest in the well-being of the organisation and can include shareholders, managers, employees, trade unions, customers, suppliers, etc. Whilst it is argued that training interventions have the potential to influence the extent to which organisations can achieve their business objectives, it is also recognised that there may be potential for conflict amongst stakeholders (Stewart 1999) with regard to such areas as training focus, expenditure, timings, content, etc. Drawing on the work of O'Donnell and Garavan (1997) as cited in Simmonds (2003, p52), each category of stakeholder will have different training goals, for example:

- 'top managers desire to see attitudes and cultural values change, particularly in the areas of disposition to change, teamwork and innovativeness
- Line managers believe that HRD should be skills based and centred on the current job.
- HRD specialists see their role primarily in terms of supporting the achievement of organisational goals, mainly in the service, advisory and consultancy areas.'

Therefore, the role of the Head of Learning and Development is critical in being able to reconcile these areas of potential conflict and to incorporate their views and opinions as part of the evaluation process. This can be achieved through encouraging participation in feedback, for example when a participant returns to the workplace, providing input regarding the content and delivery of learning and development intervention, or actually participating in the learning event itself.

7.12 BARRIERS TO EVALUATION

Many reasons or excuses can be presented for not carrying out evaluation. For example: it may be seen as time-consuming; consideration may not previously have been given to what elements of training need to be evaluated; there may be fear that the feedback will be negative, etc.

Mankin (2009, p266) and Simmonds (2003, pp168–169) identified a number of reasons why learning and development interventions are not always evaluated. These include:

- people are not convinced of the purpose or benefits of evaluation
- they feel it will be too time-consuming
- they believe that the costs of evaluating a training event will outweigh any benefits
- no training objectives have been identified
- appropriate assessment criteria have not been agreed
- people have difficulty in selecting key areas for assessment
- they are unaware of the methods of evaluation and how they can be used
- they do not have the time, expertise, or resources to analyse the learning results of any evaluation
- people feel threatened
- they may not actually want to hear any bad news
- they may feel that they are above such considerations
- the organisation or union has no agreed policy for evaluation to take place.

EXERCISE 7.6

Your training organisation has recently delivered an off-site three-day staff development programme to a public sector organisation. Your organisation usually delivers its training on-site. To ensure objectivity an independent team carries out formal evaluation within the classroom environment on the final day of delivery. Due to the fact that the programme was delivered off-site, the evaluation was carried out online and completion rates were extremely low.

Why do you think this was the case?

What could have been done differently?

7.13 TIMING OF EVALUATION

Timing of evaluation is all important and will usually be determined by the objectives of the training programme. The work of both Hamblin (1974) and Kirkpatrick (1979) provides a useful basis for gathering, analysing, interpreting and reporting evaluation data that can be considered at different levels and over varying periods of time from immediate to longer term.

Reactions to the training programme can be assessed either during or immediately after the training intervention; however, this form of evaluation tends to be superficial and influenced by a number of factors, as discussed earlier. The extent to which learning has occurred can also be assessed during or at the end of the development activity and will provide an immediate source of data to determine the effectiveness of the activity. However, transfer of learning will take somewhat longer to assess and will need to be evaluated over time once the learner has returned to the workplace. This process relies on the line manager and learner to assess the extent to which learning has occurred over the longer term.

7.14 THE ROLE OF FORMATIVE AND SUMMATIVE ASSESSMENT IN EVALUATION

How can trainers be confident that training programmes address the needs of participants and achieve programme objectives? How can they ensure that there will be transfer of learning once participants return to the workplace? How can the support of supervisors/ line managers be achieved? This can be achieved in part by conducting formative and summative assessments. Noe (2008, p198) stated that formative evaluation 'refers to the evaluation of training that takes place during program design and development. That is formative evaluation helps to ensure that (1) the training programme is well organised and runs smoothly and (2) trainees learn and are satisfied with the programme.' Formative data, such as opinions, beliefs and feelings about a programme content, design and delivery are usually gathered from a range of stakeholders, for example, employees, managers, subject experts, etc. The gathering of such data can be achieved through interviews or focus groups. The outcome of this activity can result in training programmes being adjusted to more accurately reflect learning objectives and provide participants with more appropriate content and learning activities. Whilst the invitation to stakeholders to participate in this data-gathering exercise is considered important, attention must also be paid to the practicality of the exercise with regard to resources such as costs and staffing, and time. There is also the added challenge of being able to accommodate all recommendations, and the risk of possibly alienating some stakeholders; therefore careful consideration must be given to who will be involved in the formative evaluation exercise.

In contrast to formative evaluation, summative evaluation is carried out following successful completion of the training programme and is concerned with evaluating the extent to which participants have achieved the learning outcomes, for example acquired knowledge, and developed new skills, attitudes or behaviour. Noe (2008, p199) defines summative evaluation as 'evaluation conducted to determine the extent to which trainees have changed as a result of participating in the training program'. Whereas formative evaluation was concerned with obtaining mainly qualitative data, it is argued that summative evaluation is usually more concerned with collecting quantitative data from a range of sources such as tests, assessments of performance rating, increases in sales, etc.

7.15 CONCLUSION

We can perhaps appreciate that there is a real need to evaluate training interventions. Companies are spending considerable sums on training and thus need to feel secure that they are getting a return on this investment. The classic model of evaluation developed by Kirkpatrick is still often cited as the model practitioners may initially adopt. However, as we have seen, it has limitations in that some companies do not fully understand the model and so do not use it. Equally, because of the complexity, some companies and practitioners only make use of the first of the four levels. Recognising some of the limitations, academics have proposed alternative models but, as we have seen, the model from Holton et al is arguably more complex than that of Kirkpatrick. It could, as with Kirkpatrick's model, feature in discussions in the academic journals but not be applied by practitioners and companies. To ensure that models are applied, an alternative approach would be that of Giangreco, who suggests that we improve models at Kirkpatrick's level 1. Equally, following Anderson, a useful approach might be to convince companies of the value of learning to the organisation, which in turn will persuade them to adopt models of evaluation.

Whichever approach is adopted, practitioners will need to make use of various data derived from both quantitative and qualitative methods. These may include questionnaires, interviews, and the analysis of company surveys. They will need to demonstrate that the investment from the company has resulted in a return. After all it will be difficult to persuade a CEO or shareholders to invest in training if that expenditure is not going to benefit the company in an increasingly competitive environment.

FINS PARK: ADDRESSING FUTURE CHALLENGES WITH REGARD TO THE EVALUATION OF LEARNING AND DEVELOPMENT

CASE STUDY 7.1

Fins Park is a public sector organisation with responsibility for a significant sized city in the United Kingdom. Following a recent government inspection of the management of local services, a series of significant weaknesses in the leadership and management within the organisation has been identified. It is now imperative that the organisation takes immediate action to address these identified weaknesses. Furthermore, following recent government reduction in financial budgets, the organisation has to make significant financial savings without these affecting services to their community; this might result in large-scale staff redundancies.

The Head of Learning and Development and her team were directed to undertake, as a matter of urgency, a review of the organisation's capability framework to establish the extent to which it is appropriate to meet future challenging demands. Following this exercise, an analysis of all management performance and development reviews over the past three years was carried out. It quickly became apparent that the performance and capabilities of the management and leadership teams at Fins Park were deficient in meeting the future challenges of the organisation.

Historically, leadership and management development would have been sourced from within the organisation; however, following the government report and internal review, it has become apparent that the internal resources are not fit for purpose. As a result the organisation approached a number of established leadership and management providers, with a view to selecting the most appropriate. Following a period of shortlisting, a renowned provider was appointed to deliver an accredited leadership and management programme for its senior management team.

In order to address the government's concerns, to meet the future challenges facing Fins Park and ensure that this considerable investment in leadership and management development represented value for money, discussion took place regarding how this programme was to be evaluated.

Within a short period of time, the first of several cohorts of participants commenced the programme. The programme was designed to minimise time away from work (extraction time) and required delegates to attend workshops on one Friday/Saturday per month over a period of six months. Four modules were delivered over this period of time and at the end of each module delivery an evaluation took place. This evaluation was conducted by a member of Fins Park Learning and Development Team and adopted a focus group approach.

At the end of two years, the organisation reviewed the programme and was concerned about the success of the leadership and management development. The evaluations were limited in scope and it was very difficult to determine the impact this programme had made on performance improvements. The Executive Committee, in order to continue with their investment in this programme, stressed that the Learning and Development Team needed to provide evidence that the programme was actually resulting in performance improvement. This aspect of evaluation is critical, as the programme is now due to go out for re-tender and the successful provider will need to provide details of a comprehensive evaluation process.

Questions

Drawing on appropriate academic debate and discussion, answer the following questions.

1 How effective was the focus group evaluation method adopted by Fins Park Learning and Development Team? Is there anything you would have done differently?

2 Imagine that you are an accredited leadership and management development consultancy and are planning on submitting a tender for this programme. What evaluation approach would you recommend to Fins Park?

CASE STUDY 7.2

JD GROCERS (JDG)

JDG is a large multinational supermarket chain that currently has 600 supermarkets throughout Europe with their head office based on the outskirts of London. Intense competition and growing customer expectations have resulted in JDG adopting a focused approach to customer service as part of its business strategy. As excellent customer service is integral to JDG's long-term business plans, substantial resources have been allocated to deliver a number of online customer service training programmes to their front-line staff. Initial feedback from these training interventions indicated high levels of achievement in all online tasks undertaken by participants. However, evaluation by JDG from stakeholders, such as customers, line managers,

suppliers, etc, indicated lower customer satisfaction than expected following the investment in the online training programme.

Questions

Drawing on appropriate academic debate and discussion, answer the following questions.

1   Identify and discuss the apparent inconsistency between the initial feedback indicating high levels of achievement against later feedback showing lower than expected customer satisfaction.

2   How could training evaluation be improved to address these issues?

EXPLORE FURTHER

BROWN, K.G. (2001) Using computers to deliver training: which employees learn and why? *Personnel Psychology.* Vol 5, No 2, pp271–296.

DERVEN, M. (2012) Building a strategic approach to learning evaluation. *Training & Development.* Vol 66, No 11, pp54–57.

GHOSH, P. (2011) Evaluating effectiveness of a training programme with trainee reaction. *Industrial and Commercial Training.* Vol 43, No 4, pp247–255.

MATOX, J.R. (2012) Measuring the effectiveness of informal methodologies. *Training & Development.* Vol 66, No 2, pp44–53.

CHAPTER 8

Acting Professionally and Ethically

PETER CURETON AND MAUREEN ROYCE

LEARNING OUTCOMES

By the end of this chapter, you will be able to:

- discuss the importance of ethics in learning and development practice
- explain two main philosophical bases for ethics
- discuss the place of equality and diversity in learning
- review your practice to ensure that learning is inclusive
- evaluate your own practice in continuous professional development.

8.1 INTRODUCTION

This chapter examines aspects of professional and ethical behaviour, and explores the elements that characterise a learning and development professional. We provide a working definition for ethics and consider two key philosophical divisions that are relevant. Our discussion then leads to an examination of how approaches to acting in an inclusive way need to recognise both equality and diversity in all aspects of the learning cycle. We conclude the chapter with an inquiry into continuous professional development so that learning and development specialists can be exemplars of practice, using traditional and contemporary methods.

Codes of ethics provide frameworks to guide individual conduct in everyday life. They help to educate individuals about what is considered right and wrong in a society and help them to make choices about what they do. Ethics raises questions about what actions ought, or ought not to be taken in a given circumstance. When someone is described as a good person, the criteria used to lead to this conclusion will connect with the values, beliefs and behaviours of those making such a comment. It follows that there will be a range of views about what is 'good'. The law provides rigid rules, such as you cannot take the life of another and you must pay your taxes to the government, but ethics seeks a much wider remit and deals with principles that will be viewed relatively. Are codes of ethics imposed? Is ethics associated with exerting power and influence over others or does it merely seek to place some form of limit on personal freedom to act in the interests of all?

At the time of writing this chapter there has been a renewed focus of interest in ethics in organisational settings, not least due to the activities and behaviour of some individuals in the health and financial services sectors. The awarding of high levels of financial reward to some staff despite apparent service failings or bonus payments made despite a lack of profitability and no increased shareholder value raises questions about how individuals conduct themselves at work. We judge others by our own values. When poor practice is exposed in the media, the focus will often turn to questions about the efficacy of training. Have those who are considered 'the offenders' been trained in the standards expected of them by the organisation and is their training up to date? We are sure that if you consult the media when you read this chapter that you will find similar examples about practice. As a professional, it should make you realise that we need continued awareness of ethics to guide what we consider acceptable practice.

But is ethics a matter that need overly concern learning and development professionals? In one sense, surely learning and development activities can be viewed as inherently ethical? Indeed, Jim Stewart has examined the proposition that human resource development (HRD) 'is, in and of itself, an ethical endeavour' (2007, p60). He concluded that HRD could only be considered good or bad in relation to moral choices that are made about practice. HRD can be 'good' depending on how its purpose and outcomes can be viewed and valued by different stakeholders. For example, learning can help individuals to grow their knowledge and skills at work. In turn, this means that employees do not struggle to perform their jobs, which removes a potential threat of disciplinary procedures through poor performance. Learning can enhance future employability and increase individual earnings potential by building the levels and range of their knowledge and skills. Individuals can then achieve their potential. Through processes of learning, individuals can find a position of ontological security. Ontology is a branch of philosophy that deals with perceptions of reality. There are two main ontological paradigms – realism and idealism (Blaikie 2007). A realist ontology relates to positivism and assumes that there is a single 'out-there' reality that is separate from individuals who inhabit it. Idealist ontologies locate reality in individual thoughts and experience – they assume that reality has no independent existence. This has led some writers to declare that there is no single truth, just numerous interpretations of truth. Ontological security can help individuals to find comfort in their position in an organisation, and in life: they understand where they 'fit in'. A learning and development specialist can find such security when their personal values and beliefs coincide with the demands of the role. They then become fulfilled as the employee and person they aspire to be.

Learning can also raise ethical concerns for employers. The learning curricula provided by an organisation will reinforce a company's values as they provide a knowledge framework and standards against which individual behaviour can be judged. For example, induction programmes will often include information on an organisation's background, culture and values. This means that learning and development professionals themselves interpret and act as guardians of these corporate standards. Colleagues, including senior management, will look to them to be exemplars of practice. As John Wilson has commented, 'trainers, because of their role, are privy to many of the things both positive and negative which happen in organisations . . . we all have to recognise our professional and ethical responsibilities and speak out'" (*People Management*, 3 Jan 2013).

Yet ethical behaviour is in our experience neither universally understood nor practised. For example, those who hold copyright for learning materials appear increasingly keen to pursue legal action against those who abuse the law by using materials without permission. Copyright owners are perfectly entitled to seek legal redress in cases where material is used without permission. In addition, some learning events can involve overnight stays away from home, which may not be domestically appropriate. Team development, so-called 'away days', can involve rigorous physical activities which may embarrass some participants. Learning and development specialists can struggle between being viewed as servants of senior management of an organisation, or as emancipators of people potential. We need to consider ethics beyond the confines of professional standards and explore wider issues that are needed to inform contemporary professional practice.

This chapter will provide a definition of ethics that is relevant to learning and development professionals before examining the different philosophical bases to ethics. We will then link ethics to issues of equality and diversity and extend the discussion beyond legal issues. This will conclude with a discussion on professionalism and how a learning and development professional can be recognised and sustained through processes of continuing professional development.

8.2 DEFINITION AND UNDERSTANDING OF ETHICS IN LEARNING AND DEVELOPMENT

The word ethics is derived from the Greek word ethos (εtηοσ), to identify the character or disposition of an individual, group or a society, and seeks to denote principles or sets of values that are held in common which inform our habits and behaviours. Ethics is a branch of philosophy that covers the codes by which a civilised society exists. The word is also associated with the Latin word *mores*, which is often used to describe conventions and customs, although a more accurate translation into English is to the word behaviour.

Many writers who consider ethics in their work hesitate to provide a definition, preferring to introduce words and phrases that explain its nature and what it concerns. These include moral values, responsible conduct, codes of behaviour, codes of practice, rules, principles, fairness, appropriate behaviour, and right and wrong. Yet issues of ethics tend to arise only in situations where the consequences of an individual's actions contradict the values and feelings of another. This has led some writers to suggest that this complex area of humanity can be clarified by asking oneself 'What should I do in this situation?' An example that is often used, certainly in education and training courses about ethics, asks individuals to consider how comfortable they would be to explain and justify their actions if they were interviewed by a television or radio journalist. When we have asked our learners to apply this question to difficult professional situations they have encountered, it has led to some hesitation and silences. Hindsight through reviewing our actions can add such wonderful clarity to our thinking! It is a key feature of continuing professional development that we will introduce later in the chapter.

In writing this chapter for a specific readership, we believe that it is helpful to define ethics and we propose the following definition:

> The standards that guide the behaviour of learning and development specialists to achieve positive outcomes that seek to balance the interests of organisations, individuals and wider society.

Ethical approaches are standards against which our actions and behaviours are judged by others. They will consider whether our actions are 'right' or 'wrong'. Yet this raises a key question. Who sets the rules by which actions are judged right or wrong? What is perfectly normal to one person can be most offensive to another. For example, showing the palm of your hand to stop an Australian person from crossing a busy road would be perfectly acceptable. The same gesture would be highly insulting to a Greek person. When gesturing to another in Greece, it is the back of the hand that should be used, as the palm is associated with a historical practice of spreading muck (and worse!) into the faces of criminals to humiliate them. The action in Greece implies that you think of the person as a criminal who is contemptible. So, if there are rules about conduct and behaviour, are they universal or particular? From whom do we learn the rules about how to behave with other people?

In Figure 8.1, we deconstruct the layers that underpin our behaviour. Core values provide our fundamental foundation to becoming a person. They can be traced back to our inheritance from parents and family, schools and religious teaching that gives us our initial guidance to negotiate the world, our so-called moral compass. Our values inform our beliefs. As we widen our social sphere and gain exposure to a broader range of people and experience, we develop our own individually constructed road map for life. Interacting with people who may possibly be quite different from us, and having new

Figure 8.1 Layers that underpin behaviour

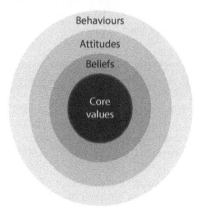

codes of behaviour imposed upon us, may challenge and threaten some of our core values. The experiences of our forebears may not be as relevant to our own lived realities. The beliefs that we develop in turn inform our attitudes, our moods and emotions. We develop ways of accommodating circumstances and if they are seen to be working we will replicate them, otherwise we will try other approaches. The ways in which others learn to understand us as a person come from the external layer of our behaviours. In existential philosophy, others judge our actions by what they observe of our lived experience; by what we *do* rather than by what we *say*. A person may make claims of being a respectful person but the behaviour of engaging in idle gossip about colleagues would not lead others to that same conclusion. Indeed, they may go further and adduce that we are not only disrespectful but rather a shallow person who makes self-claims as a whim. Each of us can reflect on the behaviours we exhibit to others, to avoid the possibility that they might form quite a different view of us than that which we intend. Further reading about interpersonal behaviours can be found at the end of the chapter.

Ethics has a key place for the practice of learning and development specialists as it is seen by staff as standards set by the organisation. It is reasonable for staff to assume that if they attend a learning session to develop their understanding or skills in a topic that the facilitator's behaviours are consistent with the espoused values contained in corporate mission statements and performance agreements. The way individuals behave in work can be a determinant of the prevailing working culture.

YOUR CORE VALUES

EXERCISE 8.1

- What are your core values?
- Who has had a significant role in instilling these in you?
- To what extent have you modified or changed these values to become your beliefs?

- What impression do you give to others by the behaviour you exhibit?
- How would you like others to regard you?
- How consistently do you role-model behaviours of an ethical learning and development specialist?

When individuals start work in an organisation, they are exposed to learning activities for their induction. Socialisation processes help them to get to know work colleagues and build relationships. Orientation helps to introduce them physically to the layout of the working environment and psychologically to understand the organisation's expectations of staff.

These expectations will include understanding elements of the performance management system as they learn how to do their job. When they are established in a role, the performance review processes will often link any required improvements to a learning plan. Learning and development therefore needs to adopt the highest ethical standards of practice or will risk losing credibility amongst peers and other stakeholders in the organisation. There is a danger that the espoused values are not witnessed in practice and raise doubts in the minds of new starters about the commitment levels of staff to the values. After all, it would not be unreasonable for them to question whether they themselves need to put into practice the behaviours that are not used by the learning and development folk.

EXERCISE 8.2

L&D AS REINFORCER OF ORGANISATIONAL CULTURE?

A private sector organisation that is set up on traditional bureaucratic lines wishes to change its culture to encourage greater working between teams. Profits have been falling over the last three years and the organisation is keen to reverse this trend. Currently, each functional area works independently and communication between departments is slow.

The senior managers believe that future prosperity will depend on exploring ways in which employees can be more creative in proposing innovative ways of working to increase both efficiency and effectiveness.

1   Propose a set of integrated learning activities that would make a contribution to the senior managers' agenda.

2   As a business partner, how might these activities need to be horizontally integrated with other people management practices?

8.3 UNITED NATIONS DECADE FOR EDUCATION FOR SUSTAINABLE DEVELOPMENT 2005–2014

Understanding of ethics in learning is not limited to organisational contexts. Ethical approaches to learning have been considered by the United Nations due to a lack of equality between peoples. What is taken for granted in Western societies as a right to education is not the case across the globe. Education can be so important to some that they are prepared to risk their lives for it. The case of Malala Yousafzai, the Pakistani girl who survived being shot in October 2012, illustrates this point (http://www.malala-yousafzai.com/). The UN project has a ten-year aim to:

> mobilize the educational resources of the world to help create a more sustainable future. Many paths to sustainability (e.g. sustainable agriculture and forestry, research and technology transfer, finance, sustainable production and consumption) exist and are mentioned in the 40 chapters of Agenda 21, the official document of

the 1992 Earth Summit. Education is one of these paths. Education alone cannot achieve a more sustainable future; however, without education and learning for sustainable development, we will not be able to reach that goal.

(From unesco.org website)

It is clear that there is a widely held view that encouraging people to learn can liberate them to be self-reliant. If those living in disadvantaged communities can acquire the knowledge and skills to build their own and their nation's future, the project will be a resounding success and lead to a more equal global society. As Nelson Mandela is reported to have said, 'education is the most powerful weapon you can use to change the world'.

EXERCISE 8.3
YOUR ORGANISATIONAL VALUES

How aware are you of the UN project?

Do you limit the delivery of learning to your employees?

What role could you play in helping the wider community, including the disadvantaged, to learn?

8.4 PHILOSOPHICAL BASES OF ETHICS

There are a number of philosophical approaches to the subject of ethics, and learning and development specialists should undertake a detailed study of the field. For our purposes, the topic is characterised by key divisions:

- Cognitivism and non-cognitivism – exploring whether it is possible or not to know moral right from wrong.
- Consequentialism and non-consequentialism – actions are or are not necessarily good or bad in themselves, but only in how they are used.

Cognitivism suggests that there are objective truths that can be known by everyone. Experience of living in the world exposes individuals to behaviours that become accepted as norms. As we can know truths about the world, such as the world is not flat and bombs kill people, statements of moral belief can be accepted as universally true or false. In contrast, **non-cognitivism** asserts that moral right and wrong are both subjective and are not universal. There are no absolute truths or codes, all that we have are our beliefs, and attitudes and behaviours, which are themselves often modified by emotional reactions. Those who subscribe to this point of view recognise the relative nature of morality, which can be exposed through working with others and becomes group norms. As individuals, we devise preferences for our behaviour which are influenced by an accepted culture; culture which is characterised by race, religion, sexual orientation and gender. As an example, some hold the view that it is wrong to use covert means to gain access to other people's telephone conversations. Others might embrace 'phone-tapping' to prevent a major terrorist incident.

In the context of learning and development, cognitivists may consider the running of a learning event for call centre workers to sell home repairs, without checking that the work was needed, to be bad in all circumstances. Non-cognitivists could argue that it is not for the call agents to decide what might be required, as closing a sale enables tradespeople to earn a living and an organisation to produce profit and pay taxes on that profit.

Consequentialism considers the outcomes of actions and how they relate to the greatest good for people. This approach seeks to secure the maximisation of the sum of human happiness, which accepts that there may be people who feel excluded or wronged. Indeed, there may be cases, for example in insisting on vaccine use for children, such as the combined measles, mumps, and rubella vaccine, where deliberate actions are taken in the pursuit of longer-term happiness for all. It is recognised that this will not be effective for all children, but as long as most people are satisfied an action can be considered ethical. This approach is associated with valuing outcomes in terms of costs and benefits. The case of the Ford Pinto illustrates this point. The costs associated with changing the design of a potentially fatal flaw in a sports car were calculated as being lower than the likely compensation for death claims. Some consider consequentialism intensely problematic as the disadvantaging of some groups for the greater good exposes all in the longer term to disadvantage, as life is valued only in economic terms. Unhappiness is often thought to be a deeper emotion than happiness, and so intense suffering by a minority will potentially outweigh any happiness that the majority might derive from being advantaged. An example of consequentialism in the realm of learning and development is so-called 'sheep-dip' training, when all members of staff are trained irrespective of an identified need.

Non-consequentialism is associated with Kant's (1724–1804) 'categorical imperative' that states 'I ought never to act except in such a way that I can also will that my maxim should become a universal law'. This means that each of us has to be willing to permit others to use the same approaches to ethics that we use: 'do unto others as you would like done unto you'. To comply with this ethical code, learning and development specialists need to challenge unacceptable behaviour and be consistent, essentially acting as a role model. This key professional behaviour in the CIPD Profession Map will be considered under professionalism later in the chapter.

The outcomes of learning and development are part of the evaluation processes that were explored in Chapter 7. To confirm the validity of a learning event, forms of testing against the behavioural objectives can be made. But, if we consider learning outcomes through an ethical lens and expose them to scrutiny over their purpose, we may raise fundamental questions about intent. Is the purpose of learning solely to build additional knowledge and skills such that individuals can be more productive? Are learning strategies simply a form of instrumentality, to achieve only an employer's purposes? This has been described by some writers as 'sweating the resources' in the quest for increased efficiencies and can lead to learning and development professionals questioning their contribution to an organisation in a teleological sense. Teleology refers to an ultimate purpose and the fundamental nature for the existence of something, in this case the role of learning and development. Does the role simply exist to serve the interests of the organisation? Is there a disconnection between espoused corporate values such as 'we will develop our people so that they achieve their full potential' and a reality that is viewed by staff as 'we will develop you only to further our corporate aims'?

We have raised many questions here and could argue that if learning and development is part of the mechanism through which an organisation achieves a consistent approach to levels of required knowledge and skills, then it *is* in the interests of all. Without a corpus of qualified, trained, and experienced workers it is difficult to see how an enterprise could survive, let alone prosper.

EXERCISE 8.4

ETHICAL STANCES

What examples of cognitivist and non-cognitivist stances might be relevant in your work?

What are the accepted 'truths' in your organisation?

Should they be challenged? Why?

How do you view the outcomes of your learning interventions?

Who are the stakeholders who benefit from this?

8.5 INCLUSIVITY – EQUALITY AND DIVERSITY

Ethical behaviour, behaving as we 'ought' to because it is the right thing to do, is one of the drivers for developing an inclusive stance towards development in organisations. In relating to the need for equality practice and a recognition of the diverse nature of the organisation and its stakeholders, learning and development practitioners require an ethical perspective, as we discussed previously. Additionally, an understanding of how legal compliance, business imperatives and changing demographics impact on the content and delivery of organisational learning will support the development of an inclusive learning culture. Inclusivity requires organisations to recognise individual diversity within learner groups, hence avoiding the 'sheep-dip' mentality of one-size-fits-all training programmes. While the Equality Act (2010) defines nine protected characteristics and organisations seek to comply with non-discriminatory practice while engaging with individuals with one or more of these characteristics, there is inevitably a concern that individuals who are not covered by the Act are either ignored or their needs not considered. Difference can be visible or invisible, protected by the law or uncovered by the law, but for the learning and development specialist the drive to achieve the best possible outcomes for each individual they engage with must be a primary objective.

Kandola and Fullerton (1998), in *Managing the Mosaic*, heralded the perceived need for organisations to respond to business drivers and create a culture and climate of equality within the workplace. In linking the diversity agenda to the business agenda, equality moved beyond a more specialist role and became part of the 'mainstream'. Mainstreaming equality into the line management structure led to a growth in the need for organisations to use learning and development tools to communicate messages about equality. Since the development of the concept of mainstreaming equality in the 1990s, its practicality and effectiveness have been praised when successful, criticised when fruitless and debated constantly. This derives from the fact that the integration of mainstreaming an equality agenda is a demanding one as it 'requires everyone in an organisation to be responsible for diversity and equality issues, thus immediately raising the policy issues into ethical and political issues for individual and group action. The aim of mainstreaming equal opportunities is to ensure its integration within an organisation rather than remain as a policy flagship championed by a small central unit' (Clifford and Royce 2008, p6). However, responsibility without knowledge or the skills to work effectively with the complexities of diversity leaves an organisation vulnerable. In an increasingly specific legal framework, attention is required to proving that individuals have been provided with the tools to be responsible. Sally Witcher defines this process as 'integrating equality considerations from the outset into how an organisation operates its policies and practices' (Witcher 2005, p1).

This definition provides both an equality and business case for mainstreaming; highlighting that for mainstreaming to truly work, equality and organisational development agendas must work hand in hand. Rees reflects this thought by stating that mainstreaming involves 'the incorporation of Equal Opportunities issues into all actions, programmes and policies from the outset' (Rees 1999, pp3–4). Witcher further comments that 'it is a means of changing organisational culture, integrating equality considerations from the outset, rather than as an afterthought' (Witcher 2005, p1). This places significant pressure on the development tools in an organisation to reach out to all parties within the stakeholder map to show that there is knowledge about behaviour and understanding about diversity of needs.

A UK survey by the CIPD (2007a, p14) found 'a damaging disconnection between the levels of authority, influence and commitment that would support diversity progress ... [which] dilutes the power organisations have to make change happen'. Learning and development plays a dual role when considering equality and diversity behaviour in organisations. It is frequently cited as a way of raising awareness or providing a framework for diverse behaviours, yet needs to question how organisational development policies themselves respond effectively to the needs of a diverse workforce. ACAS (2011) states that every staff member working for an organisation should have the same access to training regardless of whether the person has a disability or is from a minority background. However, the capacity of learning and development initiatives to instil in the workforce a set of culturally inclusive behaviours is open to doubt. An examination of how equality and diversity training is carried out reveals some of the weaknesses inherent in training delivery within a diverse workforce. Jones et al (2013) suggest that a wide variety of delivery methods are used in diversity training including classroom-based training, e-learning, videos, discussions, role-plays, simulations and exercises. However, the effectiveness of such delivery methods can be limited when trying to achieve the three categories of learning outcome identified by Kandola (2009) – awareness, attitude and behaviour. Awareness may increase, but this may not be followed through to attitude and behaviour.

It is therefore apposite to reflect on the purpose of equality and diversity training. Lai and Kleiner (2001) define it as the process by which a workforce learns about cultural, racial, lesbian/gay/bi-sexual/transgender (LGBT), and religious differences among employees; to embrace those differences to create and maintain an effective work environment. Michielsens et al (2008) explain in greater detail that in order to effectively promote equality and diversity and foster an environment whereby it is not just tolerated, but actively encouraged and valued, requires awareness-raising through communication, and commitment from senior managers which is complemented by awareness training. Bezrukova et al (2012) express the notion that the goal of equality and diversity training and development is to reduce prejudice and discrimination, enhancing the skills, knowledge and motivation to enable a person to interact with diverse people. Achieving such aims presents significant challenges,

The use of online questionnaires provides an easily administered and statistically accessible methodology for developing knowledge about diversity, but this works at a surface level and would not engage a workforce in considering the more complex ethical issues surrounding equality. The 'raising awareness' type of diversity training with a 'tick box' surface approach to learning has been criticised by those who claim that it is simply not effective enough as a tool for integrating equality and diversity within an organisation. Nancheria (2008, cited in Kumra and Manfredi 2012) states that raising awareness is ineffective, because it does not help the workforce to understand the scope of the issues involved, instead focusing on the issues of legal compliance. E-learning for awareness training has been criticised by Hayat and Walton (2012) because it lacks the ability to change a person's behaviour and attitude and it is just seen as a 'tick box' exercise to satisfy legal compliance requirements. Additionally, Kandola (2009, p149) claims that this type of diversity training is carried out simply because it is a mandatory legal requirement to do so. Whilst large numbers of staff can be accommodated quickly and cost-effectively, the outcome is that e-learning is unlikely to evoke thoughts or changes to attitudes or behaviours.

Alternatives to more traditional training methods include the use of drama enactment to bring scenarios to life. Moreno (2012) demonstrated that constructive behavioural changes in individuals and groups could occur through methods of dramatic enactment as different forms of drama can help people gain awareness and hone personal skills. However, St George et al (1999) had earlier argued that drama-based learning aims to use the sophisticated improvisational skills of professional actors to engage participants intellectually and emotionally as well as raising awareness, and develop the empathic communication skills of participants with their colleagues, clients and customers. The costs associated with such activities need to be compared with the waste of providing other, ineffective forms. Learning and development opportunities can be subject to the same cultural dominance as any other part of HR and the perceived inclusiveness of development strategy may reveal some stark differences if viewed from a radical (measuring the outcome) rather than a liberal (fairness within the process) perspective.

Evidence from the EHRC report *Barriers to Employment and Unfair Treatment at Work* (2013) suggests that learning and development methods often fail to meet the needs and aspirations of disabled employees and learners. Some employers have reservations about risks to productivity of employing disabled people and concerns about the cost and other implications of meeting the requirements of equality legislation. Taken together, these results suggest a general work culture that can be inflexible and not particularly welcoming of disabled people. The report showed that fewer disabled employees were likely to hold professional or managerial roles within organisations.

EXERCISE 8.5

INCLUSIVITY IN TRAINING

Choose both a training method and a full programme and identify the barriers a disabled person might face if participating in this approach. Think very broadly about the range of conditions that this might include.

Then redesign the method and programme so that it still achieves the learning objectives but is accessible to those with a range of disabilities.

SPOTLIGHT ON PRACTICE 8.1: EQUALITY IN DEVELOPMENT – NDCS (NATIONAL DEAF CHILDREN'S SOCIETY) SCOTLAND

NDCS Scotland has developed a template for successful transition at educational key stages and into employment. Recognising that deaf young people are statistically more likely to be unemployed, the template seeks to consolidate support and resources and to produce individualised transition plans for deaf young people. Guidance in the form of a template is included in the downloadable guide at

http://www.ndcs.org.uk/about_us/campaign_with_us/scotland/campaign_news/ a_template_for.html

8.6 PROFESSIONALISM AND PROFESSIONAL PRACTICE

In this chapter, thus far we have considered ethics and inclusivity, and have directed readers to reflect about their practice. Yet there is a central issue that we have not addressed, despite it underpinning the type of practices that we have discussed. This is the nature of professionalism and how learning and development specialists can conduct themselves in ways that are characteristic of a profession.

Distinctions between professions and trades suggest that a professional requires advanced knowledge, not just skill, to enable him or her to provide advice about novel situations. This includes the ability to reflect and draw on a significant bank of knowledge to inform a decision. There are various characteristics of a profession and here we present five that we feel are most relevant to learning and development professionals:

1   It is a specialised service that requires advanced knowledge to deal with problems primarily on an intellectual level.

2   There are occasions when there is a need to exercise confidentiality with a client or his or her manager.

3   It requires professionals to contribute to the body of knowledge through their practice and so enhance the status of learning and development.

4   Professionals are required to ensure that their knowledge and skills are up to date.

5   It is bound by a distinctive ethical code in its relationships with clients, colleagues, and the public.

The CIPD has a published code of ethical standards, part of which is shown in Table 8.1. It extends the characteristics of a professional to include two key areas – business relationships and personal integrity – and is of particular importance in ethical approaches to learning and development.

Table 8.1 Extract from CIPD Ethical Standards

Ethical Standards and Integrity
Members of the CIPD shall:
2.1   establish, maintain and develop business relationships based on confidence, trust and respect
2.2   exhibit and defend professional and personal integrity and honesty at all times
2.3   demonstrate sensitivity for the customs, practices, culture and personal beliefs of others
2.4   advance employment and business practices that promote equality of opportunity, diversity and inclusion and support human rights and dignity
2.5   safeguard all confidential, commercially-sensitive and personal data acquired as a result of business relationships and not use it for personal advantage or the benefit or detriment of third parties.

8.7 BUSINESS RELATIONSHIPS

In buying in services from third-party individuals or organisations, a learning and development professional can be exposed to issues that test personal integrity. It is common practice for organisations to use external consultants to provide specialist learning services that would be uneconomic for an organisation to resource through full-time positions. The marketing of professional services is often done through networking and recommendations by colleagues after good work. However, it must be recognised that in a competitive world, inducements may be offered to secure a business contract. Is it appropriate to accept corporate hospitality before signing a contract, or to celebrate a successful contract outcome? Most might think it acceptable to accept a cup of coffee when discussing a proposal. Yet how far could an ethical position be stretched? Would it be ethical to accept an invitation to lunch and a match at a local rugby club from a consultant who had successfully designed and managed a number of assessment and development centres for your organisation? Would your answer change if the invitation was to an international match in Paris that involved a two-night stay in a four-star hotel? Or would it change yet again if the invitation was to the Rugby World Cup 2019 in Japan?

Organisations will often have policies in place to guide behaviour. These may recognise that it is acceptable to accept small tokens such as a calendar or diary, but gifts must not be provided in expectation of material benefit to future business. Working internationally may present further problems as in some countries it may be part of the accepted business practice to exchange gifts. One of us can recall facilitating a learning event for senior managers from a Middle Eastern country when expressions of gratitude were shown by the offering of an expensive watch at the end of a course. It would have been considered very poor business etiquette to refuse. This raises issues of judgement. When is a gift not a gift?

The Institute of Business Ethics offers sound advice by considering four areas. If the intention behind the gift is to influence decisions about future business, it is not a gift but a bribe, an *inducement* to gain unfair advantage over others who compete for the business. The *scale* of the gift and how proportionate it is to the situation and the person will guide a decision about its acceptability. What might be appropriate for a senior manager may not be appropriate for a junior member of staff. Unless you are able to *reciprocate* the gift, you could find yourself beholden to the other person in the future. This could lead to pressure to change your behaviour – after all, you did accept a gift and gave nothing in return, which might suggest a power imbalance. Finally, it is never acceptable to accept cash as dealings may not always be transparent.

A test that is often used to guide thinking about the ethics of a situation can be shown through three questions to be asked personally:

- Do I mind if anyone knows?
- How comfortable would I be if this were reported in a newspaper?
- Can I honestly say that the action has not influenced my current and future actions?

REFLECTIVE ACTIVITY 8.1

Personal integrity

What is your organisation's policy on corporate hospitality?

How have you reacted to offers in the past?

How would you react now?

8.8 PERSONAL INTEGRITY AND HONESTY

To be considered a person with integrity implies that there is consistency between the claims we may make about ourselves, and the actions and behaviour that we use in dealing with others. Noelliste (2013, p13) recognises the growing interests in matters of personal integrity, suggesting that integrity is often used 'interchangeably with words such as honesty, consciousness, trustworthiness, and credibility'. She continues with advice that learning and development professionals need not only to display personal honesty, but must also encourage other members of staff to do likewise. Inappropriate or unacceptable behaviour, wherever it is seen, should be challenged.

Approaches to personal integrity can be considered from three perspectives (Trevinyo-Rodriguez 2007). These are shown in Table 8.2 and we have developed the model to include examples relevant to learning and development.

Table 8.2 Approaches to personal integrity

Perspective	Includes	Example in learning and development
Integrated self-view	Consistency in adhering to one's own motivations whatever the consequences	Refusing to run a learning event that includes outdoor activities that have the potential for people to lose their dignity
Identity view	Adherence to the principles that support your image or identity	Running a CPD event to share your own position as a lifelong learner
'Clean hands' view	Acting as a role model and being honest to foster loyalty and commitment in others	Maintaining the highest standards in all aspects of your practice

Source: adapted from Trevinyo-Rodriguez (2007)

Being honest requires more than just compliance with the law, although this is an area where learning and development professionals can be exposed to difficulties. It can be all too easy when under time pressures to simply copy an exercise to use in a learning intervention. Put simply, this is theft, as the author's copyrighted materials have been used without permission. Normally, copyright in literary work lasts until 70 years after the death of the author, and professional journals occasionally report cases involving copyright theft that have led to litigation. Such action can lead to the person being disciplined and can lead to sacking for gross misconduct. Honesty is often defined in the negative – not lying, cheating or stealing, but it is a most straightforward characteristic; it requires an individual to be genuine and sincere. But what do professionals do when their honesty is questioned?

Threats to a professional's sense of integrity can lead to whistleblowing, when a member of staff reports conduct which she considers wrong, inappropriate or illegal. Disclosures are usually made 'in the public interest' and can cover miscarriages of justice, damage to the environment or a person acting outside legal obligations. Examples of whistleblowing normally come from the public sector, but it is starting to become more prevalent in the private sector. There is protection for UK whistleblowers under the Public Interest Disclosure Act 1998 (PIDA), which applies to almost all workers and employees who ordinarily work in the UK. To seek the protection, specific procedures detailed in the Act need to be followed. In July 2012, the Organisation for Economic Co-operation and Development (OECD) published an international report: *Whistleblower protection: encouraging reporting*, as part of a series of articles titled *CleanGovBiz: Integrity in practice*. Whilst this showed improvements in protection for whistleblowers, this was limited to ten countries: Australia, Canada, Ghana, Japan, Korea, New Zealand, Romania, South Africa, the United Kingdom and the United States. The OECD does provide a range of guidance for nations on developing legislation and also for multinational organisations as a contribution towards the United Nations Convention against Corruption.

8.9 ORGANISATIONAL EXAMPLES

Where organisations can show a respect for integrity and ethics, they may benefit from increased engagement and employee identification with the organisation and its objectives. This can apply even in an organisational sector that in a global sense can be considered controversial, such as the oil industry. Studies have found that where organisations invested in environmental and community issues, there was a stronger relationship with employees and that corporate social responsibility (CSR) activities helped to moderate the views employees held about the impact of the oil industry on local communities. Development and skills advancement often play a major part of the CSR delivery where organisations are seeking to address complaints or conflict relating to the impact of their work.

An example of this is mineral mining in Africa. Despite countries being wealthy in naturally occurring mineral resources, there is continuing disappointment with the failure to translate these resources into better lives for communities, in, for example, the Democratic Republic of Congo. The mining industry in Africa has recognised that education and training is not providing the skilled people required to meet the needs for its development, operation and infrastructure. Some mining companies have joined together to sponsor initiatives to raise the standard of education and training in the indigenous populations. For the mining industry in Africa, there was a perceived need to improve the relationship with local communities and to stabilise and enhance the skills of the local population. Accordingly, the New Economic Partnership for Africa (NEPAD) and the African Mining Partnership (AMP) have created communities of practice (www.nepad.org) with the aim of modernising education and assisting in a reconstruction of an education infrastructure in a post-conflict environment.

EXERCISE 8.6

CORPORATE SOCIAL RESPONSIBILITY

Communities in the West now also face debt and levels of poverty. Consider how a multinational banking organisation could use its expertise to respond to some of the financial issues faced by an economically struggling community. What benefits to the banking organisation would you suggest help justify CSR responses of this kind?

REFLECTIVE ACTIVITY 8.2

Compliance with ethical standards

Provide examples from your practice that demonstrate your compliance with the CIPD's ethical standards.

What is your responsibility in a situation where a course member used inappropriate language to another?

8.10 ETHICS IN LEARNING AND DEVELOPMENT PRACTICE

In this section, we seek to bring together our exploration of ethics, inclusivity and professionalism and focus this in the domain of learning. Ethical issues in learning and development rarely have fundamental consequences of life and death, yet they are important in the way professionals conduct themselves. We will consider these through the four-part cycle of learning by using some examples. These are not intended to be exhaustive, but should act as reflection points about practice.

8.10.1 IDENTIFYING LEARNING NEEDS

Selecting people for learning can raise questions about equal treatment. Talent management programmes in organisations can be divisive as the quest to develop 'the best' talent may lead employers to look more favourably on a restricted number of individuals. This may exclude others, who, for whatever reason, do not have their contribution recognised in the same way.

If learning needs are typically identified through performance review processes, the kinds of learning activity may be restricted to enhancing capability at the current level. This may miss the potential to develop people for their future careers. Learning opportunities need to be accessible to all.

8.10.2 DESIGNING LEARNING

The approaches to inclusivity that we have experienced suggest that too many learning designers believe that they are developing inclusivity by making the same opportunities available for all. This is not the stance we adopt, as we recognise and celebrate the differences between us all. Whilst most learning designers will accommodate different learning styles to provide a balanced approach to learning opportunities, greater consideration needs to be given to a broader range of issues. Examples of these are given in Table 8.3.

Table 8.3 Issues of inclusivity in learning design

Ice-breaker exercises at the start of a programme are intended to relax learners and prepare them to engage in learning. However, they can have the opposite effect if individuals are expected to contribute too soon for them or if they involve too much personal disclosure.
The design of interpersonal behaviour programmes may include self-perception exercises that have the potential to make learners feel vulnerable if personal disclosures are requested.
Exercises that involve physical touch are never acceptable as it is offensive to some cultures. Even in the West it can lead to difficulties between the sexes. Taking off shoes can stray into territory that can insult some cultures.
Designing exercises that ask learners to write comments on a flipchart can embarrass those with poor handwriting, poor spelling or dyslexia.
Competitive exercises between teams can be fun, but may not be universally acceptable if individual values focus more on mutual respect.
Eastern cultures may historically be more used to education systems that adopt didactic learning methods, the so-called 'sage on the stage' through which an expert imparts her knowledge to others.

8.10.3 DELIVERING LEARNING

The business world appears increasingly to encourage working seven days a week, with long hours. Some employers have even insisted that staff check their emails daily, even whilst on annual leave. There have been examples in the financial services sector of employees dying as a result of long hours working which can be accepted as normal culture, as in the case of Moritz Erhardt, a 21-year-old bank intern who died in October 2013 after working for three days without sleep. Such pressures can find their way into learning events with very early starts or working late into the night. This may not encourage a healthy learning environment if people have responsibilities for young children or elderly parents or other care duties. Diabetics, for example, may become increasingly tired during the day. Even those in good health will experience tiredness when concentrating on new knowledge or coping with new skills. So appropriate breaks and the provision of water to avoid dehydration should be used to sequence learning content.

Most premises now have appropriate access for the visually impaired and wheelchair users. Rooms that are used for learning should be appropriately lit and uncluttered with sufficient space for ease of movement. Cramped facilities are not conducive to a healthy learning environment

However, in delivering e-learning, poor attention to the ergonomics of the equipment layout and seating can lead to eye strain and physical discomfort.

Despite the obsession of some people with their mobile devices, facilitators should insist that all equipment is turned off during an event, not just set to a silent setting. Those who have hearing difficulties may be distracted as hearing aids can still pick up when a mobile phone vibrates, or when an email announcement is received.

Finally, care needs to be exercised in the language that facilitators use. It should always be appropriate to the level of learner and not have the potential to offend. For example, patronising or over-familiar language such as 'love', 'darling' or even 'mate' cannot be considered professional. It echoes parent-child and teacher authority relationships and reinforces forms of organisational power and control. We have discussed earlier that learning and development specialists act as a proxy for the organisation, which will lead learners to make judgements about the working culture. In essence, language can be a form of bullying and can alienate learners. They may not feel confident to challenge such unacceptable behaviour and the distraction will result in a poor focus on learning opportunities.

8.10.4 EVALUATING LEARNING

Methods of validating learning, such as tests, should be appropriate to the type of learning provided. In many ways, if learners are not able to achieve acceptable test scores, the fault lies in the learning design and delivery. After all, the purpose of training is the successful completion of the stated learning outcomes, as discussed in Chapter 5. Testing should not just be restricted to an activity during an intervention; it should be linked to job performance and business results. Ways should be explored of integrating learning into performance review processes rather than having separate forms of testing which could be seen as standalone.

There is, however, a curious dilemma in learning evaluation. On one level, unless learners fully understand instructional technique, their feedback on learning processes may be of limited value. However, as active participants, they will be able to identify potential areas of improvement, certainly in terms of how relevant a session was and how much time was devoted to it. End-of-course 'reactionnaires' should be designed so that they target such areas and avoid the potential simply to give feedback on a facilitator's performance. The timing of end-of-course feedback is also important. We believe that it is better to allow the learners to reflect on their experiences and report back when they have returned to work. Whilst this will lead to a reduction in response rates, comments tend to be more meaningful.

ETHICS AND EVALUATION IN PRACTICE: FREEPORT MCMORAN GOLD AND COPPER

Operating in Indonesia, Freeport had a tarnished reputation with the local community and they had been implicated in human rights abuse in the 1990s. The largely expatriate management of Freeport had lacked sensitivity to the needs and the culture of the Indonesian people. The company had also been accused of discrimination against Indonesian nationals in both recruitment and training. The relationship was indeed a difficult one. The initial response from Freeport was reactive and fractured in that money was given to schools, or clinics, consultative bodies were formed but each of these remained isolated interventions which did little to change the overall positioning of the

organisation and the indigenous population. Prakash Sethi et al (2011) discuss the changes that followed a more integrated approach from Freeport, resulting in improved relations and reduced conflict. The approach involved a firm commitment to double and then double again the number of local people employed. This meant prioritising and creating access to training. One per cent of Freeport revenue was put aside to support community ventures which specifically targeted jobs or entrepreneurial activities. The holistic approach with clear targets combined with clear evaluation gave credibility to the interventions being made.

ETHICS IN PRACTICE

Revisit a learning intervention that you have designed, delivered and evaluated and make an assessment of areas that might expose you to a claim about your ethics.

Use the following questions as prompts:

1   Who is the target audience?

2   How could they be considered for the intervention?

3   How would they find out about it?

4   Who will benefit from the intervention?

5   In what ways could the design disadvantage people from different

    ● age groups?
    ● genders?
    ● personal values and beliefs?
    ● level of abilities?
    ● religious denominations?
    ● cultural backgrounds?

8.11 CONTINUING PROFESSIONAL DEVELOPMENT

8.11.1 RATIONALE FOR CPD

Attaining professional status after both completing programmes of study and upgrading membership is worthy of celebration. After all, many hours will have been committed to learning through study, the writing of assignments and sitting examinations. Reaching a high standard of achievement should only be considered the beginning of the pathway towards becoming a professional. In a similar vein, passing the motor car driving test indicates proficiency in controlling a vehicle, not that a person is an experienced motorist. Lifelong learning ensures that knowledge and skills stay relevant and up to date through processes of reflection from our experiences. In this section we explore a range of methods and approaches by which professionals can maintain their credentials and integrity through processes of continuous professional development.

In Chapter 5, we explored learning theories that will inform the instructional designs we introduce to learners. More recently, there has been increasing interest in the domain of learning in the use of metaphors, figurative language, to develop a clearer understanding of such a complex subject. Metaphors enable us to understand the unfamiliar by locating it within the familiar. For example, the expression 'all the world is a stage' cannot be taken literally, but implies that in public we present a form of act or theatre in the different situations we encounter throughout our lives. Metaphors that are used in the literature on learning include:

- learning as experiencing – as an individual is exposed to differing circumstances
- learning as acquisition – the gaining of knowledge in a personal store or bank for later use
- learning as participation – through engagement with others and sharing practice
- learning as knowledge-building – taking an existing idea and developing it so that it is relevant in different circumstances
- learning as reflecting – taking the time to review experiences to consider what is effective and what might need to change.

A relevant metaphor to help understanding of CPD considers learning as *becoming*. This connotes continual development throughout the life course, and throughout our working lives in particular. Becoming as a metaphor for learning is very aspirational, as it suggests a permanent need to strive and continually absorb experiences, acquire new knowledge and skills, update existing knowledge and experience working with different people. Becoming offers us the possibility that being a professional is never truly achieved, learning never ends and is arguably our teleological quest. This is important as working lives are expected to lengthen. The International Labour Organization reports that the average retirement age in 1990 was 62.2 years and currently there are pressures to increase the age to ensure that pension funds are adequate. As life expectancy of those starting retirement has increased by around five years since 1950 (when interestingly the average retirement age was 68.5), most of us can expect to continue working for much longer in the future.

With the abolition of the default retirement age in the UK, individuals can exercise their right to continue working into later life. Willingness to work must also be accompanied by willingness to learn, as many in this this age demographic have shown. For example, the phenomenon of the 'silver surfer' shows increasing competence in the use of information and communication technology by older people. CPD is a personal commitment to ensure future employability.

Most professional bodies, the CIPD included, have requirements for professionals to engage in continuous learning. To retain professional status, it is logical to expect individuals to keep their knowledge and skills up to date. There is little value in giving out-of-date advice to a client and expecting to retain respect. Even very experienced practitioners continue to learn. It is one of the characteristics of being a professional that we discussed earlier. Techniques for learning do change. The CIPD *Learning and Talent Development* survey 2012 included a table (see Table 8.4) that showed emerging methods

Table 8.4 Emerging issues in learning and development

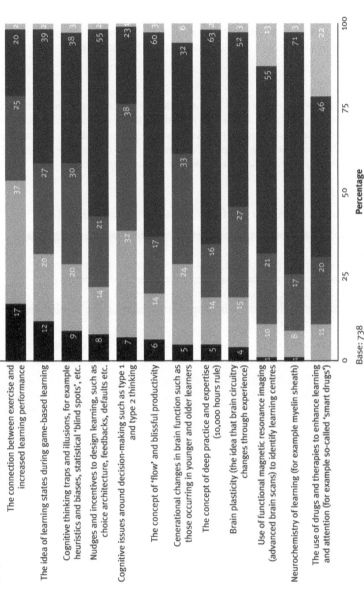

Source: 2012 Annual *Learning and Talent Development* Survey, CIPD, published in partnership with Cornerstone OnDemand.

of learning analysis. With only two of the 12 categories showing awareness above 10% by the research participants (n = 766), there are many emerging issues about which learning and development professionals are unaware.

EXERCISE 8.8

NEW ISSUES IN LEARNING AND DEVELOPMENT

Rate your knowledge of each of the 12 emerging learning analysis techniques shown in Table 8.4 on a scale from 10 (fully conversant) to 1 (no knowledge).

Learning and development professionals in particular need to address their own learning and not become 'cobbler's children' – the apocryphal story that the village cobbler was too busy to make shoes for his own children. We have noted a tendency amongst some trainers to consider that learning is for other people, not themselves. Learning and development professionals should act as role models for learning practice.

8.11.2 BENEFITS OF CPD

The CIPD includes the following as benefits to individual professionals of CPD:

- Build confidence and credibility, you can see your progression by tracking your learning.
- Earn more by showcasing your achievements. A handy tool for appraisals.
- Achieve your career goals by focusing on your training and development.
- Cope positively with change by constantly updating your skill set.
- Be more productive and efficient by reflecting on your learning and highlighting gaps in your knowledge and experience

In addition, there are benefits to employers, as responsibility for continual learning is increasingly passed to employees:

- Helps maximise staff potential by linking learning to actions and theory to practice.
- Helps HR professionals to set SMART (specific, measurable, achievable, realistic and time-bound) objectives, for training activity to be more closely linked to business needs.
- Promotes staff development. This leads to better staff morale and a motivated workforce helps give a positive image/brand to organisations.
- Adds value, by reflecting it will help staff to consciously apply learning to their role and the organisation's development.
- Linking to appraisals. This is a good tool to help employees focus their achievements throughout the year.

8.11.3 PROCESSES AND METHODS OF CPD

The start of the CPD process should be a self-assessment of your own learning needs and turning this into a specific, measurable plan. The CIPD has helpfully provided an online tool to help you make an assessment of your skills. The Profession Map can be found at: **https://myhrmap.cipd.co.uk/login.aspx?ReturnUrl=%2fDefault.aspx**. Table 8.5, also from the CIPD, will help you to consider areas for learning which should be summarised in your development plan.

Table 8.5 Questions to inform a CPD plan

Reflecting back
1. What do you consider were the three most important things (planned or unplanned) that you learned last year? Please also describe briefly how they were learned?
2. Please summarise the value you have added to your organisation/clients/customers over the last 12 months through your professional development.
3. What have been the tangible outcomes of your professional development over the last 12 months and what aspects of your work have changed as a result? Please give a brief explanation of why you have chosen to comment on these specific activities.
4. Who else has gained from your professional development and how?
Moving forward
1. How do you identify your learning and professional development needs?
2. What are the three main areas or topics you wish to develop in the next 12 months and how will you achieve these?
3. What are the key differences that you plan to make to your role/organisation/clients/customers in the next 12 months?
4. When will you next review your professional development needs?

Source: template taken from: http://www.cipd.co.uk/cpd/guidance/examples-templates.aspx

There are many activities in which a professional engages, but a question of knowledge and skills currency arises. How can we know when we need to consider refresher learning? A useful tool to help here is DIF analysis. This is a form of task analysis that uses three dimensions to assess a task – how *difficult* it is to do, how *important* the task is and how *frequently* it is required to be performed. A scale can be applied to these dimensions, as shown in Table 8.6.

Table 8.6 DIF analysis

Difficulty	Advanced	Normal for level	Basic
Importance	High	Medium	Low
Frequency	Daily	Weekly	Monthly
	Annually	Rarely	Emergency only

Difficult and important tasks that are done infrequently may need more refresher training than routine tasks that are performed often. There may be no need for refresher training for routine tasks performed regularly as competence is maintained through application. In Table 8.7 we show an example of a DIF analysis for a learning and development specialist.

Table 8.7 DIF analysis example

Topic	Difficulty	Importance	Frequency	Timing of refresher learning
Fire evacuation	Advanced	Highest	Emergency only	Twice a year
Selection interviewing	Normal	High	Twice yearly	Bi-annually
Designing a development centre	Advanced	High	Annually	Annually
Deliver an assertiveness course	Normal for level	Medium	Monthly	Bi-annually
Updating training records	Basic	Low	Monthly	Not required

The outcome of your self-assessment should be a development plan for the next 12 months in which you specify what you will learn, how you will learn it, the measure by which you will confirm that learning has been achieved and the timescale for completion. Megginson and Whitaker (2007) helpfully provide three frameworks to consider how professionals can engage in updating their knowledge and skills. We have added examples for learning and development specialists to stimulate your thinking, firstly with professional work-based activities (see Table 8.8).

Table 8.8 Professional work-based activities

Type of activity	Example in learning and development
Work project	Take responsibility for an emerging work project to increase your profile and skills
New task	
Mentoring	Seek opportunities to mentor a colleague in a different area of the business
Coaching	Become a coach to a junior colleague
Role negotiation	Discuss the relevance of your job description and your contribution with your line manager
Benchmarking	Develop networks with fellow specialists to compare and contrast practice
Shadowing	Seek the opportunity to shadow a more senior colleague to discover more about their role
360-degree feedback	Use learning evaluations to reflect about your practice and seek the views of line managers of learners
Giving/receiving feedback	Reflect on how you give feedback

Secondly, Megginson and Whitaker consider more formal types of learning, as shown in Table 8.9.

Table 8.9 Courses/seminars

Type of activity	Example in learning and development
Short courses	Use recommended and respected learning providers to advance your knowledge and skills
Qualification	Investigate ways of securing a relevant post-graduate qualification up to doctorate level
CIPD branch activities	Join specialist interest groups and make presentations to the branch having researched an emerging topic

Finally, they recognise the value of a range of informal methods under the control of learners. This area is likely to be the least-cost methods, but could be the most valuable (see Table 8.10).

Table 8.10 Self-directed informal learning

Type of activity	Example in learning and development
Biography work	Using your CV, reflect on your work history and ask: Where have you been? What have you done? Where are you now? Where do you want to be? What do you need to do to get there? How will you know that you have arrived?
Change a habit	Sometimes we may not be aware of the habits that we have and how they are seen by others: ask for feedback and practise one improvement at a time
Webgroups	Use CIPD groups such as CIPD Professional, professional communities and blogs (examples at the time of writing include evaluating training effectiveness and coaching at work) Establish a closed discussion group on Facebook or Twitter
E-learning	Use relevant e-learning packages to increase your knowledge
Action learning	Establish a group to work on a specific learning challenge, something that you have not done before such as encouraging exercise as part of a learning process
Reading	Scan HRD journals and plan to read one key HRD text a month and take one idea from it to build into your practice
Teach someone else to deepen your understanding	Learn something new, for example a new computer application and teach someone else how to use it
Networking	Use CIPD groups such as CIPD Professional, professional communities and blogs (examples at the time of writing include evaluating training effectiveness and coaching at work)
Sabbatical	Negotiate a period away from work to try something completely different

EXERCISE 8.9

PERSONAL FEEDBACK

Devise a systematic plan for you to receive feedback on your performance as an L&D specialist.

How could you incorporate this into your formal review of performance?

8.11.4 CHALLENGES OF CPD

CPD can sometimes be considered a chore, yet when we reflect about the nature of CPD, it occurs naturally through work practices. The 'chore' element is often the *recording* of the learning that has occurred. Professionals who lead busy lives may not feel that they have the time to write up their learning experiences, but retaining records is essential as a way of recognising what has been learned. In our discussions with professionals over the years, it has been interesting to use written records to look back and remind ourselves of what we have learned and possibly forgotten. This in itself is a CPD activity that can make us think about our future development plans.

Find the time after a one-to-one session with your manager to reflect on your progress and then make a brief entry in your learning log. If you have a mobile device, there are free apps that you can download for voice recognition software. This will enable you to dictate your reflection and email it ready-typed to add into a Word document. Professional bodies will occasionally ask professionals for evidence of their CPD and this method facilitates this without the process becoming a burden.

8.12 CONCLUSION

In this chapter, we located a study of ethics as relevant to the work of learning and development specialists and provided our definition. We have limited the discussion of philosophical approaches to those that are of greatest relevance and called for a deeper understanding of the topic to be undertaken. It is particularly important to us that the application of ethical approaches becomes part of the mainstream of practice, as this will advance the status and reputation of learning and development. We believe that learning is a right to which we should all have access. The learning and development function can be the architect of accessibility within organisations, whether by creating the physical opportunities for all to engage in relevant learning activities, or by building an organisational culture needed for difference to be both valued and given the necessary support to thrive.

In an increasingly global market, the more we can respect and value the differences between us, the greater understanding we will have for learning and development provision. Learning and development professionals through their engagement in continuing professional development and lifelong learning will become role models for future working. In showing the personal attributes associated with positive diversity behaviours, professionals in the field can become ethical leaders with the confidence to challenge exclusion in the many differing aspects of learning and development. This will enable them to make important contributions to their own future and that of colleagues in the organisation. The ability to understand the nature of ethical behaviour in oneself and the wider organisational community and to be able to communicate effectively how this behaviour can be integrated into every aspect of organisational learning, places a heavy burden on the learning and development professional. Influencing at director level and gaining trust from the many stakeholders involved in creating a learning environment requires knowledge, tenacity, resilience and the ability to interpret the world with an inclusive and open mind.

SPOTLIGHT ON PRACTICE 8.2

You have been asked to run a three-day skills development event for 16 junior sales staff in a mobile telephone company. For the last six months, they have worked in diverse UK city centre retail stores becoming acquainted with operations and they have shadowed more experienced staff. As they have all passed their initial probation period, they need knowledge and skills training so that they can manage staff in a shop, manage the local marketing of the company and focus on agreed sales targets. These elements are a key part of the performance management process. The event is to be held centrally at the Birmingham Head Office location in two weeks' time.

Prior to the event, one of the four regional managers, Anisa, sends you an email asking you in the strictest of confidence that you report to her personally at the end of each training day about the performance of four of her staff who will be on the course. She wants to know how they are getting on and whether you think they will be expert managers and sales people when they return to work. In addition, she wants a detailed, summative report at the end of the course, but does not want you to discuss this with your manager, Head of Learning and Development, or indeed with any of the other regional managers.

You have picked up in the organisational 'chat', gossip that Anisa's area is doing less well in terms of sales than the other three regions and there have been people management issues that have resulted in a higher number of disciplinary cases. Your informal enquiries with your HRM colleagues confirm the position. Anisa is under some pressure to improve manager effectiveness and to increase sales. No other regional manager has made the same request. You feel in an awkward position as before you became a learning and development specialist, you worked as a store manager in Anisa's region. She was very good to you and went out of her way to help with your career ambitions.

Before you get the opportunity to respond to the email, a fellow learning and development colleague answers your shared telephone. It is Anisa asking to speak with you. You feel pressurised to comply with her request, but feel that you need more thinking time.

Questions

1   How would you handle the immediate situation?

2   What ethical and professional issues does this situation present?

3   How do you respond to Anisa's request?

EXPLORE FURTHER

BLAIKIE, N. (2007) *Approaches to social enquiry*. 2nd ed. Cambridge: Polity Press.

CIPD (2007) *Diversity in business: a focus for progress*. London: CIPD Survey Report.

FENWICK, T. (2012) Older workers and continuous learning in new capitalism. *Human Relations*. Vol 65, No 8, pp1001–1020.

GOLEMAN, D., BOYATZIS, R.E., and MCKEE, A. (2002) *Primal leadership: realizing the power of emotional intelligence*. Boston: Harvard Business School Press.

INSTITUTE OF BUSINESS ETHICS (2009) *The ethics of gifts and hospitality [online]*. Available at: http://www.ibe.org.uk/userfiles/gifts_hospitality.pdf [Accessed 22 February 2014].

INTELLECTUAL PROPERTY OFFICE (2010) *Copyright: basic facts*. Newport: Intellectual Property Office.

MEGGINSON, D., and WHITAKER, V. (2007). *Continuing professional development*. 2nd ed. London: CIPD.

NOELLISTE, M. (2013) Integrity: an intrapersonal perspective. *Human Resource Development Review*. Vol 12, No 4, pp474–499.

PRAKASH SETHI, S., LOWRY, D., VERAL, E.A., SHAPIRO, H.J., EMELIEANOVA, O. (2011) *Freeport-McMoRan Copper & Gold, Inc.: an innovative voluntary code of conduct to protect human rights, create employment opportunities, and economic development of the indigenous people*. Netherlands: Springer.

RIGG, C., STEWART, J. and TREHAN, K. (2007) *Critical human resource development: beyond orthodoxy*. Harlow: FT Prentice Hall.

ROBINSON, S. and DOWSON, P. (2012) *Business ethics in practice*. London: CIPD.

TREVINYO-RODRIGUEZ, R.N. (2007) Integrity: a systems theory classification. *Journal of Management History*. Vol 13, No 1, pp74–93.

UNESCO (2013) *Education for Sustainable Development (ESD) [online]*. Available at http://www.unesco.org/new/en/education/themes/leading-the-international-agenda/education-for-sustainable-development/ [Accessed 22 February 2014].

CHAPTER 9

Themes and the Future of DDE

Jim Stewart and Peter Cureton

9.1 INTRODUCTION

Our closing chapter has two purposes. First, we attempt to identify some significant themes that emerge from the chapters of the book. Second, we predict how these themes may develop in the future and anticipate some consequences and implications for the professional practice of DDE. These purposes therefore have direct connections. Given the speculative nature of the purposes, we have not formulated or stated specific objectives for the chapter. We have also not included any reader activities. However, we hope readers will join in our speculations and that those provided here will inform and stimulate both thought and debate.

Since this is an edited text we cannot include the views of all of our contributors. In any case, given the nature of the topics covered, there is little likelihood that a consensus could have been achieved. Therefore, what we write here is our views and not necessarily those of the colleagues who authored the chapters we draw on for these conclusions and speculations. We hope none of our contributors will object to what we say here. But, they may well disagree and wish to dispute or debate our views. That will be perfectly healthy and no doubt some of you will have similar reactions as you read on. The important point is that we make our own arguments and not those of our contributors.

9.2 SOME SIGNIFICANT THEMES

It is not an easy task to draw out themes from an edited text covering this range of topics. So, what we suggest here is only one possible set of ideas. Readers are encouraged to assess these and to form their own views as a basis for testing the validity of our suggestions. This will facilitate reinforcement of learning from the book as well as provide a summary of key points for future application. We use the broad structure of the book and its associated logic to organise speculation on some significant themes. These are first the overall context of DDE followed by designing, delivering and evaluating learning and development where we attempt to apply the overall themes to the separate elements of DDE.

9.2.1 THE OVERALL CONTEXT

The context of DDE practice is ever changing. This is not a new condition but there is a clearly apparent increasing rate and impact of change. This point is illustrated by the contemporary developments in HRD mentioned in our introductory chapter and is also one referred to in many other chapters. There are a range of developments that are now and will in the future demand different responses and roles from HRD professionals and others engaging in DDE. A CIPD report published in 2013 identified seven 'megatrends' shaping the labour market and work organisations: deindustrialisation; increasing educational attainment; technology and globalisation; demographic change; increasing participation of women; decline of collective institutions; and a changing employment relationship (CIPD 2013b). All of these are of course interconnected but the latter two trends have a close relationship, particularly through the increasing proportion of SMEs active in economies across the world. The report also identifies future trends, which we will mention later in the chapter. The key point here is that DDE practice occurs in a complex external context that has impact on internal factors of work organisations, as outlined in Chapter 3.

Globalisation and developments in HRD arising from academic research and theorising result in both new sources of ideas for and changing conventions on practice in DDE. Globalisation has the effect of bringing new sites of research into influence on both theory and practice; research as well as higher education is now an international business. Developments in knowledge and theory such as those on learning discussed in Chapter 2 are now derived from research and theorising in many parts of the world. So, and as Stewart and Rogers (2012) point out, the theoretical and practice hegemony of the Anglo-American community is challenged and questioned as ideas and theory from other parts of the world are shared more widely.

These contextual factors have implications for the practice of DDE. Three seem particularly important to us, again reflecting those suggested by Stewart and Rogers (2012), and appear to be relevant to the wider practice of people development. First, the factors question the relevance and appropriateness of established approaches to designing, developing and evaluating learning and development. These arguably do not pay enough attention to changing social and cultural circumstances which can leave individual learners feeling excluded. Second is the need to utilise opportunities created for DDE through continued and continuing advances in ICT. As mentioned in our introduction and also in other chapters (eg Chapters 5 and 6 on designing and delivering learning), 'E-' and 'M-' based learning currently offer unprecedented opportunities for scale, reach and methods of learning. But what will be possible in the future? Like others, we are unable to answer that question except to say significant opportunities will continue to be created, although such opportunities will need to retain a clear focus on learning, and not use the technology simply because it is available. In common with Stewart and Rogers (2012), we see a definite need for HRD professionals to keep abreast of ICT developments. Our third and final implication is the rise of critical approaches to HRD and so to DDE. Both globalisation and ICT increase the diversity of workforces and the latter in particular is also claimed to increase employee independence. This independence will apply to learning through the rise of, for example, 'open educational resources' (OER) and 'massive open online courses' (MOOC). Globalisation and ICT both also to some extent 'free' employees from direct managerial control through, for example, 'virtual' teams spread across the globe and time zones. Associated to some extent with these factors, employees' expectations and demands of employment and employers are changing in directions not necessarily conducive to compliant behaviour. We leave it for readers to consider whether this is helpful or even desirable. However, developments such as OER and MOOC may not always be the 'good' things they appear to be. And ICT is as capable of providing alternative means of managerial control as providing locational independence to employees. So, critical HRD will have a contribution to make to debates on the purposes and means of learning and development for employees.

9.2.2 DESIGNING LEARNING INTERVENTIONS

There are a number of themes relevant to designing learning interventions. First is the need to involve wider constituencies than in the past. This means that a range of stakeholders, including managers and learners themselves, have important contributions to make. This involvement applies to the starting point of establishing learning and development needs, as discussed in Chapter 4, as well as actual design of interventions discussed in Chapter 6. Second is the need to apply current knowledge on how people learn. Learning theory may be complex and is certainly a contested field. But, developments in understanding how people learn are critical in informing design. Stewart and Rigg (2011) note lack of progress in producing a 'meta-theory' of learning and we see no immediate indications that such progress will happen any time soon. But, that is not a reason to ignore the extant range of theories. Contextual factors are another theme. External factors will have some relevance for all organisations and all interventions. For example, practitioners involved in design will be faced with increasingly diverse employees drawn from increasingly diverse ethnic backgrounds and cultures. New methods will become available through new and different technologies. But, and as discussed in Chapter 3, impacts will vary and organisations are and will remain unique. So, design of learning interventions will need to be tailored to different, varying and unique contexts. A final theme which is important to mention is the need for practitioners to demonstrate professionalism and ethicality in both their approach to designing learning interventions and in the design themselves, themes we explored in Chapter 8.

9.2.3 DELIVERING LEARNING INTERVENTIONS

The last point is perhaps even more significant when applied to delivering learning and development. There will be occasions such as formal programmes and perhaps coaching sessions when practitioners will be 'on show' to others and so their professionalism and ethicality can be more easily and directly assessed. However, it is the case that HRD professionals will retain responsibility for this aspect even if others such as consultants are actually delivering the learning and so 'on show'. Or, even if the delivery does not involve any direct human contact and relies solely on technology. And the need for demonstrated professionalism and ethicality will be even more important in the context of increasing diversity among learners since this will present new and more testing challenges.

Increasingly diverse learners present other challenges in relation to delivery. For example, facilitating learning, as discussed in Chapter 6. Cultural differences and varying experiences of education and learning mean that expectations vary. Different pedagogical approaches to which learners were exposed in their formative years can shape expectations of learning in occupational settings. So, facilitating cannot be limited to conventional or Anglo/US approaches in the way it perhaps could have been in the past. Use of technology is another factor directly relevant here. Facilitating learning through electronic learning platforms demands different approaches, techniques and skills than those relevant or effective in face-to-face settings.

Learning theory and understanding learning processes are clearly central to approaches to delivering effective learning. While design may make appropriate use of such understanding, that will count for nought if delivery ignores those same principles. Delivery of and facilitating learning will always depend for success on application of principles informed by learning theory.

Internal context factors are also important here. Varying organisational cultures, for example, are often as important as varying and mixed national cultures in determining what is expected, acceptable and effective in facilitating learning. Behaviours of DDE professionals will be judged differently in different organisation cultures. So, as with design, practitioners need sound knowledge and understanding of organisation contexts when planning and implementing learning interventions. In short, they need to be business partners.

9.2.4 EVALUATING LEARNING INTERVENTIONS

Internal factors are also highly relevant to evaluation of learning interventions. A common phrase in many organisations is 'the bottom line'. Contributing to and improving performance of the 'bottom line' is also often seen as the ultimate test and so evaluation of learning and development is important, as explored in Chapter 7. The phrase though is too often translated as profit or shareholder value. We would argue that this is a mistakenly too narrow view. It is our view that, arguably, all organisations in all sectors – private, public or voluntary – have a 'bottom line'. Practitioners therefore need, as part of their understanding of specific organisation contexts, to understand what constitutes the 'bottom line' in particular contexts. The basic premise is that all organisations have values, with one or at most two overriding all others. It may be profit or it may be minimum cost or it may be user satisfaction – or many other things. The point is that once the 'bottom line' is known then design, delivery and ultimately and in particular evaluation can all use that as a measure of success.

An additional point in relation to evaluation and the notion of the 'bottom line' is the impact of critical HRD. A basic premise and aim of critical HRD is to question the notion of a single measure of success. And more importantly, to challenge the notion that measures of success have to be limited to economic and financial indicators. As the influence of critical HRD increases, and demands and expectations of employees change, the focus and measures commonly used to evaluate interventions will also have to change. There will be a move away from economic and financial indicators such as return on investment and new ways will have to be found to assess success against social and cultural criteria. These will include indicators of value to employees and other stakeholders as well as employers and shareholders. The theme here then is one again of widening constituencies with legitimised interest in all aspects of DDE. Differences in attitudes and approaches to both work and learning between 'Generation Y' and 'Baby Boomers' provide an obvious example.

9.3 SOME SPECULATIONS ON THE FUTURE FOR DDE

This final section of the book offers some speculations on trends which may influence the practice of DDE in the immediate and near future. A starting point is to share those identified and suggested in the CIPD report mentioned earlier in the chapter (CIPD 2013b).

The CIPD report suggests four trends. The first is a reduction in the levels of staff turnover experienced by organisations. If this trend continues and employers have less and less need to develop new employees, demand for DDE may also decrease. But, this does not necessarily follow. Existing employees will continue to need development to keep up to date with developments in their industry, sector, profession and field. This is particularly the case in knowledge-based economies such as the Western developed nations and emerging, developing economies such as India. There will also be some level of turnover through retirement, for example, and probably internal promotions. Overall, though, this trend may produce some reduction in DDE activity, although we argue that knowledge and skills currency of all employees need to reflect the rate of change.

The second trend is an argued reduction in annual pay rises, or even a trend away from pay rises at all. This trend has limited implications for either demand for or the nature of DDE activities. It may, though, have three implications. First, learning and development, and perhaps especially improving employability of employees, may become a more overt part of the formal and psychological contract as well as the total reward system and package offered to employees. This is likely to increase demand for DDE and perhaps increased resources. Second and with the opposite effect, a lack of pay increases is probably associated with a lack of resource availability, as some organisations devise their learning budgets as a percentage of labour costs. That being the case, there is likely to be also reduced resources available to support DDE activities. Third, there may be pressures to find and utilise cheaper methods of undertaking DDE activities. This may be more the case if there are reduced resources available but it could also be true in the situation of increasing resource availability coupled with increased demand. This may change the focus of how learning needs are prioritised.

The CIPD's third trend is lower levels of trust in employers felt by employees. This manifests in lack of trust in managers at all levels. As the CIPD report points out, this may be associated with economic crises and wider socio-economic change but may also be a continuing trend. There are potential implications for DDE practice and practitioners. Not least of these is for demonstrated professionalism and ethical behaviour as a means of maintaining and increasing trust between practitioners and learners. But there are wider considerations. First, the use of DDE and learning interventions to repair and rebuild trust among employees may be a priority assigned to HRD practitioners. After all, many interventions, particularly for induction, reinforce dominant cultural norms. Second is the possibility of conflict between the values of the organisation that may be promoted through DDE and those of the practitioner. Third, DDE practitioners, along with other HR professionals, may be recipients of evidence of reasons for low trust, eg disconnects experienced by employees/learners between espoused and experienced organisational values. Work in critical HRD may provide approaches to help resolve conflicts of loyalty and interests experienced by practitioners in such circumstances.

The final trend is rising levels of what is commonly referred to as work intensification. In other words, more and more employees are working harder and harder. There are a number of potential implications here. First, employees may have less and less time to allocate to learning. Second and relatedly, this may lead to rising demand for 'bite-sized' learning interventions. Third, employees engaged in learning interventions may be less able and/or willing to devote as much attention as desired or expected. All of these will present challenges to practitioners but will demand responses.

In summary and to close the book, we can say that DDE cannot be seen as a simple or technical set of activities which can be undertaken by application of tried and tested prescriptions. Instead, DDE is a complex subject which requires professional knowledge, analysis of contexts, exercise of judgement and professional and ethical behaviours. Practice of DDE will continue to face many challenges and developments of theory and practice in the future, just as it has done in the past. These factors make it a compelling and fascinating subject of study as well as a satisfying and rewarding area of HR professional practice. We hope readers of this book find it a valuable aid to their understanding and ability and so a worthwhile investment of their time and effort.

References

ACAS (2011) *Delivering equality and diversity.* London: ACAS.

ADECCO (2013) *Managing the modern workforce – Part 1, The workplace revolution.* Adecco Group UK and Ireland.

AHN, D. (2012) Left- or right-brain dominant? Firms with management and leasing under one roof can be both. *Journal of Property Management.* Sep/Oct, Vol 77, No 5. pp16–19.

ALLEN, J.M. and HART, M. (1998) Training older workers: implications for HRD/HPT professionals. *Performance Improvement Quarterly.* Vol 11, No 4. pp91–102.

ANDERSON, G. (1994) A proactive model for training needs analysis. *Journal of European Industrial Training.* Vol 18, No 3. pp23–28.

ANDERSON, V. (2007) *The value of learning: a new model of value and evaluation.* London: CIPD.

ANDERSON, R.J. and ANDERSON, L.E. (2010) Professorial presentations: the link between the lecture and student success in the workplace. *Academy of Educational Leadership Journal.* Vol 14, No 1. pp55–62.

APA (2013) American Psychological Association. http://www.apa.org/ [Accessed 1 October 2013].

ARGOTE, L., GRUENFELD, D.H. and NAQUIN, C. (2001) Group learning in organizations. In: TURNER, M.E. (ed). *Groups at work: advances in theory and research.* Mahwah, NJ: Lawrence Erlbaum Associates. pp369–411.

ARGYRIS, C. (1999) *On organizational learning.* 2nd ed. Oxford: Blackwell Publishers Ltd.

ARGYRIS, C. and SCHÖN, D. (1978) *Organisational learning: a theory of action perspective.* Reading, MA: Addison-Wesley.

ARGYRIS, C., and SCHÖN, D., (1995) *Organisational learning II: theory, method and practice.* Reading, MA: Addison-Wesley

ARNOLD, J., RANDALL, R., PATTERSON, F., SILVESTER, J., ROBERTSON, I., COOPER, C., BURNES, B., HARRIS, D., AXTELL, C. and DEN HARTOG, D. (2010) *Work Psychology: Understanding Human Behaviour in the Workplace.* 5th ed. Harlow: Pearson Education Limited.

ARTHUR, W. Jr., BENNETT, W. Jr, EDENS, P.S. and BELL, S.T. (2003) Effectiveness of training in organizations: a meta-analysis of design and evaluation features. *Journal of Applied Psychology.* Vol 88, No 2. pp234–245.

ARYEE, S. and CHAY, Y.W. (1994) An examination of the impact of career-oriented mentoring on work commitment attitudes and career satisfaction among professional and managerial employees. *British Journal of Management.* Vol 5, No 4. pp241–249.

ASMUß, B. (2008) Performance appraisal interviews: preference organization in assessment sequences. *Journal of Business Communication*. Vol 45. pp408–29.

BALDWIN, T.T. and FORD, J.K. (1988) Transfer of training: A review and directions for future research. *Personnel Psychology*. Vol 41, No 1. pp63–105.

BANDURA, A. (1977a) Self-efficacy: toward a unifying theory of behaviour change. *Psychological Review*. Vol 84, No 2. pp191–215.

BANDURA, A. (1977b) *Social learning theory*. Englewood Cliffs, NJ: Prentice Hall.

BANDURA, A. (1986) *Social foundations of thought and action: a social cognitive theory*, Englewood Cliffs, NJ: Prentice Hall.

BANDURA, A. (1997) *Self-efficacy: the exercise of control*. New York: Freeman.

BARBAZETTE, J. (2006) *Training needs assessment: methods, tools, and techniques*. San Francisco, CA: Pfeiffer/John Wiley & Sons.

BARNEY, J. (1991) Firm resource and sustained competitive advantage. *Journal of Management*. Vol 17, No 1. pp99–120.

BARTEL, A. (1994) Productivity gains for the implementation of employee training programs. *Industrial Relations*. Vol 33, No 4. pp411–428.

BARTLETT, K. and KANG, D. (2004) Training and organizational commitment among nurses following industry and organizational change in New Zealand and the United States. *Human Resource Development International*. Vol 7, No 4. pp423–440.

BARTSCH, R.A. and COBERN, K.M. (2003) Effectiveness of PowerPoint presentations in lectures. *Computers and Education*. Vol 14, No 1. pp77–86.

BASS, B.M. and VAUGHAN, J.A. (1976) *Training in industry: the management of learning*. London: Tavistock Publications.

BATES, R. (2004) A critical analysis of evaluation practice: the Kirkpatrick model and the principles of beneficence. *Evaluation and Program Planning*. Vol 27, No 3. pp341–348.

BATESON,G. (1973) *Steps to an ecology of mind*. London: Paladin.

BEAUSAERT, S., SEGERS, M.R., VAN DER RIJT, J. and GIJSELAERS, W.H. (2011) The use of personal development plans (PDPs) in the workplace: a literature review. In: VAN DEN BOSSCHE, P. et al (eds), Building learning experiences in a changing world, *Advances in Business Education and Training*. Vol 3. pp235–265.

BEE, F. and BEE, R. (2004) *Learning needs and evaluation*. 2nd ed. London: CIPD.

BEEVERS, K. and REA, A. (2010) *Learning and development in practice*. London: CIPD.

BERGE, Z.L. (2007) Training in the corporate sector. In: MOORE, M.G. (ed.) *Handbook of distance education*. 2nd ed. Mahwah, NJ: Lawrence Erlbaum Associates.

BERGE, Z.L. (2008) Why it is so hard to evaluate training in the workplace? *Industrial and Commercial Training*. Vol 40, No 7. pp390–395.

BEZRUKOVA, K., EHN, K.A. and SPELL, S.C. (2012) Reviewing diversity training: where we have been and where we should go. *Academy of Management Learning & Education*. Vol 11, No 2. pp207–227.

BILLETT, S. (1995) Workplace learning: its potential and limitations. *Education & Training.* Vol 37, No 5. pp20–27.

BIRDTHISTLE, N. (2003) Educating the family business: an investigation into centres of excellence for family businesses and family business educational programmes. Conference paper presented at the 26th ISBA National Small Firms Policy Research Conference SMEs in the Knowledge Economy, November 2003.

BLAIKIE, N. (2007) *Approaches to social enquiry.* 2nd ed. Cambridge: Polity Press.

BLOOM, B. (1956) *Taxonomy of educational objectives, book 1: cognitive domain.* New York: Longman.

BOLLES, R.C. (1975) *Learning theory.* London: Holt, Rinehart and Winston.

BOND, M.H. (1988) Finding universal dimensions of individual variation in multicultural studies of values: the Rokeach and Chinese value surveys. *Journal of Personality and Social Psychology.* Vol 55, No 6. pp1009–1015.

BONET, R., CAPPELLI, P. and HAMORI, M. (2013) Labor market intermediaries and the new paradigm for human resources. *Academy of Management Annals.* Vol 7, No 1. pp341–392.

BOWER, G.H. (1961) Application of a model to paired-associate learning. *Psychometrika.* Vol 26, No 3. pp255–280.

BOYATZIS, R. (1982) *The competent manager: a model for effective performance.* New York: John Wiley & Sons.

BOYDELL, T. (1983) *A guide to the identification of training needs.* London: British Association for Commercial and Industrial Education.

BOYDELL, T. and LEARY, M. (1999) *Identifying training needs.* London: CIPD.

BPS (2011) *Design, implementation and evaluation of assessment and development centres.* London: The British Psychological Society.

BRAMLEY, P. (1996) *Evaluating training effectiveness.* Maidenhead: McGraw-Hill Publishing Company.

BREWSTER, C., SPARROW, P., VERNON, G. and HOULDSWORTH, E. (2011) *International Human Resource Management.* London: CIPD.

BROWN, J. (2002) Training needs assessment: a must for developing an effective training program. *Public Personnel Management.* Vol 31, No 4. p569.

BROWN, K.G. (2001) Using computers to deliver training: which employees learn and why? *Personnel Psychology.* Vol 54, No 2. pp271–296.

BUCKLEY, R. and CAPLE, J. (2009) *The theory and practice of training.* London: Kogan Page.

BULUT, C. and CULHA, O. (2010) The effects of organizational training and organizational commitment. *International Journal of Training and Development.* Vol 14, No 4. pp309–322.

BUNKER, K.A. and COHEN, S.L. (1978) evaluating organizational training efforts: is ignorance really bliss? *Training and Development Journal.* Vol 32, No 8. pp4–11.

BURKE, L.A. and HUTCHINS, H.M. (2007) Training transfer: an integrative literature review. *Human Resource Development Review*. Vol 6, No 3. pp263–296.

CABINET OFFICE (2006) *Capability Review of the Cabinet Office*, December 2006. London: Cabinet Office. Available at: http://www.civilservice.gov.uk/wp-content/uploads/2011/09/CabinetOffice-phase1-Dec2006.pdf [accessed 31 March 2014].

CABINET OFFICE (2009) *Capability reviews: an overview of progress and next steps*, December 2009. London: Cabinet Office. Available at: http://www.civilservice.gov.uk/wp-content/uploads/2011/09/13842-Cross-Cutting-Web_tcm6-35132.pdf [accessed 31 March 2014].

CEKADA, T.L. (2011) Conducting an effective needs assessment. *Professional Safety*. Vol 56, No 12. p28.

CERNI, T., CURTIS, G.J. and COLMAR, S.H. (2010) Executive coaching can enhance transformational leadership. *International Coaching Psychology Review*. Vol 5, No 1. pp81–85.

CHAING, C. and JANG, S. (2008) An expectancy theory model for hotel employee motivation. *International Journal of Hospitality Management*. Vol 27, No 2. pp313–332.

CHEN, R.T.-H. (2014) East-Asian teaching practices through the eyes of Western learners. *Teaching in Higher Education*. Vol 19, No 1. pp26–37.

CHIABURU, D. and MARINOVA, S. (2005) What predicts skill transfer? An exploration study of goal orientation, training and self-efficacy and organisational supports. *International Journal of Training and Development*. Vol 9, No 2. pp110–123.

CIPD (2007a) *Diversity in business: a focus for progress*. London: CIPD.

CIPD (2007b) *Equality and diversity factsheet*. London: CIPD.

CIPD (2009) *Innovative learning and talent development: positioning practice for recession and recovery*. London: CIPD.

CIPD (2010) *Employee outlook: focus on the ageing workforce*. Survey report. London: CIPD.

CIPD (2011) *The coaching climate survey report*. London: CIPD. Online version also available at: http://www.cipd.co.uk/surveys [accessed 1 March 2013].

CIPD (2012a) *From e-learning to 'gameful' employment Research Insight*. London: CIPD.

CIPD (2012b) *From steady state to ready state: a need for fresh thinking in learning and talent development. Research report*. London: CIPD. Online version also available at: http://www.cipd.co.uk/research [accessed 1 March 2013].

CIPD (2012c) *Managing a healthy ageing workforce: a national business imperative*. London: CIPD.

CIPD (2013a) *Identifying learning and talent development needs*. CIPD Factsheets [online]. Available at: http://www.cipd.co.uk/hr-resources/factsheets/identifying-learning-talent-development-needs.aspx [accessed 5 March 2014].

CIPD (2013b) *Megatrends: the trends shaping work and working lives*. London: CIPD.

CLARKE, N. (2003) The politics of training needs analysis. *Journal of Workplace Learning.* Vol 15, No 4. pp141–153.

CLEVELAND, J.N., LIM, A.S. and MURPHY, K.R. (2007). Feedback phobia? Why employees do not want to give or receive performance feedback. In: LANGAN-FOX, J., COOPER, C.L. and KLIMOSKI, R.J. (eds) *Research companion to the dysfunctional workplace: management challenges and symptoms.* Northampton, MA: Edward Elgar. pp168–186.

CLIFFORD, D. and ROYCE, M. (2008) Equality ethics and management in social work education. *Journal of Social Work Education.* Vol 27, No 1, February.

CLUTTERBUCK, D. and MEGGINSON, D. (2005) *Techniques for coaching and mentoring.* Oxford: Elsevier Butterworth-Heinemann.

COHEN, A.R., FINK, S.L., GADON, H. and WILLITS, R.D. (1995) *Effective behavior in organizations: learning from the interplay of cases, concepts and student experience.* London: McGraw-Hill Irwin.

COLLINS, E. and GREEN, J. (1992) Learning classroom settings: making or breaking a culture. In: MARSHALL, H.H. (ed). *Redefining student learning: roots of educational change.* Norwood, NJ: Ablex.

COLQUITT, J.A., LEPINE, J.A. and NOE, R.A. (2000) Towards an integrative theory of training motivation: A meta-analytic path analysis of 20 years of research. *Journal of Applied Psychology.* Vol 85, No 5. pp678–707.

CORBRIDGE, M., MACAULAY, N., BARTON, J. and HALL, D. (2013) Approaches to workplace learning: learning on-demand and workplace learning. In: HALL, D., PILBEAM, S. and CORBRIDGE, M. (eds) *Contemporary themes in strategic people management: a case-based approach.* London: Palgrave Macmillan.

CRANET (2011) *Cranet survey on comparative human resource management: international executive report 2011.* Cranfield: Cranfield University.

CROSSAN, M. and HULLAND, J. (2002) Leveraging knowledge through leadership of organizational learning. In CHOO, C.W. and BONTIS. N. (eds) *The strategic management of intellectual capital and organizational knowledge.* New York: Oxford University Press. pp711–723.

CROSSAN, M.M., LANE, H.W. and WHITE, R.E. (1999) An organisational learning framework: from intuition to institution. *Academy of Management Review.* Vol 24, No 3. pp522–537.

CROUSE, P., DOYLE, W. and YOUNG, J. (2011) Job design and the employee innovation process: the mediating role of learning strategies. *Human Resource Development International.* Vol 14, No 1. pp39–55.

DAVENPORT, T.H and PRUSAK, L. (1998) *Working knowledge: how organisations manage what they know.* Boston, MA: Harvard Business School Press.

DECHANT, K., MARSICK, V. and KASL, E. (1993) Toward a model of team learning. *Studies in Continuing Education.* Vol 15, No 1. pp1–14.

DEMING, W.E. (1986) *Out of the crisis.* Cambridge, MA: MIT Press.

DENBY, S. (2010) The importance of training needs analysis. *Industrial and Commercial Training.* Vol 42, No 3. pp147–150.

DERNTL, M. and MOTSCHNIG-PITRIK, R. (2005) The role of structure, patterns, and people in blended learning. *The Internet and Higher Education.* Vol 8, No 2. pp111–130.

DEROUIN, R.E., FRITZSCHE, B.A. and SALAS, E. (2005) E-learning in organizations. *Journal of Management.* Vol 31, No 6. pp920–940.

DERVEN, M. (2012) Building a strategic approach to learning evaluation. *Training & Development.* Vol 66, No 11. pp54–57.

DINGLE, J. (1995) Analyzing the competence requirements of managers. *Management Development Review.* Vol 8, No 2. pp30–36.

DOYLE, W. and YOUNG, J.D. (2007) Workplace learning strategies of managers in small and large firms in knowledge-based industries. *Proceedings of the University Forum on Human Resource Development.* June 27–29, Oxford, UK.

DRISCOLL, M.P. (2000) *Psychology of learning for instruction.* 2nd ed. Boston, MA: Allyn and Bacon.

DRIVER, R. (1995) Constructivist approaches science teaching. In: STEFFE, L.P. and GALE, J. (eds) *Constructivism in education.* Hillsdale, NJ: Erlbaum.

DRUCKER, P. (1995) The age of social transformation. *Atlantic Monthly.* Vol 274, No 5. pp53–80.

DUNCAN, K.D. and KELLY, C.J. (1983) *Task analysis, learning and the nature of transfer.* London: Manpower Services Commission.

EASTERBY-SMITH, M. (1986) *Evaluating management development, training and evaluation.* 2nd ed. London: Gower Publishing.

EASTERBY-SMITH, M. (1997) Disciplines of organizational learning: contributions and critiques. *Human Relations.* Vol 50, No 9. pp1085–1113.

EASTERBY-SMITH, M. and ARAUJO. L. (1999) Organisational learning: the literatures. In: EASTERBY-SMITH, M., BURGOYNE, J. and ARAUJO, L. (eds) *Organizational learning and the learning organization: developments in theory and practice.* London: Sage.

EDMONDSON, A. (1999) Psychological safety and learning behaviour in work teams. *Administrative Science Quarterly.* Vol 44, No 2. pp179–202.

EHRC RESEARCH REPORT 88 (2013) *Barriers to employment and unfair treatment at work.* ISBN 978-1-84206-483-2

ESTES, W.K. (1961) New developments in statistical behavior theory: differential tests of axioms for associative learning. *Psychometrika.* Vol 26, No 1. pp73–84.

EUROBAROMETER (2011) *Attitudes towards vocation and education training.* Special Eurobarometer 369, Wave EB75.4.

FARRELL, C. (2012) *Our (work) education crisis: Send in the MOOCs.* http://www.businessweek.com/articles/2012-09-17/our-work-education-crisis-send-in-the-moocs [Accessed 20 December 2013].

FEIGENBAUM, E.A. and FELDMAN, J. (eds) (1963) *Computers and thought.* New York: McGraw- Hill.

FENWICK, T. (2012) Older workers and continuous learning in new capitalism. *Human Relations.* Vol 65, No 8. pp1001–1020.

FERREIRA, R. and ABBAD, G. (2013) training needs assessment: where we are and where we should go. *Brazilian Administration Review.* Vol 10, No 1. pp77–99.

FINGER, M. and BRAND, S.B. (1999) The concept of the 'Learning Organization' applied to the transformation of the public sector: conceptual contributions for theory development. In: EASTERBY-SMITH, M., BURGOYNE, J. and ARAUJO, L. (eds) *Organizational learning and the learning organization: Developments in theory and practice.* London: Sage. pp130–156.

FINK, D. and DISTERER, G. (2006) International case studies: to what extent is ICT infused into the operations of SMEs? *Journal of Enterprise Information Management.* Vol 9, No 6. pp608–264.

FIOL, C.M. and LYLES, M.A. (1985) Organizational learning. *Academy of Management Review.* Vol 10, No 4. pp803–813.

FISHER, S.L. and FORD, J.K. (1998) Differential effects of learner effort and goal orientation on two learner outcomes. *Personnel Psychology.* Vol 51, No 2. pp397–420.

FLATLEY, M.E. (2007) Teaching the virtual presentation. *Business Communication Quarterly.* Vol 70, No 3. pp301–327.

FORD, J.K. and WEISSBEIN, D.A. (1997) Transfer of training: an updated review and analysis. *Performance Improvement Quarterly.* Vol 10, No 2. pp22–41.

FOSTER, P. (2002) Performance documentation. *Business Communication Quarterly.* Vol 65. pp108–14.

FRIEDMAN, T.I. (2005) *The world is flat: a brief history of the twenty-first century.* New York: Farrar, Straus and Giroux.

GAGNE, R.M. (1984) Learning outcomes and their effects. *American Psychologist.* Vol 39, No 4. pp377–385.

GARAVAN, T. and MCGUIRE, D. (2001) Competencies and workplace learning: some reflections on the rhetoric and the reality. *Journal of Workplace Learning.* Vol 13, No 4. pp144–163.

GAREIS, E. (2007) Active learning: a PowerPoint tutorial. *Business Communication Quarterly.* Vol 70, No 4. pp462–466.

GARRATT, R. (1990) *Creating a learning organization.* Cambridge: Director Books.

GARVEY, R., STOKES, P. and MEGGINSON, D. (2010) *Coaching and mentoring theory and practice.* London: Sage.

GARVIN, D.A. (1993) Building a learning organisation. *Harvard Business Review.* Vol 71, No 4. pp78–91.

GATES, S. (2004) *Measuring more than efficiency.* New York: Conference Board.

GHOSH, R. (2012) Mentors providing challenge and support: integrating concepts from teacher mentoring in education and organizational mentoring in business. *Human Resource Development Review.* Vol 12, No 2. pp144–176.

GIANGRECO, A., CARUGATI, A. and SEBASTIANO, A. (2010) Are we doing the right thing? Food for thought on training evaluation and its context. *Personnel Review.* Vol 39, No 2. pp162–177.

GIBB, S. (2002) *Learning and development: process, practice and perspectives at work.* London: Palgrave.

GIBB, S. (2008) *Human resource development: process, practice and perspectives.* 2nd ed. Basingstoke: Palgrave MacMillan.

GIBBS, G. (1988) *Learning by doing: a guide to teaching and learning methods.* Oxford: Further Educational Unit, Oxford Polytechnic.

GIST, M., STEVENS, C.K. and BAVETTA, A.G. (1991) Effects of self-efficacy and post-training intervention on the acquisition and maintenance of complex interpersonal skills. *Personnel Psychology.* Vol 44. pp837–861.

GLAISTER, C., HOLDEN, R., GRIGGS, V. et al (2013) The practice of training: the design and delivery of training. In: GOLD, J., HOLDEN, R., ILES, P., STEWART, J. and BEARDWELL, J. (eds) *Human resource development: theory and practice.* Basingstoke: Palgrave Macmillan.

GOLD, J., HOLDEN, R., ILES, P., STEWART, J. and BEARDWELL, J. (2013) *Human resource development: theory and practice.* 2nd ed. London: Palgrave Macmillan.

GOLDSTEIN, I.L. and FORD, J.K. (2002) *Training in organizations.* 4th ed. Belmont, CA: Wadsworth, Cengage Learning.

GOLEMAN, D., BOYATZIS, R.E. and MCKEE, A. (2002) *Primal leadership: realizing the power of emotional intelligence.* Boston, MA: Harvard Business School Press.

GRANT, A.M. (2007) Enhancing coaching skills and emotional intelligence through training. *Journal of Industrial and Commercial Training.* Vol 39, No 5. pp257–266.

GRATTON, L. (2008). Counterpoint. *People & Strategy.* Vol 31, No 3. p9. Cited in HARMA, P.L. and ROEBUCK, D.B., Teaching the art and craft of giving and receiving feedback. *Business Communication Conference Quarterly.* Vol 73, No 4. December 2010.

GREGORY, R.L. (1987) *The Oxford companion to the mind.* Oxford: Oxford University Press.

GRIFFIN, R. (2011) Seeing the wood for the trees: workplace learning evaluation. *Journal of European Industrial Training.* Vol 35, No 8. pp841–850.

GRIFFIN, R.P. (2010) Means and ends: effective training evaluation. *Industrial and Commercial Training.* Vol 42, No 4. pp220–225.

GUDYKUNST, W. and HAMMER, M.R. (1983) Basic Training Design: Approaches to Intercultural Training. In: LANDIS, D. and BRISLIN, R.W. (eds) *Handbook of Intercultural Training,* Vol 1. New York: Pergamon Press. pp118–154.

GURDJIAN, P., HALBEISEN, T. and LANE, K. (2014) Why leadership development programs fail. *McKinsey Quarterly.*

GUTHRIE, J.P. and SCHWOERER, C.E. (1996) Older dogs and new tricks: career stage and self-assessed need for training. *Public Personnel Management.* Vol 25, No 1. pp59–73.

HALL, D., PILBEAM, S. and CORBRIDGE, M. (2013) *Contemporary themes in strategic people management: a case-based approach.* Basingstoke: Palgrave Macmillan.

HAMBLIN, A. (1974) *Evaluation and control of training.* London: McGraw Hill.

HARMS, P.L. and ROEBUCK, D.B. (2010) Teaching the art and craft of giving and receiving feedback. *Business Communication Conference Quarterly.* Vol 73, No 4. p413.

HARRISON, R. (1988) *Training and development.* London: Institute of Personnel Management.

HARRISON, R. (1997) *Employee development.* London: IPD.

HARRISON, R. (2005) *Learning and development.* 4th ed. London: CIPD.

HARRISON, R. (2009) *Learning and development.* 5th ed. London: CIPD.

HARRISON, R. and KESSELS, J. (eds) (2003) *Human resource development in a knowledge economy.* New York: Palgrave Macmillan.

HASHIM, J. (2001) Training evaluation: clients' roles. *Journal of European Industrial Training.* Vol 25, No 7. pp374–379.

HAWKING, S.W. (2008) *A brief history of time.* New York: Bantam.

HAYAT, K. and WALTON, S. (2012) Delivering equality and diversity training within a university setting through drama-based training. *Journal of Psychological Issues in Organizational Culture.* Vol 3, No 3. p59–61.

HEDBERG, B. (1981) How organisations learn and unlearn. In: NYSTROM, P. and STARBUCK, W. (1984) (eds) *Handbook of Organisational Design.* Vol 1. Oxford: Oxford University Press.

HICKS, E., BAGG, R., DOYLE, W. and YOUNG, J.D. (2007) Canadian accountants: examining workplace learning. *Journal of Workplace Learning.* Vol 19, No 2. p61–77.

HOFSTEDE, G. (1991) *Cultures and organizations: software of the mind.* London: McGraw-Hill.

HOFSTEDE, G., HOFSTEDE, G.J. and MINKOV, M. (2010) *Cultures and organizations – software of the mind.* Revised 3rd ed. New York: McGraw-Hill.

HOLMAN, D., EPITROPAKI, O. and FERNIE, S. (2001) Understanding learning strategies in the workplace: a factor analytic investigation. *Journal of Occupational and Organizational Psychology.* Vol 74, No 5. p675–682.

HOLMAN, D., TOTTERDELL, P., ASTELL, C., STRIDE, C., PORT, R., SVENSSON, R. and ZIBARRAS, L. (2011) Job design and the employee innovation process: the mediating role of learning strategies. *Journal of Business Psychology.* Vol 27. pp177–191.

HOLTON III, E.F. (1996) The flawed four-level evaluation model. *Human Resource Development Quarterly.* Vol 7, No 1. p5–21.

HOLTON III, E.F. (2003) What's really wrong: diagnosis for learning transfer system change. In: HOLTON III, E.F. and BALDWIN, T.T. (eds) *Improving learning transfer in organisations*. San Francisco, CA: Jossey-Bass.

HOLTON III, E.F. and BALDWIN, T.T. (eds) (2003) *Improving learning transfer in organisations*. San Francisco, CA: Jossey-Bass.

HOLTON III, E.F., BATES, R.A. and RUONA, W.E.A. (2000) Development of a generalised learning transfer system inventory. *Human Resource Development Quarterly*. Vol 11, No 4. p333–360.

HONEY, P. and MUMFORD, A. (1992) *The manual of learning styles*. 3rd ed. Maidenhead: Honey.

HONEY, P. and MUMFORD, A. (2006) *The learning styles questionnaire, 80-item version*. Maidenhead, UK: Peter Honey Publications.

HOUDE, O. (2004) *Dictionary of cognitive science [electronic resource]: neuroscience, psychology, artificial intelligence, linguistics, and philosophy*. New York: Psychology Press.

HUCZYNSKI, A. and BUCHANAN, D.A. (2001) *Organisational behaviour*. 4th ed. London: Prentice Hall Europe.

HUCZYNSKI, A. and BUCHANAN, D.A. (2013) *Organisational behaviour*. 8th ed. Harlow: FT Prentice Hall

IIP (2013) Needs Analysis [online]. Available at: http://www.investorsinpeople.co.uk/resources/developing-people/define-needs [Accessed 5 March 2014].

INSTITUTE OF BUSINESS ETHICS (2009) The ethics of gifts and hospitality. Available at: http://www.ibe.org.uk/userfiles/gifts_hospitality.pdf [Accessed 5 March 2014]

INTELLECTUAL PROPERTY OFFICE (2010) *Copyright: basic facts*. Newport: IPO.

IPHOFEN, R. (1998) Understanding motives in learning: mature students and learner responsibility. In: BROWN, S., ARMSTRONG, S. and THOMPSON, G. (eds) *Motivating students*. Birmingham: Published in association with SEDA by Kogan Page.

IQBAL, M.Z. and KHAN, R.A. (2011) The growing concept of training needs assessment: a review with proposed model. *Journal of European Industrial Training*. Vol 35, No 5. pp439–466.

JENKINS, A. (1998) *Curriculum design in geography*. Cheltenham: Geography Discipline Network, Cheltenham and Gloucester College of Higher Education.

JOHNSON CONTROLS (2010) *Generation Y and the workplace*. Annual Report.

JOHNSON, M. and JOHNSON, L. (2010) *Generations, Inc.: from boomers to linksters – managing the friction between generations at work*. New York: Amacom.

JOHNSON, G. and SCHOLES, K. (1999) *Exploring corporate strategy*. 5th ed. Harlow/Essex: Pearson Education Ltd.

JOHNSON, L., SMITH, R., WILLIS, H., LEVINE, A. and HAYWOOD, K. (2011) The 2011 *Horizon Report*. Austin, Texas: The New Media Consortium.

JONES, K.P., KING, E.B., NELSON, J., GELLER, D.S. and BOWES-SPERRY, L. (2013) Beyond the business case: an ethical perspective of diversity training. *Human Resource Management Journal.* Vol 52, No 1. pp55–74.

JORDAN, A., CARLILE, O. and STACK, A. (2008) *Approaches to learning: a guide for teachers*, e-book. [Accessed 9 October 2013].

KANDOLA, B. (2009) *The value of difference eliminating bias in organisations.* Oxford: Pearn Kandola Publishing.

KANDOLA, R.S. and FULLERTON, J. (1998) *Diversity in action: managing the mosaic.* London: CIPD.

KAPLAN, R.B. (1966) Cultural thought patterns in inter-cultural education. *Language Learning.* Vol 16. pp1–20.

KASL, E., DECHANT, K. and MARSICK, V. (1993) Living the learning: internalizing our model of group learning. In: BOUD, D., COHEN, R. and WALKER, D. (eds) *Using experience for learning.* Buckingham: The Society for Research into Higher Education and Open University Press

KEMBER, D. (1999) The learning experience of Asian students: a challenge to widely held beliefs. In: CARR, R., JEGEDE, O.T., WONG, T. and YUEN, K. (eds) *The Asian distance learner.* Hong Kong, China: Open University of Hong Kong Press. pp82–99.

KENNEY, J.P.J., DONNELLY, E.L. and REID, M.A. (1979) *Manpower training and development.* London: Institute of Personnel Management.

KIM, D.H. (1993) The link between individual and organisational learning. *Sloan Management Review.* Autumn. pp37–50.

KIRKPATRICK, D.L. (1979) Techniques for evaluating training programs. *Training and Development Journal.* Vol 3, No. 6. p44–53.

KIRKPATRICK, D. (1996) Great ideas revisited. *Training and Development.* January. pp54–59.

KIRKPATRICK, D.L. (1994) *Evaluating training programs: the four levels.* San Francisco, CA: Berret-Koehler.

KLEIN, S.B. (1996) *Learning: principles and applications.* 3rd ed. New York: McGraw-Hill.

KLIMECKI, R.G., PROBST, G. and EBERL, P. (1991) System research as a management problem. In: STAEHLE, W. and SYDOW, J. (eds) (1991) *Management Research* 1, Berlin.

KLINE, J.A. (2012) That's what I said but not what I meant. Leaders and Communication. *Armed Forces Controller.* Winter 2012.

KNOWLES, M. (1973) *The adult learner: a neglected species.* Houston, TX: Gulf Publishing Company.

KNOWLES, M.S., HOLTON, E.F. and SWANSON, R.A. (1998) A theory of adult learning: andragogy. In: *The adult learner: The definitive classic in adult education and human resource development.* 5th ed. Woburn: Butterworth Heinemann. pp35–72.

KNOWLES, M., HOLTON, E.F. and SWANSON, R.A. (2005) *The adult learner: the definitive classic in adult education and human resource development.* 6th ed. New York: Elsevier, Inc., e-book. [Accessed 9 October 2013]

KNOWLES, M.S., HOLTON III, E.F. and SWANSON, R.A. (2011) *The adult learner.* 7th ed. London: Elsevier.

KOLB, D.A. (1984) *Experiential learning: experience as a source of learning and development.* New Jersey: Prentice Hall.

KOLB, D., OSLAND, J. and RUBIN, I. (1984) *Organizational psychology: an experiential approach to organizational behavior.* Englewood Cliffs, NJ: Prentice Hall.

KOLB, D.A., RUBIN, I.N. and MCINTYRE, J.M. (1974) *Organizational psychology: a book of readings.* Englewood Cliffs, NJ: Prentice Hall.

KPMG (2013) *Fast Forward: Letting Go to Grow.* KPMG.

KRAIGER, K., FORD, K. and SALAS, E. (1993) Application of cognitive, skill-based, and affective theories of learning outcomes to new methods of training evaluation. *Journal of Applied Psychology.* Vol 78, No 2. pp311–328.

KRAM, K.E. (1983) Phases of the mentor relationship. *Academy of Management Journal.* Vol 26, No 4. pp608–625.

KRUG, J. (1998). Improving the performance appraisal process. *Journal of Management in Engineering.* Vol 14, No 5. pp19–20.

KUMRA, S. and MANFREDI, S. (2012) *Managing equality and diversity theory and practice.* Oxford: Oxford University Press.

LAI, Y. and KLEINER, B.H. (2001) How to conduct diversity training effectively. *Equal Opportunities International.* Vol 20, No 5. p14–18.

LAWLER, E. (1992) *The ultimate advantage: creating the high involvement organization.* San Francisco, CA: Jossey-Bass.

LAWRENCE, T.B., MAUWS, M.K., DYCK, B. and KLEYSEN, R.F. (2005) The politics of organizational learning: integrating power into the 4i framework. *Academy of Management Review.* Vol 30, No 1. p180–191.

LEAT, M.J. and LOVELL, M.J. (1997) Training needs analysis: weakness in the conventional approach. *Journal of European Industrial Training.* Vol 21, No 4. pp143–153.

LEIMBACH, M. (2010) Learning transfer model: a research-driven approach to enhancing learning effectiveness. *Industrial and Commercial Training.* Vol 42, No 2. p81–86.

LEINO, J., TANHUA-PIIROINEN, E. and SOMMERS-PIIROINEN, J. (2012) Adding social media to e-learning in the workplace: instilling interactive learning culture. *iJAC.* Vol 5, No 3. pp18–25.

LEITCH, S. (2006) *Prosperity for all in the global economy – world class skills.* London: HM Treasury.

LEONARD-CROSS, E. (2010) Developmental coaching: Business benefit – fact or fad? An evaluative study to explore the impact of coaching in the workplace. *International Coaching Psychology Review.* Vol 5, No 1. pp36–47.

LEWIS, R.D. (1996) *When cultures collide: managing successfully across cultures*. London: Nicholas Brealey Publishing.

LINDEMAN, E.C. (1926) *The meaning of adult education*. New York: New Republic.

MADEN, C. (2011) Transforming public organizations into learning organizations: a conceptual model. *Public Organisation Review*. Vol 12, No 1. pp71–84.

MAGER, R.F. (1984) *Preparing instructional objectives*. Belmont, CA: Pitman Learning.

MANKIN, D. (2009) *Human resource development*. Oxford: Oxford University Press.

MANN, S. (1996) What should training evaluation evaluate? *Journal of European Industrial Training*. Vol 20, No 9. pp14–20.

MARCH, J. and OLSEN, J.P. (eds) (1976) *Ambiguity and choice in organizations*. Bergen, Norway: Universitetsforlaget.

MARCHINGTON, M. and WILKINSON, A. (2000) *Core personnel and development*. 4th ed. London: CIPD.

MARCHINGTON, M. and WILKINSON, A. (2012) *Human resource management at work*. 5th ed. London: CIPD.

MARSICK, V.J. and WATKINS, K.E. (2001) Informal and incidental learning. *New Directions for Adult and Continuing Education*. Vol 2001, No 89. pp25–34.

MASLOW, A. (1943) A theory of human motivation. *Psychological Review*. Vol 50, No 4. pp370–396.

MATOX, J.R. (2012) Measuring the effectiveness of informal methodologies. *Training & Development*. Vol 66, No 2. pp44–53.

MATTHEWS, P. (1999) Workplace learning: developing an holistic model. *The Learning Organisation*. Vol 6, No 1. pp18–29.

MAYO, A. and LANK, E. (1994) *The power of learning*. London: Institute of Personnel Management.

MCCAULEY, C., LOMBARDO, M. and USHER, C. (1989) Diagnosing management development needs: an instrument based on how managers develop. *Journal of Management*. Vol 15, No 3. pp389–403.

MCCLELLAND, S. (1993) Training needs assessment: An 'open-systems' application. *Journal of European Industrial Training*. Vol 17, No 1. pp12–17

MCDERMOTT, D. and NEAULT, R.A. (2011) In-house career coaching: an international partnership. *Journal of Employment Counseling*. Vol 48, No 3. pp121–128.

MCGEHEE, W. and THAYER, P. (1961) *Training in business and industry*. New York: Wiley.

MCLEOD, S.A. (2007) *Behaviorism – Simply Psychology*. Available at: http://www.simplypsychology.org/behaviorism.html [accessed 6 October 2013].

MEADOWS, P. (2003) Retirement ages in the UK: a review of the literature, Department of Trade and Industry, *UK Employment Relations*, Series 18.

MEGGINSON, D. and WHITAKER, V. (2007) *Continuing professional development.* 2nd ed. London: CIPD.

MEISTER, J. (2013) *How MOOCs will revolutionise corporate learning and development.* Available at: http://www.forbes.com/sites/jeannemeister/2013/08/13/how-moocs-will-revolutionize-corporate-learning-development/ [Accessed 20 December 2013].

MICHIELSENS, E. et al (2008) *Implementing diversity employment policies: Examples from large London companies.* London: Westminster Business School.

MITCHELL, J., HENRY, J. and YOUNG, S. (2001) A new model of workbased learning in the VET sector. Available at http://www.reframingthefuture.net/ [Accessed 25 June 2008].

MODAFF, D.P., DEWINE, S. and BUTLER, J. (2011) *Organizational communication: foundations, challenges, and misunderstandings.* 2nd ed. Boston: Pearson Education.

MOHRMAN, S., COHEN, S. and MOHRMAN, A. (1995) *Designing team-based organizations – new forms for knowledge work.* San Francisco, CA: Jossey-Bass.

MOORE, M. and DUTTON, P. (1978) Training needs analysis: review and critique. *Academy of Management Review.* Vol 3. pp532–545.

MORENO, L. (2012) Delivering equality and diversity training within a university setting through drama-based training. *Journal of Psychological Issues in Organisational Culture.* Vol 3, No 3. pp59–74.

MORGAN, G. (1986). *Images of organization.* Newbury Park, CA: Sage.

MULLINS, L.J. (1999) *Management and organisational behavior.* 5th ed. London: Financial Times, Prentice Hall.

MULLINS, L.J. (2013) *Management and organisational behavior.* 10th ed. London: Financial Times, Prentice Hall.

NADLER, L. (1970) *Developing human resources.* Houston: Gulf.

NANCHERIA, A. (2008) Company diversity programs. *Training & Development.* November. pp53–58.

NELLING, E. (2013) Student presentations in business courses: does technology enhance learning? *Business Education Innovation Journal.* Vol 5, No 1. p22.

NEWELL, A., SHAW, J.C. and SIMON, H.A. (1958) Elements of a theory of human problem solving. *Psychological Review.* Vol 65, No 3. pp155–166.

NEWTON, B., HURSTFIELD, J., MILLER, L. and BATES, P. (2005) *Practical tips and guidance on training a mixed-age workforce.* London: Department of Work and Pensions.

NICKOLS, W.F. (1995) Feedback about feedback. *Human Resource Development Quarterly.* Vol 6, No 3. pp289–296.

NOE, R.A. (2008) *Employee training and development.* 4th ed. New York: McGraw-Hill.

NOELLISTE, M. (2013) Integrity: an intrapersonal perspective. *Human Resource Development Review.* Vol 12, No 4. pp1–26.

OECD (2012) *Whistleblower protection: encouraging reporting [online].* Paris: OECD. Available at http://www.oecd.org/cleangovbiz/toolkit/50042935.pdf [Accessed 22 February 2014].

OED (2013) *Oxford English Dictionary [online].* Oxford: Oxford University Press. Available at http://www.oed.com/ [Accessed 1 October 2013].

OFLUOGLU, G. and CAKMAK, A.F. (2011) Techniques of training needs analysis in organizations. *The International Journal of Learning.* Vol 18, No 1. pp605–614.

OLAPIRIYAKUL, K. and SCHER, J.M. (2003) A guide to establishing hybrid learning courses: Employing information technology to create a new learning experience, and a case study. *The Internet and Higher Education.* Vol 9, No 4. pp287–301.

ORMROD, J.E. (1999) *Human learning.* 3rd ed. Upper Saddle River, NJ: Merrill.

ORMROD, J.E. (2011) *Human learning.* 6th ed. Upper Saddle River, NJ: Merrill Pearson.

ÖRTENBLAD, A. (2004) The learning organization: towards an integrated model. *The Learning Organization,* Vol 11, Nos 2/3. pp129–144.

OSLAND, J., KOLB, D., RUBIN, I. and TURNER, M.E. (2007) *Organizational behaviour: an experiential approach.* Englewood Cliffs, NJ: Prentice Hall.

PAUTZKE, G. (1989) *The evolution of the organisational knowledge bays: components to a theory of organisational learning.* Herrsching: Verlag Barbara Kirsch.

PAVLOV, I.P. (1928) *Lectures on conditional reflexes,* Volume I. London: Lawrence and Wishart.

PAWLOWSKY, P. (1992) Operational qualification strategies and organisational learning. In: STAEHLE, W.H. and CONRAD, P. (eds) (1993) *Management research 2.* Hennemann, Berlin. pp177–237.

PAYNE, S.C., YOUNGCOURT, A.A. and BEAUBIEN, J.M. (2007) A meta-analytic examination of the goal orientation nomological net. *Journal of Applied Psychology.* Vol 92, No 1. pp128–150.

PEARN, M. (1998) *Empowering team learning: enabling ordinary people to do extraordinary things.* London: CIPD.

PERIN, M.G. and SAMPAIO, C.H. (2003) The relationship between learning orientation and innovation. Available at: http://read.ea.ufrgs.br/read36/artigos/Article%2006.pdf [Accessed 10 February 2004]

PERSKILL, H. and RUSS-EFT, D. (2009) *Evaluation in organizations: a systematic approach to enhancing learning, performance, and change.* New York: Basic Books.

PETERSON, D.B. and LITTLE, B. (2005) Invited reaction: development and initial validation of an instrument measuring managerial coaching skill. *Human Resource Development Quarterly.* Vol 16, No 2. pp179–184.

PHAN, H.P. (2011) Interrelations between self-efficacy and learning approaches: A developmental approach. *Educational Psychology.* Vol 31, No 2. pp225–246.

POPPER, M. and LIPSCHITZ, R. (1998) Organizational learning mechanisms: A structural and cultural approach to organizational learning. *Journal of Applied Behavioural Science*. Vol 34, No 2. pp161–179.

PRAKASH SETHI, S., LOWRY, D., VERAL, E.A., SHAPIRO, H.J. and EMELIANOVA, O. (2011) *Freeport-McMoRan Copper & Gold, Inc.: An Innovative Voluntary Code of Conduct to Protect Human Rights, Create Employment Opportunities, and Economic Development of the Indigenous People*. Netherlands: Springer.

PRATT, D.D. (1992) Chinese conceptions of learning and teaching: a Westerner's attempt at understanding. *International Journal of Lifelong Education*. Vol 11, No 4. pp310–319.

PROBST, G. and BUCHEL, B.S.T. (1997) *Organizational learning: the competitive advantage of the future*. New York: Prentice Hall.

PUTNAM, L.L. (1982) Paradigms for organizational communication research: an overview and synthesis. *Western Journal of Speech Communication*. Vol 46, No 2. pp192–206.

RAVASI, D. and SCHULTZ, M. (2006) Responding to organizational identity threats: exploring the role of organizational culture. *Academy of Management Journal*. Vol 49, No 3. pp433–458.

REDDING, W.C. and TOMPKINS, P.K. (1988) Organizational communication – past and present tenses. In: GOLDHABER, G. and BURNETT, G. (eds) *Handbook of organizational communication*. Norwood, NJ: Ablex. pp5–34.

REES, T. (1999) *Mainstreaming equality – engendering social policy*. Buckingham: Open University Press.

REES, G., HALL, D. and MATTON, C. (2013) *Employee development: a journey towards competence*. In: HALL, D., PILBEAM, S. and CORBRIDGE, M. (eds) *Contemporary themes in strategic people management: a case-based approach*. Basingstoke: Palgrave Macmillan. pp156–165.

REID, M.A. and BARRINGTON, H.A. (1999) *Training Interventions: promoting learning opportunities*. London: Institute of Personnel and Development.

REID, M.A. and BARRINGTON, H. (2001) *Training interventions: promoting learning opportunities*. 6th ed. London: CIPD.

REID, M.A., BARRINGTON, H. and BROWN, M. (2007) *Human resource development, beyond training interventions*.

REYNOLDS, M. (1997) Learning styles: a critique. *Management Learning*. Vol 28, No 2. pp115–133.

REYNOLDS, A., SAMBROOK, S. and STEWART, J. (1997) *Dictionary of HRD*. Aldershot: Gower.

RICHARDSON, A. (2013) Great feedback. *Training Journal*. January.

RIGG, C., STEWART, J. and TREHAN, K. (2007) *Critical human resource development – beyond orthodoxy*. Harlow: FT Prentice Hall.

ROBINSON, S. and DOWSON, P. (2012) *Business ethics in practice*. London: CIPD.

ROGERS, C. (1969) *Freedom to learn*. Ohio: Charles and Merrill Pub. Co.

ROSENBERG, M.J. (2001) *E-learning, strategies for delivering knowledge in the digital age.* New York: McGraw-Hill.

ROSINSKI, P. (2003). *Coaching across cultures. new tools for leveraging national, corporate and professional differences.* London: Nicholas Brealey Publishing.

ROTHWELL, W.J. and KOLB, J.A. (1999) Major workforce and workplace trends influencing the training and development field in the USA. *International Journal of Training and Development.* Vol 3, No 1. pp44–53.

ROWOLD. J. (2007) Multiple effects of human resource development interventions. *Journal of European Industrial Training.* Vol 32, No 1. pp32–44.

SADLER-SMITH, E. (2006) *Learning and development for managers: perspectives from research and practice.* London: Blackwell Publishing.

SALAS, E. and CANNON-BOWERS, J.A. (2001) The science of training: a decade of progress. *Annual Review of Psychology.* Vol 52. pp471–499.

SALAS, E., TANNENBAUM, S.I., KRAIGER, K. and SMITH-JENTSCH, K.A. (2012) The science of training and development in organization: what matters in practice. *Psychological Science in the Public Interest.* Vol 13, No 2. pp74–101.

SAMBROOK, S.A. (2003) E-learning in small organisations. *Education and Training.* Vol 45, Nos 8/9. pp506–516.

SAMBROOK, S. (2006) Developing a model of factors influencing work-related learning: Findings from two research projects. In: STREUMER, J. (ed.) *Work-related learning.* Dordrecht, The Netherlands: Springer. pp95–125.

SAMBROOK, S. and BETTS, J. (2001) Report on the 2nd Conference on HRD Research and Practice across Europe: perspectives on learning at the workplace. University of Twente, University Forum for HRD, January.

SATTELBERGER, T. (1991) Die Lernende Organisation im Spannungsfeld von Strategie. In: PROBST, G. and BUCHEL, B.S.T. (1997) *Organizational learning: The competitive advantage of the future.* New York: Prentice Hall.

SCANDURA, T.A. (1998) Dysfunctional mentoring relationships and outcomes. *Journal of Management.* Vol 24, No 3. pp449–467.

SENECAL, J. and GAZDA, R. (2010) Harmonizing the virtual choir: interactive synchronous webinars for online education. *Journal of Interactive Instruction.* Vol 21, No 3. pp13–16.

SENGE, P. (1990) *The fifth discipline: the art and practice of the learning organisation.* New York: Century Business.

SHELTON, S. and ALLIGER, G. (1993) Who's afraid of level 4 evaluation? *Training and Development.* June. pp43–46.

SHRIVASTAVA, P. (1983) A typology of organisational learning systems. *Journal of Management Studies.* Vol 20, No 1. pp7–29.

SHORT, E., KINMAN, G. and BAKER, S. (2010) Evaluating the impact of a peer coaching intervention on well-being amongst psychology undergraduate students. *International Coaching Psychology Review.* Vol 5, No 1. pp27–35.

SIMMONDS, D. (2003) *Designing and delivering training.* London: CIPD.

SIMOSI, M. (2012) The moderating role of self-efficacy in the organisational culture-training transfer relationship. *International Journal of Training and Development.* Vol 16, No 2. pp92–106.

SKINNER, B.F. (1938) *The behavior of organisms: an experimental analysis.* New York: Appleton-Century.

SKINNER, B.F. (1965) *Science and human behaviour.* New York: Free Press.

SKINNER, B.F. (1953) *The behaviour of organisms.* New York: Appleton-Century-Crofts.

SLATER, S.F. and NARVER, J.C. (1995) Market orientation and the learning organization. *Journal of Marketing.* Vol 59, No 3. pp63–74.

SLOMAN, M. (2005) Learning in knowledge-intensive organisations – moving from training to learning. *Development and Learning in Organizations.* Vol 19, No 6. pp9–10.

SMITH-JENTSCH, K.A., JENTSCH, F.G., PAYNE, S.C. and SALAS, E. (1996) Training team performance-related assertiveness. *Personnel Psychology.* Vol 86. pp279–292.

SOSTRIN, J. (2011) Transforming barriers to learning and performance. *Organisation Development Practitioner.* Vol 43, No 2. pp14–21.

ST GEORGE, J., SCHWAGER, S. and CANAVAN, F. (1999) A guide to drama based training. *Employment Relations Today.* Vol 5, No 8. pp5–20.

STAEHLE, W.H. (1991) *Management. Eine verhaltenswissenschaftliche Perspektive.* 6. Aufl. München.

STAKE, R.E. (1967) The countenance of educational evaluation. *Teachers College Record.* Vol 68, No 77. pp523–540.

STAMMERS, R. and PATRICK, J. (1975) *Psychology of training.* London: Methuen.

STEINER, I.D. (1972) *Group processes and productivity.* New York: Academic Press.

STEWART, J. (1999) *Employee development practice.* London: Financial Times Management.

STEWART, J. (2007) The ethics of HRD. In: RIGG, C., STEWART, J. and TREHAM, K. (eds) *Critical human resource development: beyond orthodoxy* (pp59–77). Harlow: FT Prentice Hall.

STEWART, J. and RIGG, C. (2011) *Learning and talent development.* London: CIPD.

STEWART, J. and ROGERS, P. (eds) (2012) *Developing people and organisations.* London: CIPD.

STEWART, J., LEE, M. and POELL, R.F. (2009) The university forum for human resource development: its history, purpose, and activities [Perspectives on Practice]. *New Horizons in Adult Education and Human Resource Development.* Vol 23, No 1. pp29–33.

SUN, H. (2003) Conceptual clarifications for organizational learning, learning organization and a learning organisation. *Human Resource Development International.* Vol 6, No 2. pp153–166.

TAGGART, P. and SHEPPARD, G. (2010) *From the happy sheet to the bottom line: solving the return on investment challenge.* Northampton: Paragon Publishing.

TANNENBAUM, S.I. and YUKL, G. (1992) Training and development in work organizations. *Annual Review of Psychology.* Vol 43. pp399–441.

TARIS, T.W. and KOMPIER, M.A.J. (2005) Job demands, job control, strain and learning behaviour: Review and research agenda. In: ANTONIOU, A.S. and COOPER, C.L. (eds) *Research companion to organizational health psychology.* Cheltenham: Elgar. pp132–150.

TAYLOR, R.R. and MACKENNEY, L. (2008) *Improving human learning in the classroom: theories and teaching practices.* e-book. [Accessed 9 October 2013]

THORNDIKE, E.L. (1898) Animal intelligence: an experimental study of the associative processes in animals. *Psychological monographs: general and applied.* Vol 2, No 4. ppi–109.

TORKZADEH, G. and VAN DYKE, T.P. (2002) Effects of training on internet self-efficacy and computer user attitudes. *Computers in Human Behavior.* Vol 18, No 5. pp479–494.

TORRINGTON, D., HALL, L. and TAYLOR, S. (2005) *Human resource management.* 6th ed. Harlow: Financial Times.

TORRINGTON, D., HALL, L. and TAYLOR, S. (2011) *Human resource management.* 8th ed. Harlow: Financial Times, Pearson.

TRACTINSKY, N. and MEYER, J. (1999) Chartjunk or goldgraph? Effects of presentation objectives and content desirability on information presentation. *MIS Quarterly Review.* Vol 23. No 3. pp397–420.

TREVINYO-RODRIGUEZ, R.N. (2007) Integrity: a systems theory classification. *Journal of Management History.* Vol 13, No 1. pp74–93.

TROMPENAARS, F. (1993) *Riding the waves of culture: understanding cultural diversity in business.* London: Economist Books.

TRUEMAN, M. and HARTLEY, J. (1996) A comparison between the time-management skills and academic performance of mature and traditional-entry university students. *Higher Education.* Vol 32, No 2. pp199–215.

TSANG, E.W.K. (1997) Organizational learning and the learning organization: a dichotomy between descriptive and prescriptive research. *Human Relations.* Vol 50, No 1. pp73–89.

TUCKMAN, B.W. and JENSEN, M.C. (1977) Stages of small group development revisited. *Group and Organizational Studies.* Vol 2. pp419–427.

UKCES (2010) *The 2010 report – ambition 2020: world class skills and jobs for the UK,* Wath-upon-Dearne: UK Commission for Employment and Skills.

UNESCO (2012) *Education for sustainable development* (ESD). Available at: http://www.unesco.org/new/en/education/themes/leadingthe-international-agenda/ education-for-sustainabledevelopment/ [Accessed 3 March 2014]

URWIN, P. (2004) *Age matters: a review of existing survey evidence.* DTi Employment Relations Research Series 24.

VAUGHAN, K. (2008) *Workplace learning: a literature review*. A report prepared for Competenz, New Zealand Council for Educational Research. Available at: www. competenz.org.nz [Accessed 1 October 2013]

VELADA, R., CAETANO, A., MICHEL, J.W., LYONS, B. and KAVANAGH, M. (2007) The effects of training design, individual characteristics and work environment on transfer of training. *International Journal of Training and Development*. Vol 11, No 4. pp282–294.

WANG, G.G. and WILCOX, D. (2006) Training evaluation: knowing more than is practiced. *Advances in Developing Human Resources*. Vol 8, No 4. pp528–539.

WARR, P.B. and ALLAN, C. (1998) Learning strategies and occupational training. In: COOPER, C.L. and ROBERTSON, I.T. (eds) *International review of industrial and organizational psychology*. Vol 13. pp83–121. Chichester: Wiley.

WARR, P. and BUNCE, J. (1995) Training characteristics and outcomes of open learning. *Personal Psychology*. Vol 48, No 2. pp347–375.

WEN, W.P. and CLEMENT, R. (2003) A Chinese conceptualization of willingness to communicate in ESL. *Language, Culture and Curriculum*. Vol 16, No 1. pp18–38.

WEXLEY, K.N. and LATHAM, G.P. (2002) *Developing and training resources in organisations*. Englewood Cliffs, NJ: Prentice Hall.

WHEELAHAN, L. (2007) How competency based training locks the working class out of powerful knowledge: a modified Bernsteinian analysis. *British Journal of Sociology of Education*. Vol 28, No 5. pp637–651.

WHEELER, L. (2011) How does the adoption of coaching behaviours by line managers contribute to the achievement of organisational goals? *International Journal of Evidence Based Coaching and Mentoring*. Vol 9, No 1. p1.

WHITLEY, W., DOUGHERTY, T.W. and DREHER, G.F. (1991) Relationship of career mentoring and socioeconomic origin to managers' and professionals' early career progress. *Academy of Management Journal*. Vol 34. pp331–351.

WILLIS, P. and BRITNOR GUEST, A. (2003) Coaching – Take the ride – but avoid the bandwagon. *The Coaching Network*. Available at: http://www.coachingnetwork.org.uk/ resourcecentre/articles/ViewArticle.asp?artId=77 [Accessed 5 March 2014]

WINTER, B. (1995) Assessment centres: keeping up with and getting ahead of changing organizations. *Journal of European Industrial Training*. Vol 19, No 2. pp15–19.

WITCHER, S. (2005) Mainstreaming equality: the impact for disabled people. *Social Policy and Society*. Vol 4, No 1. pp55–64.

WORRELL, D. (1995) The learning organization: management theory for the information age or new fad? *The Journal of Academic Librarianship*. Vol 21, No 5. September. pp351–357.

ZIMMERMAN, B. (2000) Self-efficacy: an essential motive to learn. *Contemporary Educational Psychology*. Vol 25, No 1. pp82–91.

Index